Chinese Macroeconomy

This book deploys quantitative methods to focus on the operation of the Chinese economy as a whole since the reforms in 1978, by combining a range of mathematical, algorithmic and computational methods to analyze rich empirical data, seeking to demonstrate the long-term economic trends and dynamics of economic growth and fluctuations in China.

To answer the core question of how the Chinese economy became what it is, the author draws on dynamic stochastic general equilibrium (DSGE) modeling and calibration, while also exploring microfoundations to reveal optimization behavior within a context of economic change at the macrolevel. The book examines internal shocks in the Chinese economic system, including institutional changes, credit policy and monetary policy, which are all closely associated with issues of enhancing the coordination and sustainability of development and the effectiveness and efficiency of policy reforms. It also elaborates on China's close interactions with the global economy, shedding light on the dynamic effects of energy prices, the Chinese Yuan exchange rate and foreign direct investment.

This book is an essential reference for researchers and students interested in the Chinese economy, methods of microeconomic dynamics and macroeconomic theory and policy.

Ninghua Sun is Professor and Associate Dean of the School of Economics at Nanjing University, China. He specializes in macroeconomics, as well as financial derivatives and financial risk management, particularly within the context of Chinese economic development.

China Perspectives

The *China Perspectives* series focuses on translating and publishing works by leading Chinese scholars, writing about both global topics and China-related themes. It covers Humanities & Social Sciences, Education, Media and Psychology, as well as many interdisciplinary themes.

This is the first time any of these books have been published in English for international readers. The series aims to put forward a Chinese perspective, give insights into cutting-edge academic thinking in China and inspire researchers globally.

To submit a book proposal, please contact the Taylor & Francis Publisher for the China Publishing Programme, Lian Sun (Lian.Sun@informa.com).

Titles in economics include:

The Dual-Entity of Market Competition
Establishment and Development of Mezzoeconomics
Yunxian Chen

A Study of Labor Mobility in China
Sun Wenkai

Economic Growth and Income Distribution in the Development of China's Dual Economy
Wang Dihai

Fintech
Frontier and Beyond
Zhong Xu and Chuanwei Zou

Chinese Macroeconomy
Dynamic Models, Calibration and Analysis
Ninghua Sun

For more information, please visit https://www.routledge.com/China-Perspectives/book-series/CPH

Chinese Macroeconomy

Dynamic Models, Calibration and Analysis

Ninghua Sun

Routledge
Taylor & Francis Group
LONDON AND NEW YORK

First published in English 2023
by Routledge
4 Park Square, Milton Park, Abingdon, Oxon OX14 4RN

and by Routledge
605 Third Avenue, New York, NY 10158

Routledge is an imprint of the Taylor & Francis Group, an informa business

Translated by Yali Li and Jia Dai

British Library Cataloguing-in-Publication Data
A catalogue record for this book is available from the British Library

Library of Congress Cataloging-in-Publication Data
Names: Sun, Ninghua, author. | Li, Yali, translator. | Dai, Jia, translator.
Title: Chinese macroeconomy: dynamic models, calibration and analysis / Ninghua Sun; [translated by Yali Li and Jia Dai].
Description: Milton Park, Abingdon, Oxon; New York, NY: Routledge, 2023. | Series: China perspectives | Includes bibliographical references and index.
Identifiers: LCCN 2022003480 (print) | LCCN 2022003481 (ebook) | ISBN 9781032304489 (hardback) | ISBN 9781032305462 (paperback) | ISBN 9781003305651 (ebook)
Subjects: LCSH: Economic development–China–History. | China–Economic conditions. | China–Economic policy.
Classification: LCC HC427 .S76613 2023 (print) | LCC HC427 (ebook) | DDC 338.951–dc23/eng/20220125
LC record available at https://lccn.loc.gov/2022003480
LC ebook record available at https://lccn.loc.gov/2022003481

ISBN: 978-1-032-30448-9 (hbk)
ISBN: 978-1-032-30546-2 (pbk)
ISBN: 978-1-003-30565-1 (ebk)

DOI: 10.4324/9781003305651

Typeset in Times New Roman
by Newgen Publishing UK

Contents

Figures

Tables

Foreword

This is a monograph carefully composed by a highly experienced professor in the field of macroeconomics, focusing on providing quantitative answers to Chinese economic development since China began to open up and reform its economy in 1978. Although other scholars have explored the nature of the Chinese economy, the author of this book attempts to address the question: How did the Chinese economy become what it is? He agrees that a link between macroeconomic and microeconomic principles remains in reference to dynamic stochastic general equilibrium (DSGE) modeling.

Methodologically, in modern macroeconomics, DSGE models hitherto evidence their validity to answer questions regarding the behavior of a particular economic phenomenon. They are popular, as well as perplexing, in the light of rather difficult practical applications. The author does not give up on this line of research despite its initial difficulty, recording and revealing the uniqueness of Chinese economic fluctuations with these "black-box" types of models. Additionally, calibration is the tool used throughout the book to estimate the values of parameters or to test the models. In short, this book relies on calibrated models to precisely address a broad range of questions.

This work is divided into ten chapters, including an introduction. From Chapters 2 through 10, the models involve a variety of factors to quantitatively analyze the stylized facts of the Chinese economy. Fundamentally, in China, institutional factors are the keys to economic development. A number of significant institutional arrangements, including the household registration system (*hukou*), the second five-year plan (1958–1962), the great cultural revolution (1966–1976), the rural household contract responsibility system in the 1980s, the emergence of township enterprises and the innovation of state-owned enterprises in the 1990s, and the prosperity of private enterprises and the updated open economy since the turn of the millennium, have substantially led to economic fluctuations in China. This work thus begins with a basic real business cycle (RBC) model with institutional shocks. It is worth mentioning that this work focuses much attention on the urban–rural income gap in China with an extra chapter. Instead of involving institutional factors again, labor market distortions, the government investment tendency and the unbalanced development of financial markets are examined as factors that widen income disparities. Gradually, credit policy, habit formation, and monetary policy in relation to Chinese economic development are investigated. This work further elaborates on China's close connections with the global economy, shedding light on the dynamic impact of energy prices, the Chinese Yuan exchange rate and foreign direct investment. Whether by ensuring a secure political and economic order, by promoting the international trade balance or by attracting foreign investors, this work emphasizes that China was, is and will be closely interactive with the rest of the world.

Though China's economic rise has drawn much attention, it is also true that institutional obstacles, regional disparities and global issues all pose huge challenges to policymakers. The author provides prescriptions for the problems emerging through the decades of Chinese economic development. He is committed to communicating and connecting with policymakers, as well as with professionals, to exchange his research findings about the Chinese economy. Students and scholars will gain confidence to calibrate their own models based on the methodologies of this book. Moreover, this book will definitely inform and inspire whoever expects to explore the constraints or driving forces of Chinese economic growth and fluctuations.

We would like to clarify that the coherent and clear composition of this work helped facilitate our translation work tremendously. Throughout, equations, parameters, figures and tables are the most sparkling stars that illuminate or forecast the intertemporal movement, interactions and trends of economic variables. In terms of detrending the data with the Hodrick–Prescott (H-P) filter, the economic variables are translated to adapt to the context in the form of abbreviations. For instance, in Figure 4.2, LNIR represents the logarithm of urban–rural income ratio. Regrettably, due to space limitations, several chapters contributing to perfecting the techniques of calibration to further diminish the "distance" between the artificial and real economies in the Chinese version have not been translated into English. Beyond that, this translated version closely follows the original text. We appreciate your forgiveness and patience if some unwittingly made mistakes temporarily limit your understanding.

Yali Li and Jia Dai (Translators)

Acknowledgements

As the principle translators, we are very indebted to all those with whom we worked, and especially to Sun Ninghua, who was the first person to encourage us to do this work. Many thanks goes to Xiao-huang Yin, who inspired us a lot in the previous relevant project and provided invaluable advice at the outset of this translation project. We are also very indebted to Dr. Roberto J. Rioja for the benefit of more than several rounds of readings and conversations.

We particularly acknowledge a debt to our colleagues, friends and students, who contributed to the intial drafts of this monograph, including Tao Lichun (Chapters 2 and 3), Liu Qiutong (Chapters 4 and 5), Wang Jin (Chapers 6 and 7), Guo Yuwei (Chapter 8) and Xu Xiaoni (Chapters 9 and 10). Li Guanghan, Rui Xue, Bei Yan and Aaron Ohlrogge also kindly provided assistance in polishing and perfecting the manuscript, while the Department of Translation at Nanjing University of Telecommunications and Posts definitely ensured a supportive environment.

We have also been the beneficiaries of a series of excellent communications between Nanjing University Press and Routledge about the editing work. The crucial feedback assisted effectively in further perfecting this book. Our deepest thanks to them.

Yali Li and Jia Dai (Translators)
Nanjing

1 Introduction

This monograph attempts to adopt the dynamic stochastic general equilibrium (DSGE) models, calibration and numerical simulation techniques mostly used in modern macroeconomics to explore the growth and fluctuations of the Chinese economy. It aids in figuring out quantitative answers to Chinese economic development since the 1950s. Furthermore, based on such quantitative analysis, it aims to provide recommendations serving to inform policymakers about how relevant research can help to make optimal decisions.

1.1 DSGE models

DSGE models have worked as a reference in modern microeconomics going back to the debate about the microeconomic foundations of macroeconomics. In 1936, John Maynard Keynes (1883–1946) published his book titled *The General Theory of Employment, Interest and Money*. This book caused a profound shift in the major theories of economics and gave macroeconomics an outstanding place in the 1950s and 1960s. Nevertheless, the widespread "stagflation" of the 1970s triggered economists to reflect on Keynes's macroeconomic theory. In response, the New Classical school emerged in the 1970s and explained that Keynesian macroeconomics lacked the microfoundations to involve the optimization behavior of economic agents and split variables into macroeconomic and microeconomic categories.[1]

Lucas (1972) introduced the analytical framework of general equilibrium into macroeconomics, paving the way for the drive toward microeconomic foundations for macroeconomic theory. Kydland and Prescott (1982) examined economic growth and fluctuations simultaneously, initiating extensive research on business cycles, and established the theoretical framework of the real business cycle (RBC) based on the dynamic general equilibrium of macroeconomic models. These efforts promoted the DSGE theory to be a mainstream methodology in terms of offering a paradigm for macroeconomic analysis based on microeconomic foundations. Calibration was used for the first time and has gradually become an important approach to macroeconomic studies.

DOI: 10.4324/9781003305651-1

Why should stochastic factors be introduced into macroeconomic models? On the one hand, considering the real economy always subject to the influence of exogenous factors, adding stochastic factors into economic models can make the models fit well with the economic reality, examining exogenous shocks to macroeconomic equilibrium and various economic variables. On the other hand, without taking into account stochastic factors, models are reduced to dealing with the balanced-growth path.

Why should general equilibrium theory be involved into macroeconomic models? General equilibrium models can consider the optimization of enterprises, consumers, government and international trade balance simultaneously in one model to achieve the general equilibrium of a whole economic system.

Why should dynamic visions be involved in macroeconomic models? Traditionally, Keynesian economics can only perform static or comparative static analysis and cannot perform a dynamic analysis. Nevertheless, DSGE models can well analyze the problem of dynamic changes. It shifts the perspective of macroeconomic research from static equilibrium to intertemporal substitution and intertemporal equilibrium. The introduction of time into macroeconomic analysis presents a "three-dimensional" sense, and more importantly, this is much in line with economic agents' optimization behavior in reality.

1.2 Calibration

Calibration can be defined as an important part of macroeconomists' toolkit. It is effective in the sense of assigning values to parameters that arise in economic models, generating the data simulation results, such as the cyclicality and standard deviation of variables. In comparing the simulations of economic models with stylized facts of the real economy, calibration helps to provide policy recommendations. Widely used in discussing the RBC theory and other macroeconomic issues in the 1980s, calibration has gradually become the mainstream methodology in modern macroeconomics.

Economists from developed market economies such as that of the United States have calibrated the values of almost all parameters and variables while carrying out modeling. Their theoretically built artificial economies are very close to the real ones. In particular, economists' policy recommendations are based on quantitative analysis. In contrast, Chinese scholars' economic research and policy recommendations are more qualitative and less quantitative.

In a broad sense, calibration refers to the whole process of economic analysis, described as follows: First, a dynamic general equilibrium model is built by using the first-order condition and transversality condition to obtain its dynamic systems (some mathematical expressions, or dynamic recursive equation sets); second, all the parameters in the model are determined; third, the time series of the model economy is obtained and compared with that of the real economy, and the model is evaluated; finally, this model is used for economic analysis, such as impulse response analysis, and so on. In the narrow sense, it refers to the determination of the values of the parameters in the model.

Calibration originates from the natural sciences, such as physics, and is mainly used for testing measuring instruments. In *Encyclopedia Britannica*, "calibration" is equivalent to the initial point setting and scale selection for the measurement tool.[2] For instance, for the calibrated thermometer, 0 °C represents the freezing point of water, and 100 °C represents the boiling point of water (putting the thermometer into the ice–water mixture and then boiling water to determine the scale values of 0 °C and 100 °C, respectively, and then finely dividing the scale into 100 equal parts, which can then be used to measure other unknown temperatures). Only calibrated thermometers can be used to measure temperatures. Gregory and Smith (1991) claimed, after reviewing articles about macroeconomic applications, that calibrated models would dominate the empirical research of contemporary macroeconomics. More and more Chinese scholars have adopted calibration to do macroeconomic research.

International economists provide successful examples in adopting the methodologies of DSGE modeling and calibration to simulate the real economic world. Kydland and Prescott (1982) built a one-sector stochastic growth model and determined the preference parameters, technology parameters and parameters of random shocks in the system. This not only provides the determination of structural equations with empirical support but also makes the model economically and reasonably fit the real economy, providing a benchmark for future research. Prescott (1986) described the calibration method in an article based on the typical facts and micro-observations in the long-term growth of the US economy. Prescott linked the simulated economy with the long-term growth and short-term fluctuations of the US economy. This persuasively explained the real economy. Since then, as researchers have different perspectives on the real economy, the real business cycle theory has been further expanded in different dimensions, and calibration and numerical simulation have also been improved accordingly. Mehra and Prescott (1985) explained to a certain extent the phenomenon of yield premium; Parente and Prescott (1994) explained the phenomenon of income disparity globally by calibrating the difference in coefficients of technology adoption throughout different countries; Cooley and Prescott (1995) studied the impact of capital and idle resources on the US economy by studying idle resources and calibrating the average capital utilization rate; Chari and McGrattan (1997) calibrated the relative relationship between investment goods and consumer goods prices and, to a large extent, explained the income gap between countries. In addition, Hansen (1985), Dawkins, Srinivasan and Whalley (1998), Christiano and Eichenbaum (1992), Watson (1993), and others have also contributed to the development of calibration.

Calibration has gained wide acceptance in macroeconomics. However, it has many defects and needs to be improved. First, the parameter values are not reasonable. Some parameter values come from microresearch, such as the coefficient of relative risk aversion; some come from the calculation of macroeconomic statistics, such as the discount factor; some are directly derived from the model settings, such as the elasticity of the intertemporal substitution of labor and consumption derived from the setting of the utility function. Due to the different sources, statistical and calculation methods of the basic data, parameter calibration is quite arbitrary. Secondly, the Solow residual, calculated by using the production function, is used to measure technology shocks. This measurement assumes the full employment of production factors, which is inconsistent with economic facts; it can also lead to excessive fluctuations in technology and even technological regression, which is also inconsistent with the facts. Third, suitable statistics to test the degree of distance between the model economy and the real economy are not sufficient. Generally, to evaluate a calibrated model is to compare the standard deviation and correlation of the real time series with those of the model economy. However, economists have not yet found a suitable number of statistics to judge the closeness between the model economy and the real one.

Economists have constantly been improving the methodology of calibration, whether in terms of the determining values of parameters or testing models. By improving the calibration method, the function form can be made more reasonable, the parameter estimation can be more accurate, and the real economy can be better fitted.

1.3 Dynamic modeling, calibration and analysis

Since the institutionalization of the reform and opening-up, the Chinese economy has presented its own unique characteristics. It has experienced cyclical fluctuations in the course of sustainable and rapid development, and every economic fluctuation brings about the loss of economic efficiency and high operating costs. A large number of Chinese scholars have analyzed the relationship between institutional changes and economic growth and have affirmed the role of institutional changes in promoting the Chinese economy. I argue that the emergence of intermittent institutional changes is the fundamental reason for Chinese economic fluctuations. This has not been fully discussed among scholars both at home and abroad. Therefore, this book builds a basic RBC model that includes institutional factors under the DSGE framework. Through the quantitative measurement of institutional changes in China, the institutional factors can be quantified into the RBC model. Comparing the characteristics of real economic data and the simulated data, this book finds that the model can explain 94.44% of cyclical fluctuations in output, 66.07% in investment, 23.46% in labor, 21.03% in consumption, and 15.45% in capital. Through impulse response analysis, it is found that institutional shocks have a long duration of about 30 years and decline slowly, whereas technology shocks last a shorter period, about ten years.

In a vast number of developing countries, the economic policies aim to achieve sustainable and rapid economic development considering the balance between fairness and efficiency. In China, a prominent unfair phenomenon is the continuously widening of the income gap between urban and rural areas, though this unfairness acts as a result, not entirely an opportunity. A "pure" dynamic growth model is built that can well simulate the facts that labor transfers from the agricultural sector to the nonagricultural sector, that the proportion of the agricultural sector decreases gradually, and that the proportion of the nonagricultural sector increases gradually out of the whole GDP. However, the numerical simulation results are not consistent with the facts of the income gap between the urban and rural areas in China. Then a calibrated dynamic general equilibrium model that adds labor market distortions and efficiency difference of the two sectors is built to simulate the urban–rural income gap. The findings demonstrated that, under this general framework, a reasonable explanation can be provided for the formation of urban–rural income gap and its relationship with various economic institutions, economic policies, and economic variables. With the methods of parameter calibration and numerical simulation, it is found that the model could be consistent with the typical facts of Chinese economic development.

In order to explore reasons for the urban–rural income gap in China, based on the Neoclassical Growth Theory, a dynamic general equilibrium model that describes the relationships among the government investment tendency, the unbalanced development of financial markets and the urban–rural income gap is built, and the macrostatistical data are referred to for its parameter calibration. Based on the modeling, the book figures out that financial market imbalances between urban and rural areas have a bigger impact on the urban–rural income gap than that of the government investment tendency. The urban tendency of fiscal strategy promotes urban economic development on the one hand and inevitably widens the income gap between urban and rural residents on the other. At the end of Chapter 4, policy recommendations are given accordingly.

The monetary and financial system in China presents two stylized facts: One is the prosperity of informal finance (or private finance); the other is the existence of a dual-track interest rate system. These facts are interconnected and have a major impact on the process of the formulation and implementation of monetary policy, which makes the monetary policy operation of China distinctly different from that of mature market economies. Informal financing channels are not directly subject to the central bank, the People's Bank of China. Thus the two types of cost-of-capital give rise to the dual-track interest rate system. These two types, the market-oriented interest rate and the policy rate, are determined by the supply–demand relationship of loanable funds in the informal financial system and by the supervision of the central bank, respectively. Distortions of cost-of-capital remains a perennial problem. Therefore, the informal financing channels and the dual-track interest rate system are added into the DSGE model to examine the effectiveness of credit policy implementation. It is found that the credit expansion policy increases the credit supply of the banking system while inhibiting informal lending activities. The interactions of informal financing activities and banking lending weaken the regulatory effects of credit policy. The positive credit shocks reduce the enterprises' demand for loanable funds from the informal financial system, thereby lowering the market-based interest rate. This makes it possible to realize the dual effects of credit supply adjustment and capital cost adjustment, strengthening the regulatory effects of credit policy. The financial deregulation policy aimed at reducing informal financing frictions can alleviate the dependence of enterprises on banking credit and reduce the market-oriented interest rate by increasing the loanable funds supply of the informal financing channels.

It is observed that while the Chinese economy shows cycles of prosperity and recession, monetary policy is also adjusted between expansion and contraction. This requires building a macroeconomic fluctuation model with monetary policy. Before the pension insurance system, social security system and various insurance undertakings by China are truly perfected, Chinese consumers will continue to consume in a way deeply rooted in traditional cultural customs and institutional arrangements. Therefore, this book builds a money-in-utility (MIU) model by introducing habit formation. Based on calibration analysis and empirical evidences, this book comes to believe that household consumption shows strong habit formation. The MIU model with habit formation can explain 98% of real fluctuations in output and perform well to explain fluctuations in consumption, compared with the basic RBC model without introducing habit formation. Moreover, monetary shocks have a greater impact on the nominal interest rate and the inflation rate, explaining the fluctuations of 11.36% and 10.27%, respectively. The initial impact of monetary shocks is less than that of technology shocks and lasts a shorter time.

The data properties of Chinese monetary economy indicate that a path of supply of money is consistent with macroeconomic fluctuations. The econometric test found that there is Granger causality between these variables. Based on this, this book uses the VAR model to construct the money supply equation on output, introduces this equation as money supply shocks into the CIA model and thus involves monetary factors in the RBC model. The book uses the log-linearization method to solve the differential equation system and then obtains the numerical form of the differential equation system by calibrating the parameters and computing the steady-state values of variables. The data of the model economy are obtained by simulating the dynamic stochastic equations. Comparing the simulated economy to the real one, this book finds that the simulated economy can explain the real economy very well. It explains 80.5% of the fluctuations in output. In addition, through impulse response analysis and variance decomposition analysis, it is found that, though monetary policy in China has some impact on real variables such as output, it has greater impact on nominal variables such as the inflation rate and the nominal interest rate. Money tends to be neutral.

The global oil crisis in the 1970s and the following economic stagnation in some developed countries made the issue of energy prices an important topic in macroeconomic research. The scarcity and nonrenewability of energy resources make oil an important resource and a basic guarantee for the economic development of all countries in the world. The issue of energy security has become the primary factor affecting the world's political and economic order and has become the focus of the diplomatic demands of governments. It is of great practical significance to explore the transmission mechanism of energy price fluctuations and to evaluate their impact on the Chinese macroeconomy. This book involves energy price shocks in the RBC model to examine the impact of energy price fluctuations on the macroeconomy. The author calibrates the model parameters to be consistent with the stylized facts of Chinese economic development and compares the closeness of the model economy to the real economy. The results show that, after energy price shocks are introduced, the RBC model fits the real economy very closely. Compared with the technology shocks, the initial impact of energy price shocks is greater and lasts a shorter time.

Since 1997, the issue of the CNY (Chinese Yuan renminbi) exchange rate has drawn much attention at home and abroad. From 1997 to the end of the 20th century, it has been debated whether the CNY depreciated and how this depreciation impacted the exports of China. Since the beginning of the 21st century, developed areas represented by Japan, the United States, and the European Union member states have blamed the undervalued CNY according to their own interests, making it possible for China to dump Giffen goods into the international markets and expect the CNY to appreciate. There are many controversies, theoretical and practical, at home and abroad, and it will be difficult to draw a final conclusion for a while. The factors affecting the CNY exchange rate are numerous and complex. The existing theoretical models have captured some main variables, while ignoring other very important variables. This book adopts the DSGE model with the real equilibrium exchange rate of CNY under the framework of new open-economy macroeconomics. It improves the theoretical modeling and covers as many variables or parameters as possible to examine the formation mechanism of the CNY exchange rate. It finds that technological progress in sectors, foreign consumption, total exports, government noncommercial expense, real balance of foreign currency holdings, and improvement or increase in terms of trade will make the equilibrium CNY real exchange rate appreciate; the increase or acceleration of domestic consumption, domestic real currency holdings and current account balance will depreciate the CNY equilibrium real exchange rate. The conclusion of the exchange rate determination model is basically in line with economic intuition.

Economic intuition shows that, in the process of the economic transition of China, foreign direct investment has not only made up for funding gaps in the early stage of the economic takeoff but has also provided technology demonstrations, institutional examples and markets. At the same time, foreign direct investment (FDI) has also brought environmental pollution and crowding-out effect, profit outflow, unbalanced regional development and even financial risks, and many other negative effects. Therefore, it is of vital importance to explore the effects of FDI on Chinese economic growth and its fluctuations. This book first analyzes some of the stylistic facts of the Chinese macroeconomy, then builds an RBC model with FDI shocks, calibrates the model parameters to be consistent with the characteristics of Chinese economic development and compares the models. The degree of closeness between the model economy and the real economy is used to study the way and degree that FDI affects Chinese economic growth and fluctuations. The research results show that the RBC model incorporating FDI shocks can simulate Chinese real economic fluctuations. The impulse response function of FDI shocks shows that FDI shocks have a negative impact on output, domestic investment, labor etc. but has a positive impact on consumption.

1.4 Conclusion

This monograph pays a debt to the previous progress developed by both Chinese and international scholars and examines the stylistic facts of the Chinese macroeconomy by referring to the macro- and microdata of the economic reality in China. With DSGE modeling, this book attempts to demonstrate the characteristics of the Chinese economy in a transitional period and draw conclusions and policy implications by comparing calibrated models and the real economic world.

It combines quantitative analysis and calibration to improve the methodology of the calibration method. The method of constructing statistics in econometrics works as a reference to set the goodness-of-fit for model calibration. For some parameters and variables that cannot be obtained through empirical data or other research, econometric tools and methods are used to estimate the values of parameters in the structural equations. Simulations and calibrations jointly work to improve the model economy so as to make it well fit the real situation. Additionally, institutional factors are introduced into the RBC model to calibrate the effects of institutional changes on Chinese economic growth and fluctuations.

Confronting the typical issue enhancing the coordination and sustainability of development and the Chinese government's macroscopic regulatory capabilities, this book attempts to examine the long-term trends and dynamics of economic growth in the light of the rich empirical data of the Chinese economy. Specifically, it means to explore the effects of various shocks, such as institutional changes, money stock adjustment and international economic fluctuations, on the Chinese economic system. Models that conform to the characteristics of the Chinese economy will be built and made to fit the status of Chinese economic operation through the determination of parameters and the calibration of models. This monograph further strives to provide policy recommendations based on theoretical models and quantitative answers for making macroeconomic policy applicable to China.

Methodologically, this monograph mainly adopts DSGE models as important tools and involves microeconomic agents with rational expectations to link with microfoundations to analyze the dynamic and consistent optimization behavior generated during the development and change of the macrolevel. On this basis, policy recommendations are put forth. The parameters that arise in the structural equations are determined mainly through the macroeconomic data and some microresearch results, and testing is achieved mainly through calibrating the model economy, so that modeling conforms to the real economic development as much as possible.

Notes

1 Some scholars still contend that macroeconomics has no microeconomic foundations.
2 Encyclopedia Britannica Inc., *Encyclopedia Britannica* (15th edition), vol. 2, 2009, p. 382.

Bibliography

Chari, Varadarajan, Patrick Kehoe, and Ellen McGrattan. "The Poverty of Nations: A Quantitative Exploration." Staff Report 204, Federal Reserve Bank of Minneapolis, 1997.

Christiano, Lawrence J., and Martin Eichenbaum. "Current Real-Business-Cycle Theories and Aggregate Labor-Market Fluctuations." *The American Economic Review* no. 3 (1992): 430–450.

Cooley, Thomas F., and Edward C. Prescott, "Economic Growth and Business Cycles." In *Frontiers of Business Cycle Research*, edited by Thomas F. Cooley. Princeton: Princeton University Press, 1995.

Dawkins, Christina, T. N. Srinivasan and John Whalley. "Calibration." In *Handbook of Econometrics*, vol. 5, edited by James J. Heckman and Edward Learner. Amsterdam: North Holland, 1998, 3653–3703.

Gregory, Allan and Gregor Smith. "Calibration as Testing: Inference in Simulated Macroeconomic Models." *Journal of Business & Economic Statistics*, no. 3 (1991): 297–303.

Hansen, Gary D. "Indivisible Labor and the Business Cycle." *Journal of Monetary Economics*, no. 3 (1985): 309–327.

Keynes, John Maynard. *The General Theory of Employment, Interest and Money*. London: Macmillan, 1936;

Kydland, Finn E., and Edward F. Prescott. "Time to Build and Aggregate Fluctuation." *Econometrica* no. 6 (1982): 1345–1370.

Lucas, Robert E., Jr. "Expectations and the Neutrality of Money." *Journal of Economic Theory* no. 2 (1972): 103–124.

Mehra, Rajnish, and Edward C. Prescott. "The Equity Premium: A Puzzle." Journal of Monetary Economics no. 2 (1985): 145–161.

Parente, Stephen L., and Edward C. Prescott. "Barriers to Technology Adoption and Development." *The Journal of Political Economy* no. 2 (1994): 298–321.
Prescott, Edward C. "Theory Ahead of Business Cycle Measurement." *Quarterly Review*, Federal Reserve Bank of Minneapolis, no. 4 (1986): 9–22.
Watson, R. B. "Calibration Techniques for Extensometry: Possible Standards of Strain Measurement." *Journal of Testing and Evaluation* no. 6 (1993): 515–521.

2 Intermittent institutional changes and Chinese economic fluctuations

The economic transition of China essentially amounts to the course of institutional changes. During this course, institutional changes do not appear uniformly but intermittently and randomly. The emergence of intermittent institutional changes is the root of Chinese economic growth and fluctuations. This chapter builds an RBC model with institutional factors based on the DSGE theory. Using the estimated parameter values of the RBC model and the steady-state values of the systems, we can simulate dynamic stochastic equilibrium systems. Comparing the characteristics of the real economic data to the simulated data, it is found that the model can explain 94.44% of cyclical fluctuations in output, 66.07% in investment, 23.46% in labor, 21.03% in consumption, and 15.45% in capital. Comparing the institutional shocks and technology shocks on economic growth, it is found that institutional shocks have a long duration, about 30 years, and decline slowly, whereas technology shocks last a shorter period, about ten years.

2.1 Institutional changes and economic fluctuations: An introduction

Since the institutionalization of the reform and opening policy, the Chinese economy has maintained rapid growth for decades. From 1978 through 2020, the average GDP growth rate of China was as high as 9.27%, making it one of the countries with the fastest economic growth in the world. Accompanying this rapid economic growth is the stylized facts of large economic fluctuations. In 1984, the GDP growth rate was as high as 15.18%, whereas in 1990 it was only 3.84%. The range of GDP growth rate was 11.34%, and the standard deviation was 2.73%. During this period, China has experienced both hyperinflation caused by uncontrolled price rises and deflation caused by negative price growth. The average inflation rate, as measured by the Consumer Price Index (CPI) was 5.68%. In 1994, the inflation rate was as high as 24.13%. Only five years later, in 1999, China entered a deflationary phase. The price level dropped by 1.41%, the range of the inflation rate was as high as 25.54%, and the standard deviation was 6.33%. In 2020, China's GDP reaches 101.6 trillion yuan, an actual increase of 2.3% year-on-year. From the perspective of economic growth rate and inflation rate data, rapid economic growth

DOI: 10.4324/9781003305651-2

accompanied by large fluctuations is the significant feature of the Chinese economy since the reform and opening-up. What can explain these economic fluctuations?

It is observed that, in the course of the volatile high-speed growth of the Chinese economy, the economic system and institutional arrangements have been constantly changing, as well as institutional changes, and that a wave of institutional changes emerges. A series of economic systems, including the modern enterprise system, property rights system, distribution system, market price system and opening-up system, have been gradually established and improved. Economic fluctuations can be attributed to institutional shocks.

From the perspective of institutional economics, institutions play a significant role in driving economic growth. On the one hand, institutions can be used as providers of certain services, can have the characteristics of currency and can reduce transaction costs (Coase, Alchian and North, 1994; North, 1994; Ostrom et al., 1992); on the other hand, capital accumulation and technological progress are not so much the cause of economic growth but are tantamount to economic growth; institutions are the keys to economic growth and provide effective incentives for further technological progress and capital accumulation (North, 1968; North, 1991; North, 2008). In addition, when the external conditions on which institutions depend change, people modify the institutional arrangements accordingly so that their preferences can be consistent with these new institutional arrangements and obtain the benefits of the institutional changes (Bromley, 1996). The macroeconomic institutional arrangements formulated by government have a significant impact on economic growth, and institutional arrangements that conform to a country's development status can promote economic development (Guseh, 1997).

Chinese scholars have studied the relationship between economic growth and institutional changes. Lin (1989) elaborated the analytical methods of induced institutional changes and forced institutional changes from the perspective of economics and politics. Wang (1992) included culture in the category of institutional changes of China and thought about the significance of culture to the institutional reforms in China. Zhang (1992) expounded the reasons for institutional changes from the perspective of institutional equilibrium and nonequilibrium. Yang (1998), Fan (1993), Zhang and Jiang (1997), Zhou (2000) and others have studied the path of institutional changes in China.

Scholars both at home and abroad have conducted relatively sufficient research on specific ways in which institutional changes promote economic growth and institutional changes. This chapter makes it clear that institutional changes appear not uniformly but intermittently and that whenever a specific institutional change appears, it is a random event. Economic fluctuations are to a large extent explained by the intermittent appearance of institutional changes. Therefore, institutional changes can be taken as a variable and incorporated into the RBC model to examine its mechanism and effects on economic growth and fluctuations.

Kydland and Prescott (1982) and Long and Plosser (1983) were the first to put forth the RBC theory. Lucas (1982), Svensson (1985), Cooley and Hansen (1989) and others introduced money into the utility function or introduced money constraint into the RBC model for analyzing monetary policy and its effects. Gong and Semmler (2003) studied the RBC model under the nonequilibrium labor market. Bu and Jin (2002) introduced monetary factors into the exogenous labor model to build China's monetary and RBC model and analyzed the relationship between Chinese economic growth and the monetary index from 1980 through 2001. Huang (2005) regarded government expenditure as random shocks of an exogenous variable and discussed government expenditure shocks on business cycles.

This chapter will, on the basis of quantitative analysis of institutional changes in China, incorporate institutional changes into the RBC model to examine their effects on economic growth and fluctuations, figuring out the patterns of Chinese economic fluctuations.

2.2 Intermittent institutional changes: Roots of economic fluctuations in a transitional period

According to general equilibrium theory, institutions can reach an equilibrium state in a certain period of time. Institutional equilibrium is a state in which, given the negotiating power of actors and a series of contract negotiations that constitute the overall economic exchange, no actor finds that it is profitable to use resources to reestablish an agreement (North, 1994). An institutional equilibrium state does not mean that this equilibrium can be maintained forever. There are different institutional arrangements. When a change in one of the institutional arrangements changes its own equilibrium, it breaks the entire equilibrium state. The incentives for institutional changes are changes in relative prices and preferences. When the changes in relative prices enable people to commit themselves to institutional transformations so that the expected benefits outweigh the costs, the institutional equilibrium will be broken, and institutional changes will occur (North, 1994).

It can be seen that institutional changes will change the steady-state growth path of an economic system, thereby changing its real growth path. For any economic system, there is a balanced growth path under the given institutional arrangements. In the process of economic development, if there are no institutional changes, then the steady-state and balanced growth path of the economy will remain unchanged. However, if there are institutional changes conducive to economic development, the steady-state and balanced growth path of the economic system will be improved as a whole. Since the factors of production have the effect of diminishing marginal utility, when the actual diminishing marginal utility occurs, if there are institutional changes that are conducive to promoting economic development, then the economic system will maintain a high-speed growth with the overall improved steady-state and balanced growth path. The economic development speed is higher than

Figure 2.1 Economic Growth Path with Institutional Changes.

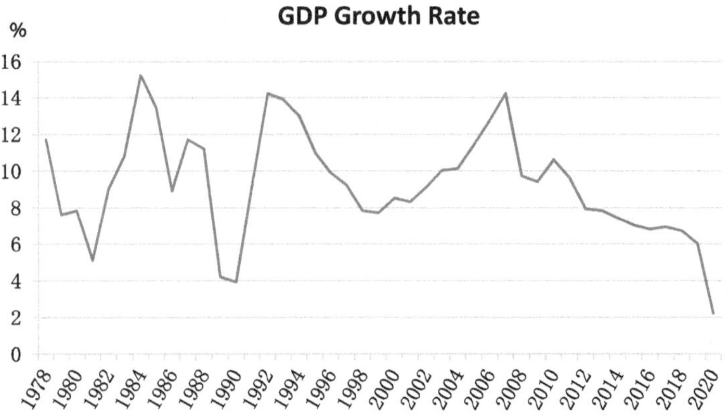

Figure 2.2 GDP Growth Rate of China from 1979 to 2010.

that before institutional changes. The real economic growth path is shown in Figure 2.1.

Since the reform and opening-up, China has experienced many institutional changes. The direction and efficiency of institutional changes have mainly explained Chinese economic fluctuations. Taking into account the process of the institutional changes and economic growth, it is found that the intermittent appearance of institutional innovations is the source of Chinese economic fluctuations. This can be illustrated by referring to the annual GDP growth rate in Figure 2.2.

It can be seen from Figure 2.2 that the Chinese economy was in a period of obvious growth from 1981 through 1985. This can be attributed to the rural household contract responsibility system. In December 1978, farmers in Xiaogang Village, Fengyang County, Anhui initiated the production responsibility system of contracting to households. In the first two years, this institutional change was not approved by central government officials until the release of the document titled "Several Issues Concerning the Further Strengthening and Improving of the Agricultural Production Responsibility System" by the Central Committee of the Communist Party of China in September 1980, with the main content of contracting to households. The agricultural production responsibility system was then established and gradually spread across the country. At the beginning of 1983, the production teams that implemented the "two-way contract" accounted for 93%. This new institutional arrangement greatly liberated and promoted the development of productive forces. The economic system reform of China began with the implementation of the household contract responsibility system.

From 1985 to 1991, a major decline in agriculture occurred due to "difficulties in selling grain" and farmers being hurt by low grain prices because of the mismatch of various institutional arrangements in the "dual-track system" of the agricultural product purchase and sale system. Generally, the GDP growth rate showed a continuous decline. But the economic growth rate in 1986 and 1987 was above 11%. This possibly owes to the release of two "No. 1 central documents" in 1985 and 1986 by the central government, which emphasized the development of agriculture. The raised prices of agricultural products improved the ability of agriculture to develop itself and the enthusiasm of farmers in production.

From 1991 to 1994, the Chinese economy ushered in another period of rising prosperity. During this period, the driving force of economic growth mainly came from the emergence of township enterprises and the innovation of state-owned enterprises. Developing township enterprises means exploring the path of industrialization with Chinese characteristics outside rural areas and traditional systems. Township enterprises are market-oriented and have the flexibility of small boats turning around easily. The rapid development of township enterprises provides not only valuable experience for the reform of the market-oriented economy in China but also a strong impetus for the in-depth advancement of reforms, enabling the reforms to be rapidly advanced to the cities. The system innovation of state-owned enterprises at this stage is reflected in the reform of "breaking the three iron rules" that began in 1992 and the corporatization of state-owned enterprises that began in 1993. The so-called breaking-the-three-iron-rules reform refers to the elimination of the "iron rice bowls," "iron posts" and "iron wages" within state-owned enterprises, which was tantamount to the reform of the labor employment, distribution and personnel system of enterprises. The reform of breaking-the-three-iron-rules was carried out under the conditions wherein the social security system and reemployment mechanism had not yet been established, which brought many social problems. Nevertheless, for the first time, this reform involved all employees of the enterprises and inspired the enthusiasm of corporate managers as well as ordinary employees. After 1993, the reform of state-owned enterprises shifted to the second stage, "corporatization transformation." In

November 1993, the Third Plenary Session of the 14th Central Committee of the Communist Party of China passed the document titled "Resolution on Certain Questions Regarding a Socialist Market Economy," which marked the transformation of the release of state-owned enterprises from the decentralization of power and the transfer of profit to the innovations of enterprise institutions. The establishment of a modern enterprise system with "clear property rights, clear rights and responsibilities, separation of government and enterprises, and scientific management" has improved the operating efficiency of state-owned enterprises. The economic downturn from 1995 to 1999 was due to the lack of efficient institutional changes at this stage.

From 2000 to 2007, the economic prosperity was mainly attributed to the prosperity of the private economy and the overall promotion of opening-up. During this period, all the institutional obstacles to the development of the private economy were eliminated, and the private economy shared the same status as the public economy. In November 2002, the report of the 16th National Congress of the Communist Party of China clearly stated that "it is necessary to encourage, support and guide the development of the nonpublic sectors of the economy. .. We should expand the areas for the market access of domestic nongovernmental capital. .. We should improve the legal system for protecting private property."[1] In February 2005, the State Council issued "Directives on Encouraging, Supporting and Guiding the Development of the Nonpublic Sector of Self-Employed, Private and Other Forms of Ownership of the Economy," the most comprehensive and systematic document to promote the development of the nonpublic sector. The rapid development of the non-state-owned economy has provided not only a sound institutional model for the reform of the state-owned economy but also a strong impetus for the formation of the market economy of China. Entering the 1990s, the opening-up strategy has been continuously upgraded, from coastal opening to inland opening, in an all-round way. On December 11, 2001, China officially became a member of the World Trade Organization (WTO). Joining the WTO marked a new stage in the course of the reform and opening-up strategy. This means not only the expansion of reform and opening-up but also that China is moving from unilaterally opening up to bilaterally and reciprocally opening up with WTO members and that China should abide by international rules instead of narrow domestic ones. After 2007, the Chinese economy was severely affected by the financial crisis in the United States and the world on the one hand and by the foreign trade industry and the external sectors facing severely insufficient market demand; on the other hand, the Chinese government has increased its intervention in the economy and adopted various measures to increase domestic demand. On the whole, the effect of institutional changes has not been significant since 2007, and the economy has moved from rapid growth to steady growth.

In short, linking the GDP growth rate of China from 1979 to 2010 with the practice of institutional changes of China since the institutionalization of reform and opening-up policy, it can be clearly seen that there is a significant correlation between the intermittent emergence of institutional changes in China and the growth and fluctuations of the Chinese economy. The following section will try to introduce institutional factors into the RBC model to formalize this relationship.

2.3 Model building

The RBC theory adds random shocks to productivity based on the Neoclassical Growth models, thereby closely combining economic growth and economic fluctuations. RBC models focus on the economic growth and fluctuations caused by the actual components of the economy (corresponding with the monetary components). The debate about the RBC theory is by no means limited to clarifying the causes of economic fluctuations (or business cycles) but to basing macroeconomics on the microfoundations and revealing the dynamic relations and interactions of various economic variables. This chapter mainly argues that the intermittent emergence of institutional changes is the source of Chinese economic growth and fluctuations. Therefore, it is reasonable to introduce institutional factors into the RBC model with assumptions as discussed next.

Assuming that the production function is constant returns to scale and that the utility function of the economic agent is of the constant relative risk aversion (CRRA) type. Technology and institutional changes in the transitional period of the Chinese economy are both regarded as exogenous random shocks and follow the first-order autoregressive process, namely AR(1). This setting considers two aspects: First, the previous section shows that since the reform and opening-up, a series of institutional changes have occurred in China. Once the reform starts, it will promote the continuation of the reform; second, this is a temporary and convenient approach, which can be improved and gradually brought closer to the future reality. However, it is worth noting that previous studies generally regarded all of the Solow residual as technical variables of random shocks. However, in economic reality, the Solow residual includes not only the technology shocks but also should include the institutional shocks. The model built in this chapter attempts to separate the influence of technology from the Solow residual in order to measure the impact of institutional factors on economic fluctuations.

Assuming that the agents in the economy are homogeneous, facing the same consumption constraint and having the same utility function, the utility function of the representative agent takes the following form:

$$E_0 \sum_{t=0}^{\infty} \beta^t U(C_t, L_t) \tag{2.1}$$

$$U(C_t, L_t) = \frac{C_t^{1-\eta}}{1-\eta} + \theta \ln(1 - \mathrm{L}_t)$$

where β^t represents the subjective discount rate of period t; C_t represents the agent's consumption of period t; L_t represents the agent's labor time of period t; η represents the CRRA $(\eta > 0)$, especially when $\eta = 1$ (the first term $\frac{C_t^{1-\eta} - 1}{1-\eta}$ of the CRRA utility function becomes $\ln C_t$, which can be regarded as a special form); θ represents the relative value with respect to consumption and labor, $\theta \in (0,1)$, reflecting the agent's preference level for consumption or labor in the utility function.

Chow and Li (2002) used Chinese macroeconomic data from 1952 to 2008 to estimate the aggregate production function and found that the Cobb–Douglas production function with constant returns to scale was in line with the reality of the Chinese economy. The production function in this chapter adopts the Cobb–Douglas form. Ostrom, Fini and Pichter (1992, p221) affirmed the important role of institutional factors in economic growth and explained that institutions were the fourth factor in economic growth. This chapter thus sets the production function purposely as follows:

$$Y_t = A_t W_t^{\gamma} K_t^{\rho} L_t^{1-\rho} \tag{2.2}$$

where A_t represents the exogenous technology variable; W_t represents the exogenous institutional variable; K_t represents the actual capital input; and ρ represents the output elasticity of capital. The production function with constant returns to scale is adopted, so the output elasticity of labor is $1-\rho$; γ represents the impact factor of institutions and reflects the elasticity of institutions to output; $A_t W_t^{\gamma}$ represents the Solow residual in the traditional sense.

The budget constraint faced by the agent in period t is:

$$Y_t = C_t + I_t \tag{2.3}$$

The capital stock evolves according to:

$$K_{t+1} = I_t + (1-\delta) K_t \tag{2.4}$$

where δ represents the depreciation rate of capital, $\delta \in (0,1]$, which reflects the depreciation of capital; I_t represents the amount of investment of period t.

Kydland and Prescott (1982), King, Plosser and Rebelo (1988), and Long and Plosser (1983) assume that technological changes over time follow the AR(1) process. Strictly speaking, whether technological changes obey AR(1) still needs to be tested. Our test on the changes in the total factor productivity (TFP) of China shows that AR(1) can well fit the changing process of technology. Therefore, it is assumed that the equation of technological changes is:

$$\ln A_t = (1-\psi_A)\ln\bar{A} + \psi_A \ln A_{t-1} + \varepsilon_{At} \tag{2.5}$$

$$\varepsilon_{At} \sim i.i.d.N(0, \sigma_A^2)$$

where $\bar{A}$ is the steady-state level of the technology shock variable A_t; ψ_A represents the regression coefficient, which represents the relationship between the current period's variables and the previous period's variables, $\psi_A \in (-1,1)$; ε_{At} represents the stochastic disturbance, obeys the white noise process and reflects the impact of exogenous random shocks on technology.

The emergence of institutional changes within a certain period of time is very similar to the emergence of a single technological change. Therefore, it is possible to imitate the equation of technological changes, assuming that the equation of the institutional changes over time is an AR(p) process, although their frequency distributions all follow a Poisson process. In addition, if the institutional changes are assumed to follow a Poisson process and this assumption is introduced into the RBC model, it will bring about the stability and existence of the solution. According to the principle of "based on data," the measurement data of institutional changes in China follow the AR(1) process in the time dimension. Therefore, the equation of institutional changes path is assumed as:

$$\ln W_t = (1-\psi_W)\ln\bar{W} + \psi_W \ln W_{t-1} + \varepsilon_{Wt} \tag{2.6}$$

$$\varepsilon_{Wt} \sim i.i.d.N(0, \sigma_W^2)$$

where $\bar{W}$ represents the steady-state value of technology shocks W_t; ψ_W represents the regression coefficient, which represents the relationship between the current period's variables and the previous period's variables, $\psi_W \in (-1,1)$; ε_{Wt} represents the stochastic disturbance, obeys the white noise process, and reflects the effects of exogenous random shocks on institutional variables.

Based on the assumptions of these equations, the programming problems faced by the representative household are:

$$\underset{(K_t, L_t)}{Max\, E_0} \left\{ \sum_{t=0}^{\infty} \beta^t \left[\frac{C_t^{1-\eta}-1}{1-\eta} + \theta\ln(1-L_t) \right] \right\} \tag{2.7}$$

with subject to:

$$C_t + K_{t+1} - (1-\delta)K_t = A_t W_t^{\gamma} K_t^{\rho} L_t^{1-\rho}$$

$$\ln A_t = (1-\psi_A)\ln\bar{A} + \psi_A \ln A_{t-1} + \varepsilon_{At}, \varepsilon_{At} \sim i.i.d.N(0, \sigma_A^2)$$

$$\ln W_t = (1-\psi_W)\ln \overline{W} + \psi_W \ln W_{t-1} + \varepsilon_{Wt}, \varepsilon_{Wt} \sim i.i.d.N(0, \sigma_W^2)$$

K_0 given

This is the RBC model that includes institutional shocks. This chapter obtains the equilibrium solution of the model by solving the decentralized equilibrium. Through the Lagrange equation that maximizes the utility of the representative household, the corresponding first-order condition can be obtained, and the following conditions can be obtained:

$$\rho \frac{Y_t}{K_t} + (1-\delta) = R_t \tag{2.8}$$

R_t represents the return ratio of real capital of period t. In terms of the economic implications of the equation, R_t includes not only the capital/output ratio corresponding to the current period but also the capital surplus after the capital depreciation in the previous period.

$$\theta L_t = (1-\rho)(1-L_t) Y_t C_t^{-\eta} \tag{2.9}$$

$$C_t^{-\eta} = \beta E_t (R_{t+1}) \tag{2.10}$$

$$\beta E_t \left(\left(\frac{C_t}{C_{t+1}} \right)^{\eta} R_{t+1} \right) = 1 \tag{2.11}$$

The first-order condition represented by equation 2.11 can be called the Euler equation, which means that the ratio of the agent's intertemporal consumption marginal utility is equal to the product of the agent's subjective discount rate times the real rate of return on capital. Equations 2.8–2.11 together constitute a nonlinear differential equation set. The existence of the solution of the group requires the following boundary conditions: First, initial capital input K_0, $K_t \mid_{t=0} = K_0$; second, the transversality condition of the economy: $\lim_{i\to\infty} E_t \beta^i C_{t+i}^{-\eta} K_{t+i+1} = 0$[2]; third, in steady state, the labor supply of the agent is a constant.

Log-linearly process the constraint condition and the first-order condition around the steady state, and obtain:

$$\overline{Y} \cdot y_t = \overline{C} \cdot c_t + \overline{I} \cdot i_t \tag{2.12}$$

$$\overline{K} \cdot k_{t+1} = \overline{I} \cdot i_t + (1-\delta)\overline{K} \cdot k_t \tag{2.13}$$

$$y_t \approx a_t + \gamma w_t + \rho k_t + (1-\rho) l_t \tag{2.14}$$

$$a_t = \psi_A a_{t-1} + \varepsilon_{At} \tag{2.15}$$

$$w_t = \psi_W w_{t-1} + \varepsilon_{Wt} \tag{2.16}$$

$$l_t \approx (1-\overline{L})(y_t - \eta \cdot c_c) \tag{2.17}$$

$$E_t\left[r_{t+1} + \eta(c_t - c_{t+1})\right] = 0 \tag{2.18}$$

$$\overline{R} \cdot r_t = \rho \frac{\overline{Y}}{\overline{K}}(y_t - k_t) \tag{2.19}$$

After the equation is processed by log-linearization, eight equations and eight variables, as shown from equations 2.12–2.19, are obtained, where k_t and c_t are endogenous control variables; a_t and w_t are exogenous state variables; y_t, r_t and l_t are system state variables. The economic system involving the economic programming problem can be approximated represented by these eight stochastic linear equations.

2.4 Quantitative analysis of institutional changes and parameter calibration

The introduction of institutional variables into the RBC model will inevitably involve the problem of how to measure institutional changes. Chinese scholars have done some research on this. Lu and Hu (1993) first proposed the marketization index measurement; Gu (1997) and Jiang and Song (1995) discussed the relative process of marketization of the Chinese economy and its estimation; Fan and others (2001) and Fan and Wang (2003, 2004) studied the relative progress and measurement of marketization in various regions of China. These documents on the marketization degree and marketization index in China have already involved the measurement of the development and innovation of the market economy system of China. Kang et al. (2007) and Li et al. (2008) used the proportion of nonstate industrial value-added to industrial value-added as a measure of the property rights system of China. Kang et al. (2007) pointed out that, after the reform and opening-up, the transformation from the planning system to the market economy system was generally carried along four avenues: the government's functional identity conversion and withdrawal from microeconomic activities, the denationalization of the economy, further economic openness, and the cultivation of product markets. Jin (1998, 2001) constructed an institutional changes index from these four aspects of the economic transition to investigate the institutional changes in China.

This chapter draws on the research by Jin (2001), introduces four institutional variables, then uses gray dynamic relation theory to measure the correlation between these four variables and macroeconomic fluctuations, and finally establishes a representative and comprehensive institutional index based on their respective correlations. The four institutional variables are discussed here.

First, the *non-nationalization rate* (*NNR*) indicator reflects the diversification degree of economic components and the active degree of the non-state-owned economy. The proportion of the gross value of nonstate industrial output (or value added) in the gross industrial output value (or value added) represents the degree of denationalization. The calculation equation is:

$$NNR = \frac{\text{gross value of non} - \text{state industrial output}\left(\text{or value added}\right)}{\text{gross industrial output value}\left(\text{or value added}\right)}$$

Second, the *marketization degree* (*MD*) indicator reflects the breadth and depth of marketization in the process of resource allocation. The calculation formula is:

$$\begin{aligned} MD = {} & \text{marketization index of production factors} * 60\% \\ & + \text{marketization index of economic parameters} * 40\% \end{aligned}$$

The marketization degree of investment is adopted to measure the marketization index of production factors represented by the proportion of free investment (including the use of foreign capital, self-financing investment and other investments) in gross fixed asset investment in the whole society; the marketization of weighted prices is adopted to measure marketization index of economic parameters, obtained by the proportion of the price of freely priced commodities in the prices of all commodities in the whole society, of which the weight is the quantity corresponding to the price. Due to the limited data, the prices of agricultural products are used here as a substitute.

Third, *fiscal revenue share in GDP* (*RS*) is an inverse indicator. The larger the indicator value is, the greater the country's administrative power will be. This indicator reflects the size of the country's share in the distribution of economic benefits. The calculation equation is:[3]

$$RS = \frac{\text{fiscal revenue}\left(\text{tax income is not included}\right)}{\text{GDP}}$$

Fourth, the *index of economic openness* (*ID*) uses the weighted number of the index of the opening of international trade to measure the degree of economic openness. The calculation equation is:

$$ID = \frac{\text{total volume of imports and exports}}{\text{GDP}}$$

Due to the incompleteness of various statistical data, it is impossible to measure the institutional changes of the period from the establishment of PRC to the reform and opening-up. The period discussed in this chapter is defined from 1978 through 2011. This chapter uses the gray dynamic relation theory to measure the influence of various variables, and the corresponding correlation coefficient can be obtained. The value of the relational degree is between 0 and 1. The larger the value, the greater the influence of the indicator on the institutional indicator will be. Observed from the average of these four measurement indicators, *ID* has the greatest impact on the Chinese economy, followed by *MD*, *NNR* and *RS*, in sequence, which conforms to the real Chinese economy. Certainly, this does not rule out that the influence of one of these indicators on the economy in a particular period deviates from its average value.

In order to convert these four measurement indicators into a comprehensive indicator, the weighted average method is used for calculation, and the equation is:

$$\mathrm{W}_t = \frac{NNR_t \times NNRf_t + RS_t + RSf_t + MD_t + MDf_t + ID_t \times IDf_t}{NNRf_t + RSf_t + MDf_t + IDf_t}$$

where NNR_t, RS_t, MD_t and ID_t, respectively, represent the number of non-state-owned rate, fiscal revenue share, marketization degree, and degree of opening-up; NNR_{ft}, RS_{ft}, MD_{ft} and ID_{ft}, respectively, represent the impact factor of each corresponding indicator of period t, so that more comprehensive institutional measurement values can be obtained, namely, the measurement values of institutional changes from 1978 through 2011. In the process of institutional changes in China, key institutional changes often occur at certain times, but their impact on economic growth lasts a long time. Therefore, when the four measurement indicators are weighted into a comprehensive indicator, the characteristics of its volatility will be weakened. With the H-P filter, detrending of data is done to obtain periodic fluctuation data.

The institutional changes in China have shown a wave-like uplift trend. The accumulation of institutional changes has led to an increase in indicator data, but volatility is also evident in the process of growth. This chapter mainly focuses on whether this volatility can have an impact on the economy.

It is necessary to calibrate the parameters of the eight stochastic linear equations as 2.12 through 2.19, use the iteration method to solve the numerical solutions of the equations, and finally test the accuracy of the model based on these numerical solutions.

2.4.1 Estimation of output elasticity, technological and institutional shocks

Supposing the production function is a Cobb–Douglas form with constant returns to scale and replacing it with $Z_t = A_t W_t^{\gamma}$ to obtain the following production function:

$$Y_t = e^{Z_t + \mu . T} K_t^{\rho} L_t^{1-\rho} \tag{2.20}$$

where T represents the time variable trend, $T = 1,2, \dots$, and μ is the parameter value of the variable T. In order to eliminate the linear dependence between the regression variables, the production function is transformed by the intensive form of output and capital and log-linearly processed. Real output, capital stock and labor data are calculated at constant prices in 1978. In the selection of capital stock, the calculation method of Lei (2009) is used here, and capital stock in period t is calculated as:

$$K_t = K_{t-1} + RGI_t \times \frac{NI_t}{GI_t} \tag{2.21}$$

where RGI_t represents the real gross investment; NI_t and GI_t represent the net investment and the gross investment calculated at the current year's price; based on the obtained data, the estimated production function is as follows:

$$\ln\frac{Y}{L} = 3.028 + 0.5116\ln\frac{K}{L} + 0.0305T \tag{2.22}$$

Both the parameters and the model pass the test. The measurement result shows that the output elasticity of capital ρ is 0.5116 and that the output elasticity of labor is 0.4884.

According to equation 2.22, the time series of the Solow residual can be further obtained:

$$\ln Z = \ln\frac{Y}{L} - 0.5116\ln\frac{K}{L} - 0.0305T \tag{2.23}$$

According to the established institutional shock data series from 1978 to 2011, ψ_W, the first order autoregressive coefficient of technology shocks, is 0.9228 according to equation 2.6, and its standard deviation σ_W is 5.5123%.

The influence coefficient of institutional variables γ will be obtained by data calibration. It is first of all set as a specific value and is finally determined through subsequent data simulation. It is calibrated as 0.248.

Use the predetermined $Z_t = A_t W_t^{\gamma}$ to get:

$$\ln A = \ln Z - \gamma \cdot \ln W \tag{2.24}$$

With the time series data of technology shocks that can be obtained from the preceding equation and with the autoregressive equation 2.5, the first-order autoregressive coefficient of technology shocks ψ_A can be calculated as 0.7608, and its standard deviation σ_A is 2.8176%.

2.4.2 *Estimation of values of other parameters*

On the basis of the constant consumer price index in 1978, the average growth rate of the consumer price index of China from 1978 to 2011 was 5.39%. Therefore, the discount factor β of the model can be set as 94.70%. In steady state, based on $\beta = \frac{1}{\bar{R}}, \bar{R} = 1.056$, According to Huang (2005), when the labor supply is normalized as 1, in the steady state, labor supply $\bar{L} = 0.542$; according to the research on the consumption and savings behavior of Chinese residents by Chen et al. (2005), the constant relative risk aversion coefficient (CRRA) $\eta =$ 0.77; the annual depreciation rate of foreign countries is 0.1, and while analyzing Chinese economic fluctuations, Chinese scholar Chen (2006) set the depreciation rate as 0.1, and Lei (2009) selects the depreciation rate as 0.09732. Based on the existing research, the annual depreciation rate δ is set as 0.09732.

In summary, the calibrated values of parameters are shown in Table 2.1.

2.5 Empirical results

According to the calibrated parameters of this model, the numerical iteration method can be used to obtain a numerical equation set, and then the MATLAB program can be used to solve the standard deviation of variables

Table 2.1 Values of Model Parameters

ρ	η	δ	β	ψ_A	σ_A
0.8951	0.77	0.09732	94.70%	0.7608	2.82%
Ψ_W	σ_W	$\bar{A}$	$\bar{W}$	$\bar{R}$	$\bar{L}$
0.9228	5.51%	1	1	1.056	0.542

Base Data	*Variable L, I, C* $\bar{L} = 0.542$ $\bar{R} = 1.056$	*Variable L, I, C* $\bar{L} = 0.562$ $\bar{R} = 1.166$	*Variable L, I, C* $\bar{L} = 0.542$ $\bar{R} = 1.166$	*Variable L, I, C* $\bar{L} = 0.542$ $\bar{R} = 1.156$
Capital	15.45%	42.23%	43.76%	45.38%
Consumption	21.03%	35.46%	37.12%	38.28%
Output	94.44%	68.30%	71.14%	75.25%
Labor	23.46%	23.41%	26.32%	27.15%
Investment	66.07%	106.46%	114.50%	114.02%

Table 2.2 Cyclical Characteristics of Simulated Economy

Parameters	*Real Economy*		*Simulated Economy*		*Kydland–Prescott Radio*
	Standard Deviation (%)	*Corresponding Correlation Coefficient with Output*	*Standard Deviation (%)*	*Corresponding Correlation Coefficient with Output*	
Capital	4.0908	0.2404	0.6321	0.685	15.45%
Consumption	3.4318	0.6412	0.7217	0.8465	21.03%
Output	2.6546	1	2.507	1	94.44%
Labor	4.0178	0.1179	0.9426	0.9896	23.46%
Investment	9.8366	0.6614	6.499	0.9924	66.07%

under the equilibrium condition and the correlation coefficients between these variables. See Tables 2.2 and 2.4.[4] Comparing with the actual data of macroeconomic variables, it can be judged whether the RBC model with institutional shocks can well simulate the real economy.

In Table 2.2, the real and simulated economic data of the macroeconomic variables, including capital, consumption, output, labor and investment, are all obtained by using the H-P filter to detrend. The Kydland–Prescott ratio is obtained with the standard deviation of the variables under the model economy divided by the standard deviation of the corresponding variables under the real economy, reflecting the effectiveness of the model. In the case when the Kydland–Prescott ratio is less than 100%, the larger the ratio, the better the fit of the model to the economic reality.

From this simulation of the five variables, investment fluctuations are quite drastic, reaching 6.4990%, which are far greater than the output fluctuations of 2.5070%, and labor fluctuations are 0.9426%, which are much smaller than investment fluctuations and output fluctuations, followed by consumption fluctuations and capital fluctuations in sequence.

Judging from the situation reflected by the Kydland–Prescott ratio, the output ratio is the largest at 94.44%, indicating that the model can explain 94.44% of cyclical fluctuations in output. Similarly, the model can explain 66.07% of cyclical fluctuations in investment, 23.46% in labor, 21.03% in consumption and 15.45% in capital. The reasons why the model can provide a better explanation for output and investment fluctuations are that, on the one hand, the model assumes that consumption is the sum of household consumption, government consumption and net exports, while consumption in the real economy is only household consumption, which leads to a weak explanation for consumption fluctuations; on the other hand, it shows that, when considering the impact of institutional factors, investment has a greater impact on the economy. The investment in China is greatly affected by the government's macroeconomic policies; that is, the government has had a great impact on Chinese economic growth and fluctuations through mandatory institutional changes.

Table 2.3 Different Kydland–Prescott Ratio: Sensitivity Analysis of Changing Variables and Parameter Measurement Method

	Base Data $\overline{L}=0.542$ $\overline{R}=1.056$	*Variable L, I, C* $\overline{L}=0.562$ $\overline{R}=1.166$	*Variable L, I, C* $\overline{L}=0.542$ $\overline{R}=1.166$	*Variable L, I, C* $\overline{L}=0.542$ $\overline{R}=1.156$
Capital	15.45%	42.3292%	43.7632%	45.3816%
Consumption	21.03%	35.4620%	37.1164%	38.2757%
Output	94.44%	68.2996%	73.1444%	75.2465%
Labor	23.46%	23.4077%	26.3237%	27.1479%
Investment	66.07%	106.4579%	114.5040%	114.0161%

It is noticed that the number of the Kydland–Prescott ratio is related to the measurement method of variables and parameters. For this reason, a sensitivity analysis of the Kydland–Prescott ratio under the condition of changing the measurement method of variables and parameters is made, as shown in Table 2.3. The "variable labor, investment, and consumption" in Table 2.3 means the following: The measurement of consumption has changed from the previous household consumption expenditure to the final consumption expenditure; the measurement of investment has changed from the previous gross fixed capital formation to gross investment calculated based on Lei's (2009) capital calculation method; the labor measurement has been changed from the previous total number of employees to the proportion of the number of employees to the total number of employees. The reasons for changing the variables and parameters include the following: First, the final consumption expenditure is widely used by Chinese scholars to measure consumption; second, the change of investment data is made mainly to be consistent with the calculation method of capital stock K, that is, to calculate both capital and investment according to the calculation method of Lei (2009); third, the change in labor is mainly because labor has been normalized as 1, so the employment ratio is used instead of the number of employees to be measured; fourth, according to the calculation equation of return on invested capital, $\overline{R}=\left(\sum_{t=1978}^{2011}\frac{(1-\alpha)Y_t}{K_t}\right)/34+1-\delta$, the estimated value of $\overline{R}$ is about 1.166; fifth, $\overline{L}$ is set as 0.562 mainly because the employment rate in China has basically stabilized at 0.562 in recent years; finally, regarding the value of $\overline{R}$, Chinese scholars have not yet reached a consensus. The value range is basically in the interval of 1.06–1.2. This chapter has tried all the values of this interval and found that $\overline{R}$ set as 1.156 has a higher degree of fit.

From the sensitivity analysis in Table 2.3, it can be seen that, by changing the variables and parameter measurement methods, the Kydland–Prescott ratio will change to varying degrees and that the degree of fitting to capital and consumption will be significantly improved from 15%, 21%, respectively, to 45%, 38%. The fitting of investment is also closer to 1, increased from 66%

Table 2.4 Relation Between Real Economy Variables and Output

Variable/Lags	*−4*	*−3*	*−2*	*−1*	*0*	*1*	*2*	*3*	*4*
Capital	−0.53	−0.84	−0.79	−0.24	0.2	0.35	0.41	0.2	0.1
Consumption	−0.44	−0.13	0.32	0.54	0.63	0.546	0.19	−0.13	−0.23
Output	−0.69	0.24	0.59	0.71	1	0.68	0.22	−0.23	−0.39
Labor	−0.12	−0.13	−0.38	0.64	0.78	−0.01	−0.37	−0.36	−0.26
Investment	−0.65	−0.06	0.14	0.52	0.67	0.51	−0.07	−0.24	−0.29

Table 2.5 Relation Between Simulated Economy Variables and Output

Variable/Lags	*−4*	*−3*	*−2*	*−1*	*0*	*1*	*2*	*3*	*4*
Capital	−0.07	−0.28	−0.51	−0.34	0.69	0.58	0.16	−0.11	−0.2
Consumption	−0.09	−0.28	−0.47	−0.23	0.85	0.44	0.01	−0.16	−0.18
Output	−0.12	−0.24	−0.31	0.05	1	0.05	−0.31	−0.24	−0.12
Labor	−0.12	−0.22	−0.25	0.13	0.99	−0.05	−0.38	−0.25	−0.1
Investment	−0.12	−0.2	0.21	0.16	0.98	−0.11	−0.47	−0.25	−0.09

to 106% and 114%, which conform to the stylized facts of large investment fluctuations in China, and accuracy is improved.

Comparing the correlation coefficients of capital, consumption, labor, investment and output in the real economy and the model economy over the same period, it can be found that the correlation coefficients corresponding to each variable are in the same order and that each macroeconomic variable and output are positively correlated, which also shows that the fluctuations of fixed asset investment, consumption and output are all highly consistent, which is very consistent with the relationships among variables in the real economy.

From Tables 2.4 and 2.5, we can also compare the cyclical relationship between output and model economic variables or real economic variables. Consumption, investment, capital, labor, and output are all pro-cyclical. The autocorrelation relation between the different lag phases of each variable can show that the model economy is very consistent with the real economy and that the model has good predictability.

Through the data simulated by the model parameters, the impulse response figures of the different variable fluctuations can be established. Figure 2.3 shows the impulse response of institutional fluctuations, and Figure 2.4 shows the impulse response of technological fluctuations.

Theoretically, technology and institutions are both exogenous shocks, but as seen from Figures 2.3 and 2.4, the impulse responses of the two are quite different. First of all, the initial impact of technology shocks is greater than that of institutional shocks. This is reasonable because technology can quickly transform into real productivity, which will have a significant impact on the economy, ultimately reflected in output fluctuations, and the effect of

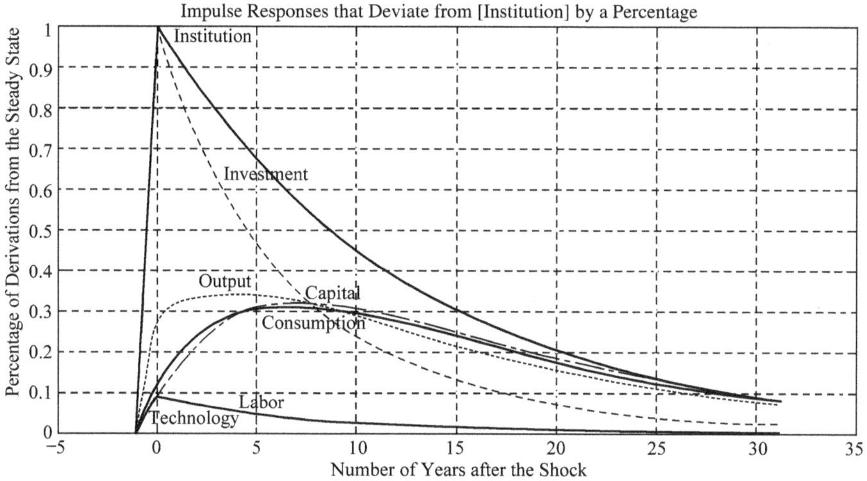

Figure 2.3 Impulse Responses to Institutional Shocks.

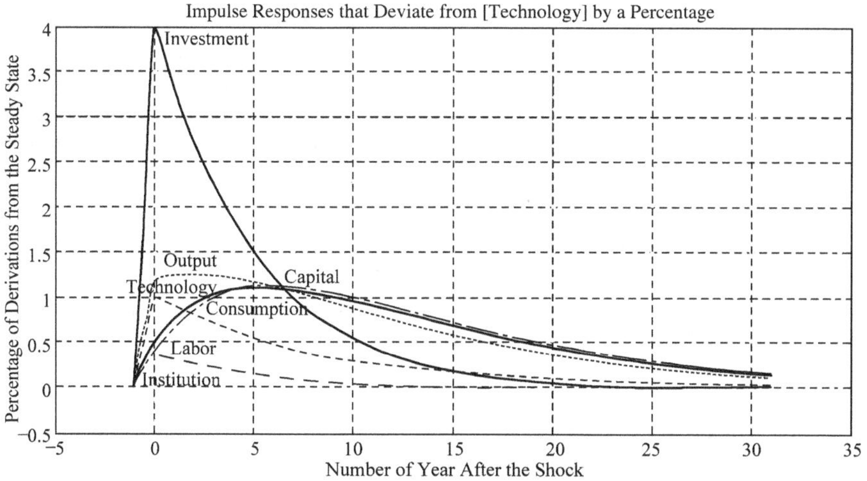

Figure 2.4 Impulse Responses to Technology Shocks.

fluctuations are thus obvious. Nevertheless, institutional shocks need to be transmitted in the economic system according to a certain mechanism; this transmission process is relatively slow, and the effects on output fluctuations are not as obvious as those of technology shocks. Second, from the perspective of the duration of the random shocks on output, institutional shocks can last for nearly 30 years, but technology shocks last for only ten years. This is also very consistent with theoretical expectations. Finally, from the perspective of the decline process of the shocks, the institutional shocks present a steady decline, but technology shocks decline more rapidly.

2.6 Conclusion

Since the establishment of the People's Republic of China in 1949, the Chinese economy has developed tortuously. There have been many large fluctuations in the process of economic development. These fluctuations happened during important institutional arrangements as the second five-year plan (1958–1962), great cultural revolution (1966–1976), reform and opening-up and Deng Xiaoping's talks in the South in 1992. Therefore, institutional changes are the keys to explaining Chinese economic fluctuations. This chapter built an RBC model with institutional factors based on DSGE modeling, incorporated the institutional factors into the theoretical framework of economic growth and economic fluctuations, and adopted the theory of gray dynamic relation to measure institutional shocks. On the basis of quantification, a calibration method is used to solve the impact factors of institutions, and finally an economic cycle model containing institutional shocks is built, and the economic data is simulated by computer technology. Comparing the simulated economic data and the real economic data can test the accuracy and steadiness of the model.

The results show that the RBC model involving institutional factors has a good degree of fit to the real economy and can well explain the output fluctuations and investment fluctuations of China. The model can explain 94.44% of cyclical fluctuations in output, 66.07% in investment, 23.46% in labor, 21.03% in consumption and 15.45% in capital.

Through the numerical simulation of the dynamic economic system, simulated economic data can be generated. By simulating the cyclical relationship between various variables of the economic data and the output and the relationship between the various variables in real economy, it can be seen that the simulated economy and real economy seems to be highly consistent, of which consumption, investment, capital, labor and output are all pro-cyclical. This illustrates the accuracy of the model and the role of institutional factors in explaining economic fluctuations.

The impulse response analysis of the exogenous random shocks of the model shows that the initial impact of institutional shocks is less than that of technology shocks but that the former can last a long time, about 30 years, and then present a steady decline; while the decline of technology shocks is relatively fast, about ten years. This illustrates it is necessary to introduce institutional factors in the model.

The RBC model with institutional factors that was built in this chapter provides a reference for macroeconomic policymaking to a certain extent. That is to say, policymaking must take into account the long-term impact of such policies and minimize the adverse economic fluctuations caused by institutional changes. In order to promote long-term and stable economic growth, institutional changes should be brought forth in a timely manner.

This chapter assumes that institutional changes are based on the fact that China is confronted with a transitional period in its economic development. In such a period, either the institutional environment or various specific institutional arrangements keep on changing, just like technological changes. Although institutional changes, viewed individually, are like leaps now and again, the continuous results of frequent changes in multiple institutional arrangements and their sustained effects on economic growth can be regarded as continuous. The assumed institutional changes path represented by equation 2.6 imitating the technological changes equation in the classic writings is also a temporary and immature assumption. If possible, in future research, this assumption should be changed to make the model perform perfectly.

Notes

1 Full text of Jiang Zemin's Report at the 16th Party Congress on November 8, 2002: http://language.chinadaily.com.cn/2013-11/26/content_17132209_7.htm
2 If the discounted marginal utility of the infinite bound is greater than 0, that is, $\lim_{i\to\infty} E_t\beta^i C_{t+i}^{-\eta} > 0$, the agent has the possibility of improving personal utility at the end of life. The optimization behavior of an economically rational man must be to abandon capital accumulation and use it for consumption, thus making $\lim_{i\to\infty} K_{t+i+1} = 0$. This transversality condition means that the agent's utility level in the infinite bound cannot be further improved.
3 In the process of numerical processing, it is necessary to obtain the positive index value through numerical conversion.
4 The MATLAB program is rewritten on the basis of the program provided by Uhlig (1997).

Bibliography

Bromley, Daniel W. *Economic Interests and Institutions: The Conceptual Foundations of Public Policy*. Translated by Chen Yu, Guo Yufeng and Wang Chun. Shanghai: Shanghai People's Press, 1996.

Bu, Yongxiang, and Jin Yan 卜永祥, 靳炎. "Real Business Cycle in China: A Basic Model and Its Extension" 中国实际经济周期: 一个基本解释和理论扩展. *The Journal of World Economy* no.4 (2002): 3–11+80.

Chen, Kunting, and Gong Liutang 陈昆亭, 龚六堂. "Numerical Simulation for the Chinese Economy in a Sticky-Price Model" 粘滞价格模型以及对中国经济的数值模拟—对基本RBC模型的改进. *The Journal of Quantitative & Technical Economics* no. 8 (2006): 106–117.

Chen, Xuebin, Yang Ling and Fang Song 陈学彬, 杨凌, 方松. "The Micro-Foundation Studies of Monetary Policy Effects: An Empirical Analysis of Residents' Consumption–Savings Behaviors" 货币财政政策的微观基础研究——我国

居民消费储蓄行为的实证分析. *Fudan Journal* (Social Sciences Edition) no. 1 (2005): 42–54.
Chow, Gregory C., and Kui-Wai Li. “China Economic Growth: 1952–2010.” *Economic Development and Culture Change* no. 1 (2002): 247–256.
Coase, Ronald, Armen Alchian, and Douglass C. North. *Property Rights and Institutional Changes*. Translated by Liu Shouying. Shanghai: Shanghai Joint Publishing Company, 1994.
Cooley, Thomas F., and Gary D. Hansen. “Inflation Tax in a Real Business Cycle Model.” *American Economic Review* no. 7 (1989): 733–748.
Fan, Gang 樊纲. “Public Choice and Reform Process” 公共选择与改革过程. *Comparative Economic & Social Systems* no. 1 (1993): 17–24.
Fan, Gang, and Wang Xiaolu 樊纲, 王小鲁. “Marketization Index for Various Provinces of China” 中国各地区市场化相对进程报告. *Economic Research*, no. 3 (2003): 9–18+89.
Fan, Gang, and Wang Xiaolu 樊纲, 王小鲁. *Marketization Index for Various Provinces of China in 2004* 中国市场化指数——各地区市场化相对进程 2004 年度报告. Beijing: Economic Science Press, 2004.
Fan, Gang, Wang Xiaolu and Zhang Liwen 樊纲, 王小鲁, 张立文. “Marketization Index for Various Provinces of China in 2000” 中国各地区市场化进程2000年报告. *Journal of Chinese Academy of Governance* no. 3 (2001): 17–27.
Gong, Gang, 龚刚 and Willi Semmler. “Real Business Cycles with Labor Market Disequilibrium” 非均衡劳动力市场的真实经济周期模型. *China Economic Quarterly* no. 4 (2003): 591–604.
Gu, Haibing 顾海兵. “The Latest Estimates and Forecasts of the Marketization of the Chinese Economy” 中国经济市场化程度的最新估计与预测. *Management World* no. 2 (1997): 52–55.
Guseh, James S. “Government Size and Economic Growth in Developing Countries: A Political-Economy Framework.” *Journal of Macroeconomics* no. 1 (1997): 175–192.
Huang, Zelin 黄赜琳. “A Study on Business Cycle and the Effects of Fiscal Policy in China: An Empirical Study on a RBC Model with Three Sections” 中国经济周期特征与财政政策效应—一个基于三部门RBC 模型的实证分析. *Economic Research Journal* no. 6 (2005): 27–39.
Jiang, Xiaowei, and Song Hongxu 江晓薇, 宋红旭. “Exploration the Degree of the Market Economy of China” 中国市场经济度的探索. *Management World* no. 6 (1995): 33–37.
Jin, Yuguo 金玉国. “The Macro-Institutional Analysis on Chinese Economic Growth from 1984 to 1995” 1984—1995年中国经济增长的宏观制度解析. *Statistical Research* no. 5 (1998): 13–15.
———. “The Contribution of Macroeconomic Institutional Changes to Chinese Economic Growth in the Transition Period” 宏观经济制度变迁对转型时期中国经济增长的贡献. *Finance and Economics* no. 2 (2001):24–28.
Kang, Jijun, Zhang Zongyi, and Fu Yunying 康继军, 张宗益, 傅蕴英. “Chinese Economic Transition and Growth” 中国经济转型与增长. *Management World* no. 1 (2007): 7–17+171.
King, Robert G., Charles I. Plosser, and Sergio T. Rebelo. “Production, Growth and Business Cycles: I. The Basic Neoclassical Model.” *Journal of Monetary Economics* no. 2–3 (1988): 195–232.
Kydland, Finn E., and Edward F. Prescott. “Time to Build and Aggregate Fluctuations.” *Econometrica* no. 6 (1982): 1345–1370.

Lei, Hui 雷辉. "Research on the Capital Deposit Measurement and Investment Efficiency of China" 我国资本存量测算及投资效率的研究. *Economist* no. 6 (2009): 75–83.

Li, Fuqiang, Dong Zhiqing, and Wang Linhui 李富强, 董直庆, 王林辉. "An Empirical Study of the Institution Rule, Factor Contribution and Determinants of Chinese Economic Growth" 制度主导、要素贡献和我国经济增长动力的分类检验. *Economic Research* no. 4 ((2008): 53–65.

Lin, Yifu林毅夫. "An Economic Theory of Institutional Change: Inducible and Coercive Change" 一个制度变迁的经济学理论: 诱致性和强制性变迁. *Cato Magazine* September 1989.

Long, John B., and Charles I. Plosser. "Real Business Cycles." *Journal of Political Economy* no. 1 (1983): 39–69.

Lu, Zhongyuan, and Hu Angang 卢中原, 胡鞍钢. "The Impact of Market-oriented Reform on the Economic Operation of China" 市场化改革对我国经济运行的影响. *Economic Research* no. 6 (1993): 49–55.

Lucas, Robert E., Jr. "Interest Rates and Currency Prices in a Two-Country World." *Journal of Monetary Economics* no. 3 (1982): 335–359.

North, Douglass C. "Sources of Productivity Change in Ocean Shipping, 1600–1850." *The Journal of Political Economy* no. 5 (1968): 953–970.

———. *Structure and Change in Economic History*. Translated by Chen Yu and Luo Huaping. Shanghai: Joint Publishing Company, 1991.

———. *Institutions, Institutional Change and Economic Performance*. Translated by Liu Shouying. Shanghai: Joint Publishing Company, 1994.

———. *Understanding the Process of Economic Change*. Translated by Zhong Zhengsheng and Xing Hua. Beijing: Renmin University of China Press, 2008.

Ostrom, Vincent, David Feeny, and Hartmut Picht, eds. *Rethinking Institutional Analysis and Development: Issues, Alternatives & Choices*. Translated by Wang Cheng. Beijing: Commercial Press, 1992.

Svensson, Lars E. O. "Money and Asset Prices in a Cash-in Advance Economy." *Journal of Political Economy* no. 5 (1985): 919–944.

Wang, Dingding 汪丁丁. "General Theory of Institutional Innovation" 制度创新的一般理论. *Economic Research* no. 5 (1992): 69–80.

Yang, Ruilong 杨瑞龙. "The Three-Stage Theory of the Transformation of the Institutional Change Modes of China" 我国制度变迁方式转换的三阶段论-兼论地方政府的制度创新行为. *Economic Research* no. 1 (1998): 3–10.

Zhang, Jun 张军. "Capital Formation, Industrialization and Economic Growth: Understanding the Economic Reform in China" 资本形成、工业化与经济增长：中国的转轨特征. *Economic Research* no. 6 (2002): 3–13+93.

Zhang, Jun, and Jiang Linqi. "Changes in China's Rural Public Goods Supply System" 中国农村公共品供给制度的变迁：理论视角. *World Economic Papers* no. 5 (1997): 3–14.

Zhang, Shuguang 张曙光. "Analyzing Institutional Equilibrium and Institutional Reform" 论制度均衡与制度变革. *Economic Research* no. 6 (1992): 30–36.

Zhou, Yean 周业安. "The Institutional Changes of China in an Evolutionary Perspective" 中国制度变迁的演进论解释. *Economic Research* no.5 (2000): 3–11+ 79.

3 Labor market distortions, efficiency difference and the urban–rural income gap

Since the institutionalization of the reform and opening-up policy, the income gap between urban and rural areas in China has gradually widened. Firstly, a "pure" dynamic growth model is built, and it does well in simulating the stylized facts that during the process of reform and opening-up, the labor transfers from the agricultural sector to the nonagricultural sector, that the proportion of agricultural sector decreased gradually and that of nonagricultural sector increased gradually out of the whole GDP. However, the numerical simulation results do not match with the typical facts of the urban–rural income gap. Then we resort to a calibrated dynamic general equilibrium model, adding the distortions of the labor market and the efficiency difference of the two sectors. The results can be modified to explain the kinds of economic institutions, economic policies and economic variables under this general framework. With the methods of parameter calibration and numerical simulation, it is found that the model can be consistent with the stylized facts of Chinese economic development.

3.1 The urban–rural gap

Achieving sustainable and rapid economic development in the balance between fairness and efficiency is the main goal of the economic policies of the vast number of developing countries. One of the prominent unfair phenomena in Chinese economic life is the continuous widening of the urban–rural income gap, although this unfairness acts as a result, not entirely as an opportunity.[1] The per capita net income of the agricultural sector of China increased from CNY 113.6 in 1978 to CNY 17 131.5 in 2020, while the disposable income of urban residents rose from CNY 343.4 in 1978 to CNY 43 833.8 in 2020. The gap between the two also widened from the original CNY 229.7 to CNY 8172.5.[2] The residents' Gini coefficient rose from 0.298 in 1978 to 0.468 in 2020. The internationally recognized Gini coefficient cordon is 0.35–0.4. The Gini coefficient between urban and rural China reached 0.401 in 1987 and began to exceed the internationally recognized cordon. Except for a small decrease in the early 1980s and in the mid- and later 1990s, the Gini coefficient of the other years increased at a relatively obvious rate

DOI: 10.4324/9781003305651-3

(Wang Wenjun, 2007). The difficulty in increasing farmers' income and the widening of the urban–rural income gap has seriously affected the quality of Chinese economic growth and social harmony. A large number of poor people in China are concentrated in rural areas. Therefore, studying the relationship between the urban–rural income gap and related economic policies is of great significance to narrowing the gap and reducing the poverty population in China.

Chinese scholars are very concerned about the phenomenon of urban–rural income gap and have carried out a great deal of research. Cai (1998), Lu and Chen (2004), Yao (2005), Lu (2006), Cheng, and Li (2007), Yin et al. (2007) and others used econometric methods to explore the causes of the widening urban—rural income gap in China. They generally believe that urbanization and city-biased policies are the reasons. Cai and Yang (2000), Cai et al. (2003), Liu et al. (2004) and Lin (2004) used the tools and methods of institutional analysis to analyze the impact of institutional factors such as the household registration system and the welfare system on the formation of labor market distortions and the resulting urban—rural income gap. For them, labor mobility has not narrowed the income gap for three main reasons: First, there are many institutional obstacles, and the flow cost is very high, so that part of the urban wages of rural labor in excess of rural income is offset by the flow cost; second, the wage income of the rural labor employed in urban areas has been fixed at a relatively low level for a long time; third, rural labor cannot enter the planning control departments with high wages and high benefits. Guo (2005) and Wei and Fu (2004) tried to use the endogenous economic growth model and labor transfer model to study the relationship between economic factors such as human capital, fertility rate and population mobility and the urban—rural income gap in China. Unfortunately, a mathematical model of the urban—rural income gap involving the factors affecting the formation and mechanism of the urban—rural gap has not yet been built.

Recently, the representative literature on income disparity research is mainly shown as the following. Barro and Sala-i-Martin (1992) studied the income disparity of the 48 neighboring states in the United States. They argued that if the growth rate of the economy with a low initial economic development level surpassed that with a high initial level of economic development, different economies would reach convergence. But after studying 98 countries around the world, the conclusion was that only under the same conditions—that the enrollment rate and the proportion of government expenditure in the gross national product were the same—would there be an economic convergence.

Parente and Prescott (1994) believed that the country-to-country differences in technology adoption in time and space are responsible for the huge differences in the income gap worldwide. They believed that the technological progress of a country depended on the world knowledge available to it and the amount of the obstacles to the country's adoption of technology.

Mapping the US political system, the degree of corruption and other factors to such obstacles and aligning the model economy to be consistent with the reality of stable growth in the United States, they explained the situation that Japan surpassed the United States after World War II and that Japan's per capita GDP developed by leaps and bounds. Parente and Prescott (1999a, 1999b) improved these ideas and found that the behavior that hindered the effective use of advanced technology to increase production stemmed from monopoly. The supplier that provided the technology monopolized the technology by virtue of its own technological advantages. There was a similar monopoly relationship between developed and developing countries in the world. Developed countries had advanced technology, while developing countries were lacking in technology. The vast majority of the population in developing countries was concentrated in the agricultural sector. Therefore, the need for the agricultural sector to increase income through improved technology will inevitably involve the stock of available technologies and obstacles. Based on this, they explained why there are widespread income differences between developed and developing countries worldwide. In the numerical experiments of their model, it was found that if such obstacles were eliminated, the output of backward countries would triple without increasing input. Subsequently, Parente and Prescott (1999b, 2004) published a general theoretical framework for studying income disparity among countries. In such a framework, through simple numerical experiments, it was found that factors such as savings rate, human capital and technological progress alone are not sufficient to explain the huge income gap between countries. It was found that the institutional and political factors that hindered the use of technology and the use of human capital are the main reasons for the huge income disparity. By introducing these institutional and political factors into the model and calibrating the stylized facts of long-term growth in the United States, it was found that such a theory can well explain the huge income gap between countries.

Chari et al. (1997) used Neoclassical Growth Theory to analyze the income gap between countries around the world and argued that the distortions of capital investment affected the rate of return of capital in each country, which in turn affected investment decisions. Such distortions could extend to corruption, ineffective bureaucracy and resistance to the adoption of new technologies. They used the price dispersion between investment goods and consumer goods to measure investment distortions and introduced an exogenous random shock representing "good government" and "bad government," explaining the income disparity experienced by 126 countries around the world in the course of 26 years of economic development. Gollin and Rogerson et al. (2002, 2007) studied the technological progress in the agricultural sector. It was found that due to the relatively fixed demand for agricultural products in the whole society, surplus labor in the agricultural sector would flow to the nonagricultural sector for the agricultural sector's "push" as the economy developed. Such mobility led to a decrease in the number of laborers in the agricultural sector and a decline in income, while the nonagricultural sector would continue to rise in income due to the increase in social demand and the expansion of employment. Through applying the calibration model to the economic development of the United Kingdom for more than 200 years, it was found that such a theory could not only fit the trajectory of British economic development well but also explain the income gap between urban and rural areas within the framework of economic growth as a useful tool. Restuccia (2002) and Restuccia and Rogerson (2003) also applied the Neoclassical Growth Theory to explain the income gap between countries. They believed that capital accumulation in two sectors confronted different obstacles and that the industrial sector was much more impacted by the obstacles. The income gap of different groups in economic development stemmed from the differences of their industries, and the differences of industries came from the differences in the obstacles to capital accumulation and the resulting differences in total factor productivity (TFP).

As previously shown, Chinese literature differs from that of the international one in two aspects. First, international scholars, mainly on the basis of the Solow model, introduce consumer behavior and various distortion factors of economic development by expanding the production sector and building the neoclassical general equilibrium model to explain the income gap between countries or between different sectors of a country. Chinese scholars mainly use econometric models or quote classical theoretical conclusions and lack generalized research on the relationship between institutional barriers, market distortions respectively and the formation of income disparity. Second, international scholars introduce the behaviors of consumers and production sectors, so that the macroanalysis of income disparity has a microfoundation support, and at the same time the neoclassical production function is used as the basis for its theory. The neoclassical mode of production conforms to the typical facts of economic development, which is not only the cornerstone of neoclassical theory but also the foothold of economic development theory. Chinese scholars have not yet considered the microfoundation issues of macroanalysis.

Based on the Neoclassical Growth model, this chapter attempts to abstract the Chinese economy into a general equilibrium system including three economies including the consumption sector, the urban modern industrial sector and the traditional rural sector. Consumers pursue the maximization of utility. The modern industrial sector adopts modern production technologies to produce means of production, while the traditional agricultural sector adopts relatively inferior technologies to produce means of livelihood. The calibration methods and numerical simulation techniques are adopted to make the model simulate the operation of Chinese real economy as accurately as possible and explore the causes of the urban–-rural income gap in China. This chapter then attempts to provide feasible policy recommendations for narrowing the urban–-rural gap. The literature on the analysis of the urban–-rural gap in China has not yet used the general equilibrium, calibration and numerical simulation methods. Therefore, methodologically, this chapter presents a new approach.

3.2 A pure dynamic growth model[3]

3.2.1 Model building

Assuming that the instantaneous utility function of the representative household is:

$$U(c_t,a_t)=\begin{cases} a_t, & if\ \ a_t<\bar{a} \\ \ln(c_t)+\bar{a}, & if\ \ a_t\geq\bar{a} \end{cases} \tag{3.1}$$

The utility function divides household consumption into agricultural products a_t and nonagricultural products c_t. The final products produced by the agricultural sector a_t are mainly used to meet the basic living needs of residents. When the production of the agricultural sector cannot meet people's basic living needs $\bar{a}$, the resources of the entire economy will be concentrated in the agricultural sector. Once the production of the agricultural sector is able to meet people's basic living needs, the means of production will flow out from the agricultural sector to the nonagricultural sector to meet people's needs beyond the basic living needs. In an economy that develops infinitely, the aggregate utility function of the household is:

$$\sum_{t=0}^{\infty} N_t\beta^t U(c_t,a_t) \tag{3.2}$$

where β represents the subjective discount factor of households, and N_t represents the number of households in the economy in period t, assuming the same in each period. It is also assumed that the growth rate of the family is the exogenous given growth rate η.

This chapter intends to investigate the urban–-rural income gap that has emerged in the process of Chinese economic development. According to the typical facts, the main source of rural income is in the agricultural sector, and the final products of the agricultural sector are intended to meet people's basic needs, while the main source of urban income is in the urban sector, mainly the secondary and tertiary industries. Therefore, in the model, the secondary and tertiary industries are merged into nonagricultural industries. The final products of the nonagricultural sector are to meet people's needs for investment, consumption and service. For a long time, the agricultural sector maintained its traditional production methods. The rent of rural land is much lower than that of urban land. Therefore, in the model, it is assumed that the agricultural sector only uses labor as a factor, while the nonagricultural sector's factors of production include labor and capital. Capital here is defined as physical capital. Capital in a broad sense, including human capital, technological capital and knowledge capital, is all included in the total factor productivity. This, on the one hand, can reduce the disputes arising from different calibers in the estimation of the model. On the other hand, it also emphasizes the income gap caused by the difference in exogenous technological progress between the agricultural and the nonagricultural sectors.

The agricultural products produced by the agricultural sector are not only used to meet their own basic living needs, but also sold to the nonagricultural sector to meet the living needs of the nonagricultural sector. The income of the agricultural sector only comes from the wage income of agricultural employment. The income of nonagricultural employment comes not only from the wage income of the employment but also from the interest income of the capital element.

The agricultural sector uses labor N and land L to produce agricultural products. The production function is:

$$Y_{a,t} = E_a\left(1+\gamma_a\right)^t N_{a,t}^{\mu} L_t^{\phi}, \qquad 0<\mu,\phi<1 \tag{3.3}$$

where γ_a represents the technical progress index of the agricultural sector, which is an exogenous variable and is the same in each period. E_a represents other factors affecting the technological progress of the rural sector except for fixed technological progress, which depends on government policies, weather, land fertility etc. Assume that the amount of land is given in each period and is the same. $0<\mu<1$ shows labor's diminishing marginal returns. Products from the rural sector are only used for basic household consumption, namely:

$$a_t N_t \le Y_{a,t} \tag{3.4}$$

In the nonagricultural sector, labor (N) and capital (K) are used to produce nonagricultural products, and its production function adopts the equation of Gollin et al. (2002, 2007), which is:

$$Y_{n,t} = E_n\left(1+\gamma_n\right)^t N_{n,t}^{\theta} K_{n,t}^{1-\theta}, 0<\theta<1 \tag{3.5}$$

where γ_n represents the progress of exogenous fixed technology in the nonagricultural sector; E_n means that factors such as government policies, FDI, and technology import are taken into consideration. Since the labor input in the nonagricultural sector can be calculated in advance by subtracting the labor in the agricultural sector from the total labor, the number of labors in the nonagricultural sector can be regarded as an exogenous variable or a known variable in this dynamic system. Therefore, this dynamic system can also be approximately regarded as a single-sector economic growth model with a capital accumulation progress.

Since the final products of the nonagricultural sector can be used not only for consumption but also for investment, the nonagricultural sector is subject to the following resource constraint:

$$(c_t + i_t) N_t \leq Y_{n,t} \tag{3.6}$$

Capital stock in the economy evolves according to:

$$(1-\delta) K_t + I_t = K_{t+1} \tag{3.7}$$

where δ represents the rate of capital deprecation, which is given exogenously by the economy. Capital stock in the entire economy is subject to the constraint:

$$K_{n,t} \leq K_t \tag{3.8}$$

3.2.2 Equilibrium solution of the model

The representative household's dynamic programming problem is:

$$\begin{aligned}
&\max \ \sum_{t=0}^{\infty} \beta^t \left[\ln(c_t) + \bar{a} \right] \\
&s.t. \quad \bar{a} \leq E_a (1+\gamma_a)^t n_{a,t}^{\mu} l_t^{\phi} \\
&(c_t + i_t) \leq E_n (1+\gamma_n)^t n_{n,t}^{\theta} k_{n,t}^{1-\theta} \\
&(1-\delta) k_t + i_t = k_{t+1} \\
&k_{n,t} \leq k_t \\
&n_{a,t} + n_{n,t} \leq 1 \\
&k_0 \ given
\end{aligned} \tag{3.9}$$

The equilibrium solution of this dynamic programming problem can be expressed as $\{c_t, n_{a,t}, n_{n,t}, k_{t+1}\}_{t=0}^{\infty}$.

In the model, if the production of the agricultural sector cannot meet people's basic living needs, there will be no surplus means of production and therefore no means of production in the agricultural sector (mainly referring to labor) flowing to the nonagricultural sector. It can be seen that the model attributed the motivation of industrial development in the process of economic development to the "push" of the agricultural sector. The "push" is mainly derived from technological innovations in the agricultural sector, such as crop rotation, irrigation and land fertility (Love, 1997, p358) and is represented by the combined effects of E_a and γ_a.

To solve this dynamic programming problem, the agricultural and the nonagricultural sectors' income levels are:

$$\text{Income}_{a,t} = \mu E_a (1+\gamma_a)^t n_{a,t}^{\mu} \tag{3.10}$$

$$\text{Income}_{n,t} = E_n (1+\gamma_n)^t n_{n,t}^{\theta} k_{n,t}^{1-\theta} \tag{3.11}$$

In the following calibration experiment, the ratio of equations (3.11) and (3.10) is used to describe the urban-–rural income gap in the model economy.

3.2.3 Model calibration and numerical experiments

The model economy is calibrated to conform to the general level of Chinese long-term development since the reform and opening-up. Since the variables examined in the model economy are all variables that have been unitized by the population, the number of people employed in the agricultural and nonagricultural sectors is measured by the distribution of the total population of the society between the two sectors. By referring to Gollin et al. (2002), people's basic living needs $\bar{a}$ are normalized as 1, the output elasticity of labor in the nonagricultural sector is set as 0.4, and the output elasticity of labor in the agricultural sector is set as 0.6. By referring to Chen et al. (2004), the subjective discount factor is set as 0.98, and the capital depreciation rate is set as 0.1. Since this numerical experiment is used as a benchmark for future research, we first set the efficiency coefficients of the two sectors as 1 and set the exogenous technical growth rate of the agricultural sector as 0.1, which is lower than that of the nonagricultural sector 0.2. Up to now, the calibration of some key parameters in the benchmark model has been completed, as shown in Table 3.1.

Based on the calibration of the model parameters, the model just built is used to numerically simulate the economic growth since the reform and opening-up. The year 1978 is set as the base year of the model, and the initial capital stock is normalized as 1.

First, the calibrated model economy is used to calculate the value of each economic variable when the model economy reaches a steady-state level, shown as in Table 3.2 (the simulation software is R 2.6.1).

It can be seen that when the model economy reaches a steady growth state, the per capita output of the agricultural sector will be constant at 1, while the

Table 3.1 Calibrated Values of Parameters

$\bar{a}$	E_a	γ_a	E_n	γ_n	μ	θ	β	δ
1	1	0.1	1	0.2	0.6	0.4	0.98	0.1

Table 3.2 Steady-State Values of Economic Variables

$\bar{y}_a$	$\bar{n}_a$	$\bar{y}_n$	$\bar{n}_n$	$\bar{c}$	$\bar{k}$
1	0	2.095	1	1.092	0.754

per capita output of the nonagricultural sector will be constant at 2.095. This shows that even if the urban–-rural income gap is examined in the context of a long-term development, the ratio of the per capita output between the two sectors will not continue to expand or shrink but will gradually converge to a stable ratio, and this ratio is 2.095 in the model economy.

The model economy and the calibrated parameters are used to simulate Chinese economic development after the reform and opening-up. The distribution of labor, output of agricultural sector and output of nonagricultural sector from 1979 to 1997 are shown in Table 3.3.

It can be seen from Table 3.3 that the preceding dynamic growth model well simulates the labor transfer from the agricultural sector to the nonagricultural sector in the process of Chinese economic reform and the stylized facts of the gradual decrease of the proportion of the agricultural sector in the national economy and the gradual increase of the proportion of the nonagricultural sector in the national economy. However, the urban–-rural income ratio in the model economy that this chapter is mainly concerned with is far from the stylized facts. With the development of the economy, the urban–-rural income ratio has shown an explosive expansion trend, and this trend will not be reversed or relieved in the long run. This situation has not been tested empirically in the reality of Chinese economic development.[4] From this point of view, the conditions of the model are too "pure" to describe Chinese economic facts. In the next section, labor market distortion and the efficiency difference between the agricultural sector and the nonagricultural sector will be introduced into the model to well explain the economic reality.

3.3 A model with labor market distortions and efficiency difference

From the perspective of the dynamic general equilibrium, if there is no government intervention in urban and rural labor, capital and other factors, capital and labor will flow freely between the urban and rural areas, thereby tending to make urban and rural factor payments (salaries and interest, etc.) equalized, namely, no urban–-rural income gap. Therefore, when there is a clear income gap between the homogeneous labor in the urban and rural areas of China, it means that there is government intervention or institutional barriers, as well as market distortions and misallocation of production factors caused by such interventions or institutional barriers. In fact, the formation of the urban–-rural income gap is a historical process with different markets and institutional distortion factors in different periods.

Table 3.3 Agricultural and Nonagricultural Labor and Output in Simulated Economy from 1979 to 1997[a]

Year	*1979*	*1981*	*1983*	*1985*	*1987*	*1989*	*1991*	*1993*	*1995*	*1997*
I	0.853	0.621	0.452	0.329	0.239	0.174	0.127	0.092	0.067	0.049
II	0.147	0.379	0.548	0.671	0.761	0.826	0.873	0.908	0.933	0.951
III	0.578	0.477	0.394	0.326	0.270	0.223	0.184	0.152	0.126	0.104
IV	0.843	3.791	16.239	85.126	588.333	5710.27	81796.2	1778968	59381878	3056374183

Note *I. Labor in the agricultural sector; II. Labor in the nonagricultural sector; III. Output in the agricultural sector; IV. Output in the nonagricultural sector.*

a Due to the obvious divergence in the output of the nonagricultural sector, it is unnecessary to list the simulated data after 1998.

Under the planned economic system from 1952 to 1978, the newly established People's Republic of China was faced with a severe situation of political isolation and economic blockade. The central government implemented the development strategy of giving priority to the development of heavy industries, which is mainly achieved through three specific institutional arrangements: the unified purchase and marketing system of agricultural products, the people's commune system and the household registration system. At the beginning, the government purchased agricultural products in the market at low prices. After 1953, the purchase became more and more difficult; then the government implemented a unified purchase and marketing policy. The government monopolized the purchase of all agricultural products and controlled the prices of food and other agricultural products through a ticket system (Cai and Yang, 2000). Under such a system, there is an obvious "scissors gap" between industrial and agricultural products, and the living expenses of urban residents are significantly lower than that of rural residents. In order to prevent the rural population from flowing into the cities, the government used the people's commune system and the household registration system to restrict population mobility. This is the initial institutional root of the unequal exchange of urban and rural products and the formation of the urban–-rural income gap.

At the beginning of the reform and opening-up from 1979 to 1985, the household contract responsibility system was implemented in the rural areas, which unprecedentedly stimulated farmers' enthusiasm for production. At the same time, the government reformed the price system and gradually liberalized the prices of agricultural products. The market for production factors gradually developed, and labor and capital begun to flow between the urban and rural areas. These reform measures reduced the income gap between the urban and rural areas in a short period of time.

Since 1986, rural labor has been continuously transferred to the cities, and the efficiency of resource allocation has been continuously improved. However, the household registration system, employment policy and welfare system and other institutional obstacles restricting the flow of rural labor still exist. In order to maintain a higher employment rate for local urban residents and give priority to urban population employment, local governments have implemented various discriminatory policies against rural populations. For instance, local companies employing migrant workers are charged a certain management fee and are encouraged with rewards while employing local laid-off workers; urban residents can enjoy housing subsidies, education subsidies, medical security, and old-age security benefits, while rural populations are excluded; various ways are adopted to increase the migration cost of surplus rural labor to move to cities.[5] This dual urban–-rural system makes the remuneration for employment at the same labor significantly different in the urban and rural areas. In the model, the wage difference between the two sectors is introduced to summarize these institutional obstacles, as represented by the labor market distortion index ϕ.

In addition to these factors that lead to the income gap between urban and rural areas, the differences in the modes of production between the urban and rural areas, as well as the differences in the acquisition of advanced technology, human capital and other high-quality production factors between the two sectors, have caused inconsistencies in the stages of economic development between the urban and rural areas. Such inconsistencies will intensify with the acceleration of economic development, thereby exacerbating the urban–rural income gap. The current rural land system (the household contract responsibility system) leads to "land fragmentation" and greatly restricts the mechanization and large-scale operation of agriculture. The differences in mode of production between the urban and rural areas and the differences in the use of final products have made urban and rural incomes nonsynchronized in terms of growth methods and speeds. Most capital and technology are concentrated in the urban sector, while the rural sector's mode of production is still labor-intensive, remains small-scale and does not rely on technological progress. The scale and speed of technological progress and capital accumulation in the rural sector are far below that of the urban sector. All these factors make the progress of exogenous technology in the urban and rural areas significantly different. A variable is added to the production function of the agricultural sector to measure the inequality between the two sectors due to institutional factors, that is, the efficiency difference index π_a.

Based on Restuccia et al. (2008), the variables of the labor market distortion, the exogenous technological progress difference between the two sectors caused by policy and institutional factors, are introduced. That means friction factors preventing the full play of production factors and production efficiency are added to the competitive equilibrium economy, which makes the model economy closer to the real economy.

3.3.1 The Model

Assume that the instantaneous utility function of the representative household is:[6]

$$U(c_a, c_n) = \begin{cases} c_a, & \text{if } c_a < \bar{a} \\ (1-a)\ln(c_n) + a\ln(c_a - \bar{a}), & \text{if } c_a \geq \bar{a} \end{cases} \tag{3.12}$$

This utility function first distinguishes household consumption into agricultural products and nonagricultural products and assumes that the utility function is a simplified Stone–Geary utility function. The final products produced by the agricultural sector (c_a) are mainly used to meet the most basic living needs of residents. When the production of the agricultural sector cannot meet people's basic living needs, the resources of the entire economy will be concentrated in the agricultural sector; once the production of the agricultural sector can meet people's basic living needs, the means of production will flow from the agricultural sector to the nonagricultural sector and will be used to produce to meet people's other needs. Such a utility function not only captures the basic product characteristics in the consumption process of Chinese residents but also reflects the structural transformation characteristics of the agricultural and the nonagricultural sectors.

The agricultural sector uses labor (N) and land (L) to produce agricultural products. The production function is:

$$Y_a = E_a(1-\pi_a)N_a^{\mu}L^{1-\mu} \qquad 0<\mu<1 \tag{3.13}$$

where π_a represents the efficiency difference index of the agricultural sector relative to the nonagricultural sector. It is an exogenous variable whose magnitude mainly depends on the negative impact of institutions and policies on the agricultural sector. E_a represents the exogenous fixed technological progress of the agricultural sector, which explains other factors affecting the technological progress of the rural sector except the preceding influences and depends on exogenous conditions such as weather, land fertility and social demand for agricultural products. Assume that the land is given and remains unchanged. $0<\mu<1$ indicates that the marginal productivity of labor is diminishing. Products from the rural sector are only used for basic household consumption, namely:

$$c_aN \le Y_a \tag{3.14}$$

In the nonagricultural sector, labor $(N)$and capital $(K)$are used to produce nonagricultural products, and the production function is:

$$Y_n = E_nN_n^{\theta}K_n^{1-\theta} \qquad 0<\theta<1 \tag{3.15}$$

E_n represents the exogenous fixed technological progress of the nonagricultural sector, which is mainly affected by factors such as government policies, FDI, technology import and other factors. The production function of the nonagricultural sector is a neoclassical production function that considers constant returns to scale.

The nonagricultural sector is subject to the following resource constraint:

$$c_nN \le Y_n \tag{3.16}$$

The available capital stock of the whole society in each period is K, and the amount of capital used by the nonagricultural sector in production is subject to the following constraint:

$$K_n \le K \tag{3.17}$$

The wage level of the agricultural sector is w_a, and the wage level of the nonagricultural sector is w_n. Under the conditions of competitive equilibrium, the wage difference between the two sectors (labor market distortions) is:

$$w_n = (1+\phi)w_a \tag{3.18}$$

Suppose that ϕ is a given exogenous variable. This equation means that, on the one hand, the outflow of surplus labor in the agricultural sector is determined by the difference in wage levels between the two sectors; on the other hand, even for employment in the nonagricultural sector, the wages of rural labor will still be lower than the wages of labor already employed in the nonagricultural sector.

3.3.2 Equilibrium solution of the model

The optimization behavior of the household is:[7]

$$\begin{aligned} &\max U(c_n, c_a) = (1-a)\ln(c_n) + a\ln(c_a - \bar{a}) \\ &s.t.\ c_n + p_a c_a \le y = w_a n_a + w_n n_n + r k_n \end{aligned} \tag{3.19}$$

If the price is given as $\{p_a, w_a, w_n, r\}$, the optimal decision of the preceding representative household is $\{c_a, c_n\}$, and the solution is:

$$c_a = ay/p_a + (1-a)\bar{a} = \bar{a} + a(y/p_a - \bar{a}) \tag{3.20}$$

$$c_n = (1-a)y - (1-a)p_a\bar{a} = (1-a)(y - p_a\bar{a}) \tag{3.21}$$

From the intuitive perspective, equation 3.20 indicates that after meeting their basic living needs, the representative household will use the remaining actual income to consume additional agricultural products according to the utility function coefficient a, whereas equation 3.21 indicates that the representative household uses the remaining income to consume nonagricultural products according to the proportion $1 - a$.

According to the nature of the household's instantaneous utility function, if the final consumer goods produced by the agricultural sector cannot meet the basic needs of residents, the entire economy can only use all resources to produce agricultural products. At this time, the development of the nonagricultural sector is almost stagnant. When the products of the agricultural sector can meet the final consumption of residents, the remaining resources (labor) in the agricultural sector will flow to the nonagricultural sector to produce nonagricultural products, and with the technological advancement of the agricultural sector, more production resources (labor) will flow into the nonagricultural sector.

With the gradual flow of labor from the agricultural sector to the nonagricultural sector, the nonagricultural sector's previously slow developing production activities due to the lack of labor gradually prospered, and people's utility needs gradually expanded from the original basic daily necessities to other manufactured products and services.

If the price is given as $\{p_a, w_a\}$, the production function of the agricultural sector is:

$$y_a = E_a(1-\pi_a)n_a^{\mu} \qquad 0<\mu<1 \tag{3.22}$$

The optimal decision of the agricultural sector can be expressed as:

$$\max: p_a E_a(1-\pi_a)n_a^{\mu} - w_a n_a$$

The amount of labor required by the agricultural sector thus determined is:

$$n_a = \left[p_a E_a(1-\pi_a)\mu / w_a\right]^{1/(1-\mu)} \tag{3.23}$$

$$\text{Similarly,} \, w_a = p_a E_a(1-\pi_a)\mu n_a^{\mu-1} \tag{3.24}$$

Similarly, if the price is given as $\{w_a, r\}$, the production function of the nonagricultural sector is:

$$y_n = E_n n_n^{\theta} k_n^{1-\theta} \qquad 0<\theta<1 \tag{3.25}$$

The optimal decision of the nonagricultural sector is:

$$\max: E_n n_n^{\theta} k_n^{1-\theta} - w_n n_n - rk$$

The first-order conditions, respectively, are:

$$r = E_n(1-\theta)k_n^{-\theta} n_n^{\theta} \tag{3.26}$$

$$w_n = E_n \theta k_n^{1-\theta} n_n^{\theta-1} \tag{3.27}$$

According to equations 3.26 and 3.27, the nonagricultural sector has a certain proportional relationship between labor income and capital income, and this proportional relationship is determined by the nonagricultural sector's neoclassical mode of production:

$$(1-\theta)w_n n_n = \theta r k_n \tag{3.28}$$

Competitive equilibrium can be expressed as follows: First, if a price $\{p_a, w_a, w_n, r\}$ is given, the consumption strategy of $\{c_a, c_n\}$ can maximize the utility of the representative household; second, if the prices $\{p_a, w_a\}$ and $\{w_a, r\}$ are given, the investment strategy combination of n_a and $\{n_n, k_n\}$ can respectively make the producers' income in the agricultural and nonagricultural sectors maximized; third, under the condition expressed as equation 3.18, labor is similar between the two sectors; fourth, market clearing. Namely, the following conditions need to be satisfied:

$$\begin{cases} n_a + n_n = 1 \\ y_a = p_a c_a \\ y_n = c_n \\ y = y_a + y_n \end{cases} \tag{3.29}$$

To solve this programming problem, the following can be obtained:

$$y_a = \left[p_a E_a (1-\pi_a)\mu / w_a^{\mu}\right]^{1/(1-\mu)} \tag{3.30}$$

$$y_n = \left[E_n \theta / (1+\phi)^{\theta} w_a^{\theta}\right]^{1/(1-\theta)} k_n = \left[E_n \theta / w_n^{\theta}\right]^{1/(1-\theta)} k_n \tag{3.31}$$

The income ratio between the agricultural sector and the nonagricultural sector can be expressed as:

$$\frac{y_a}{y_n} = \frac{\left[p_a E_a (1-\pi_a)\mu / w_a^{\mu}\right]^{1/(1-\mu)}}{\left[E_n \theta / w_n^{\theta}\right]^{1/(1-\theta)} k_n} = \frac{\left[p_a E_a (1-\pi_a)\mu / w_a^{\mu}\right]^{1/(1-\mu)}}{\left[E_n \theta / (1+\phi)^{\theta} w_a^{\theta}\right]^{1/(1-\theta)} k_n} \tag{3.32}$$

This shows that the income gap between urban and rural areas is inversely proportional to the relative prices of agricultural products and nonagricultural products p_a, the exogenous technological progress of the agricultural sector E_a, and the wage level of the agricultural sector w_a, and it is proportional to the exogenous technological progress of the nonagricultural sector E_n, the wage level of the nonagricultural sector w_n, the capital stock invested in the nonagricultural sector k_n, the efficiency difference between the agricultural sector and the nonagricultural sector π_a, and the degree of distortion of the labor market ϕ. As for the labor output elasticity of the agricultural sector μ and the labor output elasticity of the nonagricultural sector θ, the following numerical simulations are used to examine their impact on the urban–rural income gap.

3.3.3 Model calibration

The model is calibrated so that the model economy is in line with the long-term process of real economic development in the past decades since the reform and opening-up. Based on the previous parameter calibration, the new parameters are calibrated here. The wage levels of employed population in the two sectors are measured by the per capita net income of rural residents and the per capita disposable income of urban residents in the real economy.[8] The relative price index of agricultural products and nonagricultural products measures the relative price relationship of final products between the two sectors, so it can be expressed as the ratio of the production price index of agricultural products and the ex-factory price index of industrial products. These data come from the statistical yearbooks of past years. $\bar{a}$ is set as 1 because the Chinese population is unitized in the model economy, and the products produced by the agricultural sector are intended mainly to meet the basic living needs of all Chinese people. The values of variables and parameters are shown in Table 3.4.

After determining the values of the preceding parameters and variables in the steady growth state, the labor market equilibrium conditions expressed as equation 3.29 obtained previously are used to calibrate exogenous technological distortion due to policy or institution changes; the labor market wage premium and discount equation 3.18 is used to calibrate the difference in wage levels between the two sectors in the model economy due to the household registration system or other factors. Through the calibration process of these two equations, we can assign all the factors describing the income gap between the agricultural sector and the nonagricultural sector in the model economy to the role of empirical research, so that we can comprehensively investigate according to equation 3.32 the income gap between the agricultural sector and the nonagricultural sector, between rural areas and urban areas.

From the perspective of numerical experiments, the reasonable values of the model parameters are determined first; further, through numerically changing the variables, the main reasons that affect the income gap between urban and rural areas in China and the extent of their impact are explored. The economic meaning of some parameters and their numerical simulation values are shown in Table 4. The remaining variables and parameters that need to be determined are the efficiency difference between agricultural sector and nonagricultural sector (π_a), the distortion of the labor market between the two sectors (ϕ), the wage level of the agricultural sector (w_a) and the capital

Table 3.4 Calibrated Values of Exogenous Variables

Parameters	*Economic Meaning*	*Value*
p	Relative price of agricultural products and non-agricultural products	0.9
E_a	Total factor productivity of agricultural sector	1.1
E_n	Total factor productivity of non-agricultural sector	1.2
μ	Output elasticity of labor of agricultural sector	0.6
θ	Output elasticity of labor of non-agricultural sector	0.4

deposit of the nonagricultural sector (k_n). This chapter analyzes their impact on the entire model economy through the method of assignment.

First, a benchmark model economy is taken into account, where the values of π_a and ϕ are set as 0, and w_a and k_n are set as 1. Through calculation, the income ratio between urban and rural areas is 3.677:1. Therefore, in an ideal economy with the free flow of factors and without externality, there are still differences in income between the urban and rural areas. The main reason is that the final products produced by the agricultural sector have a fixed or upper bound on the utility satisfaction of people. The increase in the output of the agricultural sector will not lead to an increase in the selling price of the agricultural sector. Therefore, the income of the agricultural sector in the process of economic development is relatively fixed. In contrast, since the utility of the nonagricultural sector's final products for people will increase with the increase in demand, the increase in the output of the nonagricultural sector will increase the income of the nonagricultural sector. Additionally, the income of the nonagricultural sector also includes the income of capital interest; thus, with economic development, the income of the nonagricultural sector will gradually increase. This reveals the natural source of the income gap between the agricultural and the nonagricultural sectors.

By taking this simulation model economy as a benchmark and changing the values of π_a, ϕ, w_a and k_n, the impact of these variables and parameters on the urban–-rural income gap is examined. The results of the 0 numerical simulation are shown in Tables 3.5–3.8. (the numerical simulation is calculated by R 2.6.1).

Numerical simulation results show that, relative to the benchmark model economy, when π_a, ϕ ,w_a, and k_n, respectively, grow algebraically, k_n's impact on the income between urban and rural areas is the largest, followed by w_a

Table 3.5 Changing π_a and Keeping the Other Three Variables Fixed

π_a	ϕ	w_a	k_n	y_n / y_a
0.1	0	1	1	1.015
0.2	0	1	1	0.958
0.3	0	1	1	0.908
0.4	0	1	1	0.865

Table 3.6 Changing ϕ and Keeping the Other Three Variables Fixed

π_a	ϕ	w_a	k_n	y_n / y_a
0	0.1	1	1	1.408
0	0.2	1	1	1.890
0	0.3	1	1	2.640
0	0.4	1	1	3.881

Table 3.7 Changing w_a and Keeping the Other Three Variables Fixed

π_a	ϕ	w_a	k_n	y_n / y_a
0	0	2	1	1.928
0	0	3	1	2.703
0	0	4	1	3.435
0	0	5	1	4.138

Table 3.8 Changing k_n and Keeping the Other Three Variables Fixed

π_a	ϕ	w_a	k_n	y_n / y_a
0	0	1	2	2.164
0	0	1	3	3.246
0	0	1	4	4.328
0	0	1	5	5.411

and ϕ, and π_a's impact is the smallest. Economically, that k_n has the greatest impact on the urban--rural income gap indicates that capital income brought about by capital accumulation mainly occurs in the nonagricultural sector and that capital goods are not limited to physical capital but also include human capital, intellectual property rights, patents and other nonmaterial capital. Therefore, when the capital stock (k_n) increases, the expansion of the urban--rural income gap will be the quite significant. The gap in capital stock can be regarded as one of the main factors leading to the income gap.

w_a's impact on the urban--rural income gap is positive. It does not seem to be in line with economic intuition at first glance, but it can be explained. When the wage level of the agricultural sector increases year by year, the willingness and speed of agricultural labor transfer will decrease, and the labor in agriculture will be crowded. At the same time, the scarcity of urban labor has intensified.[9] In that case, the redistribution of labor in the two sectors has widened the income gap between urban and rural areas.

ϕ's impact on the urban--rural income gap is positive. This is relatively intuitive because the most direct manifestation of the labor market distortion is to restrict the free flow of labor or to restrict the role of the price mechanism in disguised form through other channels.

π_a has the smallest impact, and its impact is negative. The reason is that, for a populous country like China, the food issue of 1.3 billion people is the primary issue. The lower the efficiency of agriculture (the larger π_a is), the fewer the resources and labor transferred to the nonagricultural sector, and the smaller the urban--rural income gap. π_a's increase will also reduce agricultural income, and the impacts on the urban and rural areas will offset each other, so the total impact of π_a is small.

After examining the impact of some explanatory variables on the urban--rural income gap, it is found that the impact of the output elasticity of labor of the two sectors on the urban--rural income gap is theoretically uncertain and numerically unstable, so it is necessary to perform the sensitivity analysis of the output elasticity of labor in the two sectors, which is verified through two sets of numerical experiments. The results show that the labor output elasticity of the nonagricultural sector has a unilateral impact on the income gap between the two sectors: As θ increases and the income gap widens, the labor output elasticity of the agricultural sector does not have a unilateral impact on the income gap between the two sectors. $\mu = 0.6$ is a threshold value. At a value less than this threshold, the income gap will be narrowed as μ increases; at a greater value than this threshold, the income gap will be widened as μ increases.[10]

3.4 Conclusion

This chapter first uses a two-sector dynamic growth model under the condition of perfect competition to simulate Chinese economic development since the reform and opening-up, and the parameters are calibrated to be consistent with the typical facts of Chinese economic development, through which to calculate the value of each economic variable when the model economy reaches a steady state. It is found that when the model economy reaches a steady growth state, the per capita output of the agricultural sector will be constant at 1, while the per capita output of the nonagricultural sector will be constant at 2.095. This shows that even if the urban--rural income gap is examined in the context of long-term development, the ratio of the per capita output between the two sectors will not continue to expand or shrink but will gradually converge to a stable ratio, namely 2.095.

On the basis of parameter calibration, the numerical simulation of Chinese economic growth is carried out, which shows that the dynamic growth model well simulates the stylized facts of the labor transfer from the agricultural sector to the nonagricultural sector, the gradual decrease of the proportion of the agricultural sector and the gradual increase of the nonagricultural sector out of the whole GDP. However, because the model analyzes the complicated economic reality under a "pure" competitive equilibrium framework, the simulation results are not consistent with the real urban--rural income gap data.

From the perspective of economic practice, the formation of the urban--rural income gap is a historical process, with different market distortion factors and institutional distortion factors in different periods. Since the reform and opening-up, rural labor has been continuously transferred to the cities, and the efficiency of resource allocation has been continuously improved. However, the household registration system, employment policy and welfare system and other institutional obstacles restricting the flow of rural labor still exist. This urban--rural dual system makes the remuneration for employment in the urban and rural areas significantly different.

The labor market distortion index is introduced to summarize these institutional obstacles. In addition, the differences in modes of production between urban and rural areas, as well as the differences in the acquisition of advanced technology, human capital and other high-quality production factors between the two sectors, have caused inconsistencies in the stages of economic development between the urban and rural areas. The current rural land system leads to land fragmentation and greatly restricts the mechanization and large-scale operation of agriculture. The scale and speed of technological progress and capital accumulation in the rural sector are far below that of the urban sector. The efficiency difference index between the two sectors is introduced to summarize the two sectors' differences in total factor productivity.

In this way, a general equilibrium model, with varying degrees of distortions between the two sectors, is adopted to analyze the formation of the urban--rural income gap. We come to the conclusions that the urban--rural income gap is inversely proportional to the relative prices of agricultural products and nonagricultural products, the exogenous technological progress of the agricultural sector and the wage level of the agricultural sector, but that it is proportional to the exogenous technological progress of the nonagricultural sector, the wage level of the nonagricultural sector, the capital stock of the nonagricultural sector, the efficiency difference between the agricultural sector and the nonagricultural sector, and the degree of distortions of the labor market. By using the methods of parameter calibration and numerical simulation, it is found that the model could match the typical facts of Chinese economic development. This chapter makes the following policy implications obvious: In order to achieve the goal of reducing the urban--rural income gap, the distortions of the labor market, the efficiency difference between the agricultural sector and the nonagricultural sector, and the institutional barriers that separate urban and rural areas should be removed as much as possible to make various production factors freely flow between urban and rural areas.

Notes

1 According to Lu and Chen (2004), the decomposition of the income gap shows that China's regional income gap is related to the huge urban–rural income gap.
2 These data are collected from *China Statistical Yearbook 1978* and *China Statistical Yearbook 2006*.
3 This model does not consider factors that violate competitive equilibrium, such as labor market distortions and efficiency difference between the agricultural sector and the nonagricultural sector, so it is a "pure" model.
4 The real urban–rural income ratio ranges from 2 to 3.3.
5 For example, the education expenses of migrant workers' children, job placement expenses of migrant workers' spouses, expenses of migrant workers' housing rental or purchase etc. are all not ensured.

6 Here the static general equilibrium analysis is adopted to reduce the complexity of the model.
7 According to the assumption of equation 3.12, and the variables shown from equation 3.12–3.17 are divided by *N*. Assume that the price of nonagricultural products (c_n) is set as 1, and in general equilibrium, the amount of land is fixed, so it is reasonable.
8 According to the research of the Agricultural Survey Team of the National Bureau of Statistics (1991), the net income of rural residents comprehensively reflects the income and expenditure of the entire household and can be used to measure the disposable income of rural residents.
9 For instance, many cities face a shortage of migrant workers.
10 Due to limited space, specific results are not reported here. Interested readers can contact the author for more information.

Bibliography

Barro, Robert J., and Xavier Sala-i-Martin. "Convergence." *The Journal of Political Economy* no. 2 (1992): 223–251.

Cai, Fang 蔡昉. "Urban–Rural Income Gap and Critical Point of Institutional Change" 城乡收入差距与制度变革的临界点. *Social Sciences in China* no. 5 (2003): 16–25+205.

Cai, Fang, Du Yang, and Wang Meiyan 蔡昉, 都阳, 王美艳. *The Political Economy of Labor Mobility* 劳动力流动的政治经济学. Shanghai: Shanghai Joint Publishing Company, 2003.

Cai, Fang, and Yang Tao 蔡昉, 杨涛. "The Political Economy of Urban–Rural Income Gap" 城乡收入差距的政治经济学. *Chinese Social Sciences in China* no. 4 (2000): 11–22+204.

Cai, Jiming 蔡继明. "Comparative Productivity and Relative Income Differences of Urban and Rural Areas in China" 中国城乡比较生产力与相对收入差别. *Economic Research* no. 1 (1998): 11–19.

Chari, Varadarajan, Patrick Kehoe, and Ellen McGrattan. "The Poverty of Nations: A Quantitative Exploration." Staff Report 204, Federal Reserve Bank of Minneapolis, 1997.

———. "Business Cycle Accounting." Staff Report 328, Federal Reserve Bank of Minneapolis, 2006.

Chen, Kunting, Gong Liutang, and Zou Hengfu 陈昆亭, 龚六堂, 邹恒甫. "Numerical Experiments of Basic RBC Method for Simulating the Chinese Economy" 基本RBC方法模拟中国经济的数值试验. *The Journal of World Economy* no. 2 (2004): 41–52.

Cheng, Kaiming, and Li Jinchang 程开明, 李金昌. "Analysis of Mechanism and Dynamic Econometric Relationships Between Urban Bias, Urbanization and Urban–Rural Inequality" 城市偏向、城市化与城乡收入差距作用机制及动态分析. *The Journal of Quantitative and Technical Economics* no. 7 (2007): 116–125.

Gollin, Dauglas, Stephen L. Parente, and Richard Rogerson. "The Role of Agriculture in Development." *The American Economic Review* no. 2 (2002): 160–164.

———. "The Food Problem and the Evolution of International Income Levels." *Journal of Monetary Economics* no. 4 (2007): 1230–1255.

Guo, Jianxiong 郭剑雄. "Human Capital, the Birth Rate and the Narrowing of the Urban–Rural Income Gap" 人力资本、生育率与城乡收入差距的收敛. *Chinese Social Sciences in* China no. 3 (2005): 27–37+205.

Hansen, Gary D., and Edward C. Prescott. "Malthus to Solow." *The American Economic Review* no. 4 (2002): 1205–1217.

Li, Shi, and Luo Chuliang 李实, 罗楚亮. "Re-estimating the Income Gap Between Urban and Rural Households in China" 中国城乡居民收入差距的重新估计. *Journal of Peking University* (Philosophy and Social Sciences) no. (2007): 111–120.

Lin, Guangbin 林光彬. "The Hierarchical System, Market Economy and the Expansion of Urban–Rural Income Gap" 等级制度、市场经济与城乡收入差距扩大. *Management World* no. 4 (2004): 30–40+50.

Liu, Shejian, and Xu Yan 刘社建, 徐艳. "A Study on the Cause of the Gap Between Urban and Rural Households' Income and Distribution and Countermeasures." 城乡居民收入分配差距形成原因及对策研究. *Journal of Finance and Economics* no. 5 (2004): 93–103.

Liu, Shenglong 刘生龙. "The Relationship Between Income Inequality and Economic Growth" 收入不平等与经济增长的关系. *Economic Science* no. 3 (2007): 16–25.

Love, David R. F. "A Dynamic General Equilibrium Model of Industrialization When Manufactures Are Unnecessary." *Journal of Development Economics* no. 2 (1997): 357–385.

Lu, Ming, and Chen Zhao 陆铭, 陈钊. "Urbanization, Urban-Based Economic Policies and Urban-Rural Inequality" 城市化、城市倾向的经济政策与城乡收入差距. *Economic Research* no. 6 (2004): 50–58.

Lu, Yunhang 陆云航. "Factor Accumulation, Government Policies and the Urban–Rural Income Gap" 要素积累、政府政策与我国城乡收入差距. *Contemporary Finance and Economics* no. 4 (2006): 5–13.

Parente, Stephen L., and Edward C. Prescott. "Barriers to Technology Adoption and Development." *The Journal of Political Economy* no. 2 (1994): 298–321.

———. "Monopoly Rights: A Barrier to Riches." *The American Economic Review* no. 5 (1999a): 1216–1233.

———. "Barriers to Riches." The Third Walras-Pareto Lecture, University of Lausanne, 1999b.

———. "A Unified Theory of the Evolution of International Income Levels." Staff Report 333, Federal Reserve Bank of Minneapolis, 2004.

Restuccia, Diego. "Barriers to Capital Accumulation and Aggregate Total Factor Productivity." Working Paper, University of Toronto, 2002.

Restuccia, Diego, and Richard Rogerson. "Policy Distortions and Aggregate Productivity with Heterogeneous Plants." Working Paper DR070803, University of Toronto, 2003.

Restuccia, Diego, Dennis T. Yang, and Xiaodong Zhu. "Agriculture and Aggregate Productivity: A Quantitative Cross-Country Analysis." *Journal of Monetary Economics* no. 2 (2008): 234–250.

Stokey, Nancy L., Robert E. Lucas, and Edward C. Prescott. *Recursive Methods in Economic Dynamics*. Cambridge, MA: Harvard University Press, 1989.

Wang, Wenjun 汪文君. "The Income Gap of Chinese Residents" 我国居民收入差距. *Modern Agriculture* no. 11 (2007): 169–171.

Wei, Wei, and Fu Yong 韦伟, 傅勇. "Urban–Rural Income Gap and Population-Flow Model" 城乡收入差距与人口流动模型. *Journal of Renmin University of China* no. 6 (2004): 16–22.

Yao, Jun 姚耀军. "An Empirical Analysis of Financial Development and Urban–Rural Income Gap in China" 金融发展与城乡收入差距关系的经验分析. *Journal of Finance and Economics* no. 2 (2005): 49–59.

Yin, Xiguo, Chen Gang, and Cheng Shiqi 尹希果, 陈刚, 程世骑. "Reevaluation of the Relationship Between Financial Development and Urban–Rural Income Gap in China: An Empirical Study Based on Panel Unit Root and VAR Models" 中国金融发展与城乡收入差距关系的再检验——基于面板单位根和VAR模型的估计. *Modern Economic Science* no. 1 (2007): 15–24+124.

4 Government investment tendency, financial market imbalance and the urban–rural income gap

In this chapter, the formation of the urban–rural income gap in China will be further examined. In reference to Neoclassical Growth Theory, a dynamic general equilibrium model is built to capture the relationship between the government investment tendency, financial market imbalances and the income gap. Chinese macrostatistical data are referred to for parameter calibration and numerical simulation. Based on the model study, this chapter comes to believe that the factors of financial markets have a much bigger influence compared with the government's fiscal investment. Particularly, the fiscal investment strategy's propensity for urban areas promotes urban economic development on the one hand and inevitably widens the income gap on the other. Policy recommendations are given at the end of this chapter.

4.1 Reflections on the urban–rural income gap

Whether income distribution is fair or not is a major economic issue related to social stability and people's well-being. According to the World Bank, in 2019, the Gini coefficient of China was 0.465, while the Gini coefficient of India, a country with a large population, was only 0.39. China has entered a stage of economic development where the disparity between the rich and the poor is very wide, and the antagonism between different income classes has affected social harmony and economic growth stability. The report of the 18th National Congress of the Communist Party of China pointed out that "we should adjust the pattern of national income distribution, tighten its regulation by secondary distribution and work hard to narrow income gaps so that all the people can share in more fruits of development in a fair way."[1] The widened urban–rural income gap remains one of the main reasons for income distribution unfairness. In 1978, the income gap of urban–rural residents was CNY 209.8; in 2002, CNY 5227.2; in 2010, CNY 13190.4; and in 2020, CNY 26702.2. The income gap multiplied rapidly.[2]

An economic intuition and a preliminary analysis explain that the widening of the urban–rural income gap mainly stems from the fiscal expenditure difference and financial market imbalance.

DOI: 10.4324/9781003305651-4

First of all, one of the major functions of public finance is income distribution, and the role of fiscal expenditure policy in regulating household income distribution is unique and incomparable to any other policies. The analysis of statistical data shows that the proportion of fiscal expenditure on agriculture and rural areas in the total national fiscal expenditure since 1992 is less than 10% in most years, and the highest proportion is only 10.69%. In contrast, the proportion of fiscal expenditure on nonagricultural in the total national fiscal expenditure is as high as 89%. Nonagricultural industry generally locates in the urban areas, such as the main services and industries, while agriculture is still dominant in the rural areas. The fiscal expenditure's propensity for urban areas encourages investment that drives employment and consumption, and urban people can enjoy public services at low cost; in the rural areas, infrastructure construction receives little government support and requires villagers to raise funds. The urban tendency of fiscal spending directly and indirectly leads to urban residents enjoying more public resources than rural residents, urban living standards being higher than rural ones, urban economy developing significantly faster than rural counterparts, and the income disparity between peasants and town people inevitably widening.

Secondly, in the past 60 years or more since the establishment of the People's Republic of China (PRC) in 1949, the financial market has prospered with the financial supervision system improved, more financial institutions emerging and financial instruments constantly innovated, but the imbalance between urban and rural financial markets has been deteriorating. Unlike the urban areas, the types of financial institutions in rural areas are limited, with banks as the representative credit institutions; financial products are not rich, limited to mainly loans. Nevertheless, in taking out a loan, meeting the various conditions required by financial institutions due to the fragmentation of production is simply very hard. With the lack of suitable investment channels, it is difficult and rarely successful for peasants to take out loans. As a result, financial services in rural areas are actually dominated by savings. The various financial institutions pursuing profit will promote the flow of deposits from rural areas to urban areas. This imbalance in the development of rural and urban financial markets has resulted in the inability of rural residents to efficiently use financial institutions to expand their reproduction and increase their income, while residents in urban areas can continuously expand their investment, which also widens the urban–rural income gap.

In terms of these two aspects, this chapter argues that it is necessary to study the relationship between the government investment tendency, financial market imbalance and the income gap, as well as the direction and degree of the influence of fiscal and financial factors on the urban–rural income gap.

Regarding the urban–rural income gap, scholars at home and abroad have conducted much research. For instance, the urban–rural income gap theory can be traced back to the proposal of the Kuznets curve. In 1955, Simon Kuznets, an American economist, based on the analysis of historical data of the United States, Britain and Germany, proposed an inverted U-curve to describe the relationship between income gap and economic growth. According to the inverted U-curve, the income gap will gradually widen at the primary stage of economic development, and only after the economy has reached a certain level will the income gap narrow with economic development, which overturns the customary notion that the income gap simply narrows with economic development.

Scholars focused on whether the Kuznets curve derived from empirical data in Europe and the United States applied to China. For example, Wang (2006) tested this theory in terms of the relationship between China's openness to the outside world and the urban–rural income gap. He used the ratio of urban residents' consumption level to rural residents' consumption level and established a regression equation to examine the impact of economic openness degree index, the degree of urbanization, and the institutions and policies related to the urban–rural income gap. The empirical results show that the impact of economic openness on the urban–rural income gap in China has gone through an inverted U-curve process.

After clarifying the relationship between the urban–rural income gap and economic development, more scholars focus on which factors influence the urban–rural income gap and provide the basis for identifying corresponding polices. This chapter focuses on a brief literature review of the representative ones that are more closely related to the research done in this chapter.

First, under the principle of distribution according to one's work, wage income is the most fundamental source of income, and the formation of an income gap is inevitably related to the level of wages. Gollin et al. (2002) assumed that the representative household with infinite life only consume two types of products—nonagricultural products and agricultural products—and they developed a two-sector Neoclassical Growth model involving the agricultural sector and the nonagricultural sector. It is found that, as the economy grows, surplus labor in the agricultural sector flows from the agricultural sector to the nonagricultural sector. On the one hand, the quantity and income of labor in the agricultural sector decrease. On the other hand, the labor flowing to the nonagricultural sector not only increases the employment in the nonagricultural sector but also increases the demand for nonagricultural products, which brings about a continuous rise in income. They refer to the UK historical data to calibrate the model and well explain the facts of the UK economic development. Gollin et al. (2002) undoubtedly provide a new direction for the study of the urban–rural income gap, and, based on this method, Sun, Du and Hong (2009) adopted a general equilibrium model involving labor market distortion and the efficiency difference between the two sectors to model the urban–rural income gap in China. The results show that a reasonable explanation for the formation of the urban–rural income gap and its relationship with various economic institutions, policies and variables can be provided under this generalized framework. With parametric calibration and numerical simulation, it is found that the proposed model can pass the test of stylized facts of the Chinese economy.

Second, regarding the relationship between fiscal factors and the urban–rural income gap, Pradhan et al. (2000) studied the microimpact of macroadjustment policies in India based on the empirical data of rural–urban income, expenditure and poverty in India and concluded that Indian government policies do affect the formation of the urban–rural income gap. Drawing on Barrow's endogenous economic growth model of government expenditure and the Cobb–Douglas production function, Mo and Zhang (2010) built an endogenous model with government fiscal expenditure in which labor and capital can flow freely between the urban and rural areas. After empirical tests, it is found that, for a one percentage point increase in the ratio of government fiscal expenditure to GDP, the coefficient of the urban–rural income gap will increase by 0.4068%. In other words, under the current dual economic structure and institutional framework, increasing fiscal expenditure will widen the urban–rural income gap. Hence, fiscal expenditure should show the propensity for the development of agriculture and peasants.

Finally, regarding the relationship between financial factors and the urban–rural income gap, Galor and Zeira (1993) assumed that the economy was an intertemporal open economy: The representative individual survives for only two periods. There are differences in initial wealth; people with high initial wealth are more likely to be financed through the credit market than those with low initial wealth, and people who obtain financing can invest in human capital in the first period and thus produce with greater efficiency in the second period. In this way, the difference in financial market development has an impact on economic output from the perspective of wealth distribution. According to their research, financial development has a positive linear relationship with income inequality, i.e., the higher the level of financial development, the greater the income level gap. Greenwood and Jovanovic (1990) built a dynamic model to discuss the relationship between financial development and income distribution, which assumed that, in the initial stage, the poor have different wealth from the rich; both have to pay a certain amount in costs and operating expenses to enter the financial market, and the poor have to rely solely on wage income because they cannot afford this expense. Only after reaching a certain level of financial development can the poor afford to enter the financial market for financial investment activities. They argue that, in the early stage of financial development, the number of participants in the financial market is small, so the participants will obtain higher investment returns, and thus the development of the financial market will widen the income gap. After a period of financial development, the poor also gradually participate in financial market activities, so that they also share the development opportunities brought by borrowing capital, and, due to the increase in the number of participants, the investment returns obtained by the rich remain relatively unchanged or decrease, so that the income gap between the poor and the rich continues to narrow until it converges to an equilibrium level and then stops changing. They conclude that the relationship between financial development and income distribution follows an inverted U-shaped trajectory. In contrast to Jeremy and Boyan, Yao (2005) used the proportion of bank credit to GDP as an indicator of measuring financial development, analyzed the relationship between financial development and the urban–rural income gap and argued that further financial development will significantly widen the income gap. In response to Yao, Cao et al. (2007) proposed that the relationship between financial development level and urban–rural income disparity should not be analyzed in general but that each region should be empirically analyzed separately. They adopted the vector error correction (VEC) model to study the relationship between financial development and the urban–rural income gap in Jiangsu Province after reform and opening-up from the perspective of the scale and efficiency of financial development. They concluded that, in the long run, there is a stable negative relationship between financial development scale and urban–rural income gap in Jiangsu, while the development efficiency of the financial market is positively related to the urban–rural income gap.

The literature review on the income gap reveals the following aspects: First, most domestic empirical analyses are conducted by time series regression using econometric methods, the existing studies using calibration methods are still very limited, and the only calibration studies are mostly focused on the labor market. There is no literature regarding the calibration analysis of fiscal expenditure or financial market development, not to mention in-depth and comprehensive literature regarding the calibration analysis of combining fiscal expenditure and financial market. Second, most of the international studies take the neoclassical production function as their theoretical basis and study the income problem from the perspective of consumer and manufacturer optimization, which adds the microfoundations to the macroeconomic analysis, while domestic studies rarely consider this point. Hence this chapter attempts to build a dynamic general equilibrium model including consumers, production sectors and government based on Neoclassical Growth Theory, and introduces the financial market imbalance index and fiscal expenditure propensity for urban areas to involve government and financial market factors in the model of urban–rural income research. With calibration and numerical simulation, the direction and degree of the impact of these two factors on the income gap will be calculated.

4.2 Stylized facts of the Chinese economy

This chapter selects Chinese economic data from the *China Statistical Yearbooks* from 1990 to 2010 mainly because the relevant economic data before 1990 is missing. To study the impact of the government investment tendency and financial market development imbalance on the urban–rural income gap, for the sake of data consistency and the *China Statistical Yearbooks* urban–rural gross deposit/loan ratio works to estimate the difference in urban–rural financial markets' development. The urban–rural fiscal expenditure ratio works to estimate the propensity of fiscal expenditure. An

H-P filter is applied to all data to eliminate the trend component of the series and retain only the fluctuation component.

The fluctuation figures of the urban–rural income ratio, the urban–rural fiscal expenditure ratio, the urban–rural gross deposit/loan ratio are shown in Figures 4.1–4.6. After applying the H-P filter to all variables in Eviews 6.0, the results of the analysis are shown in Tables 4.1–4.2.

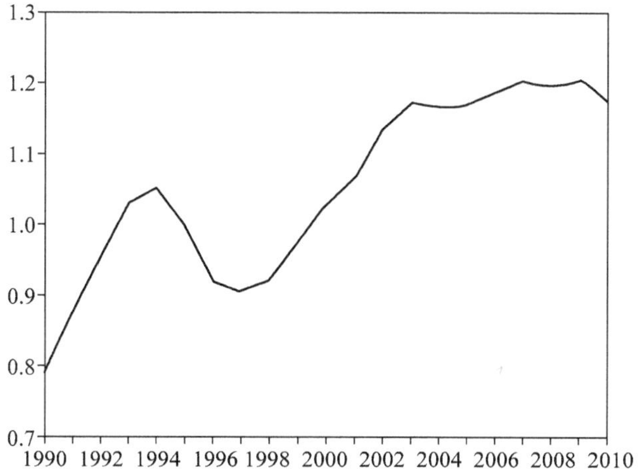

Figure 4.1 Changes in the Urban–Rural Income Ratio.

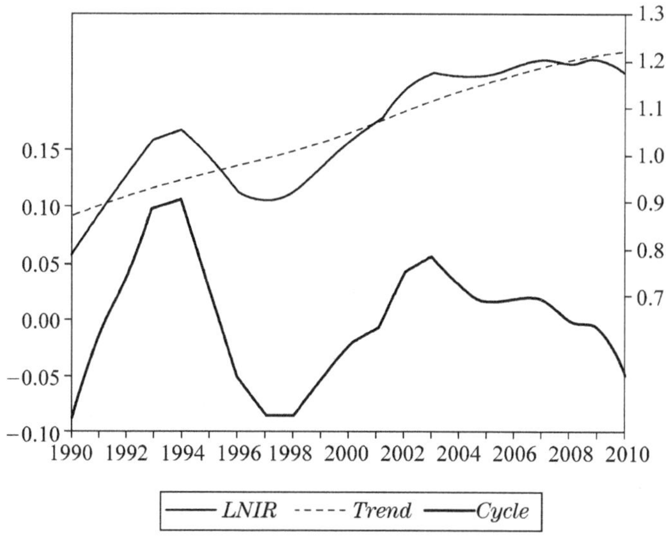

Figure 4.2 Changes in the Urban–Rural Income Ratio Using H-P Filter.

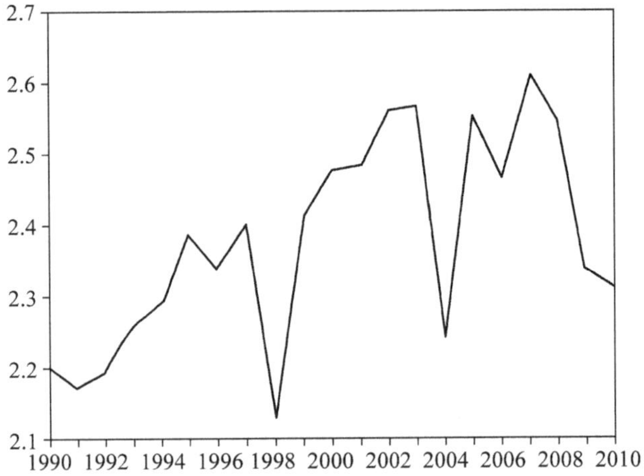

Figure 4.3 Changes in the Urban–Rural Government Investment Ratio.

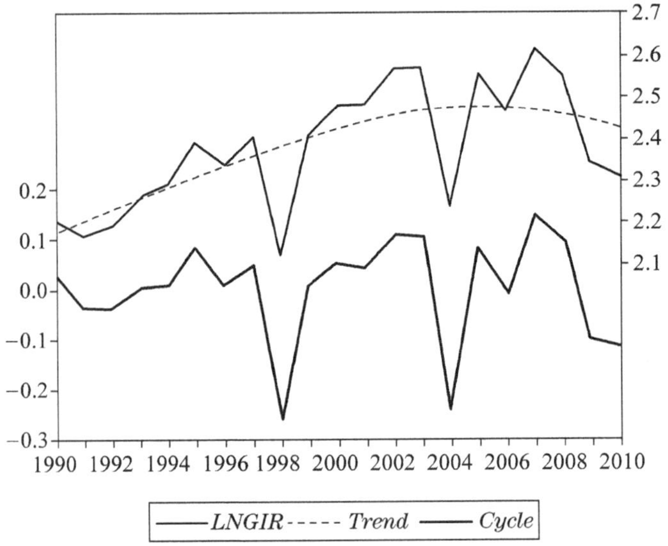

Figure 4.4 Changes in the Urban–Rural Government Investment Ratio Using H-P Filter.

By analyzing these tables and figures, it can be seen that the fluctuations of the urban–rural income ratio are smaller than those of the urban–rural gross deposit/loan ratio and of the urban–rural fiscal expenditure ratio, and all three ratios are procyclical. Additionally, it is clear that during the period from 1990 to 1998 when the urban–rural income ratio fluctuated the most sharply,

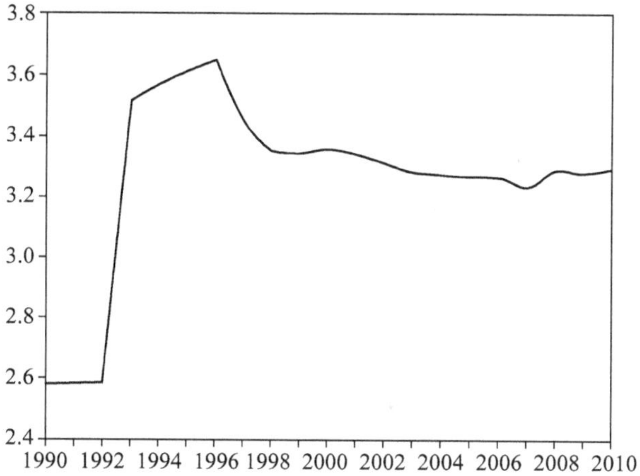

Figure 4.5 Changes in the Urban–Rural Deposits and Loans.

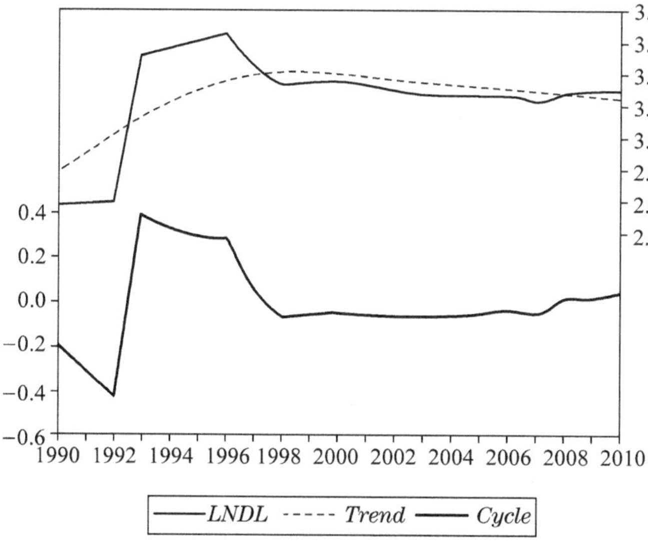

Figure 4.6 Changes in the Urban–Rural Deposits and Loans Using H-P Filter.

the urban–rural fiscal expenditure ratio and the ratio of urban–rural gross deposit/loan ratio fluctuated correspondingly with a larger magnitude, and the fluctuation trend of the H-P-filtered urban–rural income ratio was generally consistent with the fluctuation trend of the urban–rural fiscal expenditure ratio and the urban–rural gross deposit/loan ratio. The correlation coefficient between the urban–rural fiscal expenditure ratio and the urban–rural income

Table 4.1 Basic Characteristics of Economic Variables[a]

	Urban–Rural Income Ratio	*Urban–Rural Fiscal Expenditure Ratio*	*Urban–Rural Gross Deposit-Loan Ratio*
Standard Deviation	0.360	1.610	1.164
Autocorrelation Coefficient	0.867	0.406	0.742

a The data are collected from the *China Statistical Yearbooks* over the years, and all the data have been log-linearized and H-P-filtered.

Table 4.2 Correlation Coefficient of Urban–Rural Government Investment Ratio, Urban–Rural Gross Deposit–Loan Ratio and Urban–Rural Income Ratio from 1990 to 2010, cor($x(t)$, $y(t + k)$)

	−3	*−2*	*−1*	*0*	*1*	*2*	*3*
Urban–Rural Fiscal Expenditure Ratio	0.816	0.850	0.879	0.903	0.933	0.957	0.975
Urban–Rural Gross Deposit–Loan Ratio	−0.113	0.185	0.380	0.331	0.553	0.601	0.655

ratio is 0.903, indicating that the urban–rural fiscal expenditure ratio and the urban–rural income ratio are highly correlated. The correlation coefficient between the urban–rural gross deposit/loan ratio and the urban–rural income ratio is 0.33, and the impact on the urban–rural income ratio becomes more obvious over time. There may be two reasons for this phenomenon: First, the current period's deposits and loans are generally prepared for the next period's investment or production activities, so the correlation between the current period's deposits and loans and the current period's residents' income is not as high as the correlation between the current period's deposits and loans and the next period's urban and rural residents' income. Second, due to the problem of data availability, this chapter chooses the urban–rural gross deposit/loan ratio to estimate the value of the difference between urban and rural financial market development, which ignores the role of nonbank financial institutions, whose influence on residents' income is increasing in the development of modern financial markets.

4.3 Dynamic growth model with fiscal and financial factors

First, a two-sector model including government and financial markets is built, of which the decision makers are consumers and production sectors, while government and financial markets are introduced into the model only as influencing factors. The rural areas in China are dominated by the agricultural sector, and agricultural products are used to meet the basic needs of people, while the industries in urban areas are mainly secondary and tertiary, and nonagricultural products are used to meet the needs of the residents for a higher quality of life. Given the distinguishability of agricultural and nonagricultural products, the production sectors in the model are divided into the agricultural sector and the urban economic sector, which is dominated by the secondary and tertiary industries. It is assumed that households are homogeneous and that economic decisions reflect the decisions of the representative household. Both the product market and the market of production factors are perfectly competitive; with each period, the market clears. Households sell capital services and labor to the market in return for rents and wages. There are only two production sectors: the urban and rural production sectors. Both sectors use production technology with constant returns to scale, and households choose the quantities of agricultural and nonagricultural products to maximize utility.

The utility function of the representative household is set as:

$$E_t \sum_{t=0}^{\infty} \beta^t U(C_{a,t}, C_{c,t}) \quad 0 < \beta < 1$$

$$U(C_{a,t}, C_{c,t}) = a \ln(C_{a,t}) + (1 - a) \ln(C_{c,t}) \tag{4.1}$$

where $C_{a,t}$ represents the products consumed by the representative household in period t, which are produced in the agricultural sector (agricultural products). $C_{c,t}$ represents the products consumed by the representative household in period t, which are produced in the urban economic sector (nonagricultural products). β represents the subjective discount rate. The household's disposable income needs to be allocated between agricultural products $C_{a,t}$ and nonagricultural products $C_{c,t}$. a in the utility function $U(C_{a,t}, C_{c,t})$ represents the ratio of utility generated in agricultural product consumption to total utility, and $(1 - a)$ represents the ratio of utility generated in the nonagricultural products' consumption to total utility. Classifying all products other than agricultural products consumed by households as nonagricultural products, including industrial products, services etc., coincides with the urban–rural issue studied in this chapter.

Due to the regional development difference in China, for a long time the vast number of rural areas still follow the traditional production methods to carry out production activities—"living at the mercy of the elements." Also, due to the capital market entry barriers, on the one hand, it is difficult for peasants to expand and reproduce through borrowing and financing; on the other hand, peasants' free or idle capital can only be deposited in banks to obtain fixed returns. Therefore, it is assumed in the model that the agricultural sector uses only two elements, labor and land, to produce and that the production function takes the form of the Cobb–Douglas production function; then the production function of the agricultural sector in period t can be expressed as follows:

$$Y_{a,t} = A_{a,t} T_{a,t}^{\theta} L_{a,t}^{1-\theta} \quad 0 < \theta < 1 \tag{4.2}$$

where $A_{a,t}$ represents the stochastic technological progress shock in the agricultural sector in period t, an exogenous variable whose magnitude is mainly influenced by natural factors such as institutions, land fertility and weather on agricultural technology. $A_{a,t}$ is assumed to be a factor that grows at a fixed rate. $T_{a,t}$ represents the total amount of available rural land in period t, and $L_{a,t}$ represents the labor engaged in agricultural production in period t. Owing to the assumption that the production sector is under constant returns to scale, the sum of the output elasticity of land and output elasticity of labor is 1, and the quantity of land is considered constantly given.

Assuming that agricultural products are only used for consumption, then the total consumption of agricultural products by the whole society cannot be greater than the total output of the agricultural sector; i.e., the agricultural sector in period t is subject to the following resource constraint:

$$C_{a,t}L_t \leq Y_{a,t} \tag{4.3}$$

L_t represents the population of the whole society, which is here simplified accordingly so that L equals the number of labor in the labor sector plus the number of labor in the urban economic sector. This will be defined eventually.

The endogenous growth theory suggests that economic growth is determined by a series of endogenous variables on which that government fiscal policy has a significant impact. Education expenditure and general public service expenditure account for a large proportion of total fiscal expenditure, which not only lead to the development of education and service industries but also improve the knowledge literacy and labor efficiency of the labor. So by referring to Barro's (1990) endogenous growth model of government expenditure, the production function in the urban economy is set as:

$$Y_{c,t} = A_{c,t}K_{c,t}^{\mu}(\upsilon_g L_{c,t})^{1-\mu} \quad 0 < \mu < 1 \tag{4.4}$$

$A_{c,t}$ represents the exogenous technological progress in the urban economic sector in period t. μ is the capital output elasticity parameter, $0 < \mu < 1$, indicating the diminishing marginal utility of capital. $K_{c,t}$ represents the capital invested in production in the urban economic sector in period t. $L_{c,t}$ represents the amount of labor in the urban economic sector in period t. It is worth mentioning that υ_g represents the ratio of urban financial expenditure to rural financial expenditure, which is used as a measure of the fiscal expenditure's propensity for urban areas. Although the country has attached great importance to the "three rural issues" in recent years and has increased financial investment in rural areas, the overall financial investment in urban areas is still much larger than that in rural areas, and υ_g reflects this urban–rural difference of fiscal expenditure. This difference is even more obvious if the long-term trend since the reform and opening-up is considered.

For a long time in the rural areas, the capital was conservatively used for some historical reasons. And the traditional production method led to the risk-averse investment behavior of peasants. In addition, the financial market development in rural areas seriously lagged behind that in urban areas, and the lack of credit system in rural areas made the traditional credit institutions evolve into merely deposit institutions. What's more, the money deposited by peasants flowed to urban areas through credit institutions. Therefore, in the model it is assumed that peasants deposit all their money in banks and receive returns with a fixed interest rate $\bar{r}$. Banks then lend all the money to urban citizens for investment at the rate $\bar{r}$. A financial market imbalance parameter φ is introduced to represent the difference in capital utilization between the nonagricultural and agricultural sectors. All of the K_a owned by peasants is finally transformed into productive capital K_c in the urban economic sector through credit from the financial sector.

$$k_c = (1+\varphi)k_a \tag{4.5}$$

Equation 4.5 shows that the capital stock of the agricultural sector contributes to that of the urban economic sector. This is consistent with the hypothesis that residents of the primary sector deposit their excess funds in banks that are fully transformed into loan capital in the urban sector, reflecting the difference in capital ownership between urban and rural residents due to the urban–rural financial markets' development imbalance in China, as well as the process of capital flow from rural areas to urban areas.

The identical equation of total labor and capital in the economy is:

$$\begin{aligned} K_{c,t} + K_{a,t} &= K_t \\ L_{c,t} + L_{a,t} &= L_t \end{aligned} \tag{4.6}$$

The products of the urban sector are used not only for the consumption of the whole society but also for reinvestment of the urban sector. But the consumption of these nonagricultural products cannot be greater than the total production of nonagricultural production, and the urban sector in period t is subject to the following resource constraint:

$$C_{c,t}L + I_t \le Y_{c,t} \tag{4.7}$$

The capital stock of the whole society evolves according to:

$$K_{t+1} = (1-\delta)K_t + I_t \quad 0 < \delta < 1 \tag{4.8}$$

where δ represents the capital depreciation rate, given exogenously by the economy, and the initial capital K_0 is given.

By unitizing the variables, the instantaneous optimal decision behavior of the representative household can be described as:

$$\max U(c_a, c_c) = a\ln(c_a) + (1-a)\ln(c_c) \tag{4.9}$$

$$st. \quad c_c + p_a c_a \leq y = w_a l_a + \bar{r} k_a + w_c l_c + r_c k_c \tag{4.10}$$

Assume that the nonagricultural products' price is 1, p_a represents the relative price of agricultural products versus nonagricultural products. w_a represents the wage level of the agriculture sector. w_c represents the wage level of the urban economic sector. r_c represents the rate of equity returns of urban economic sector. Given the prices $\{p_a, w_a, w_c, \bar{r}, r_c\}$, the optimal decision of the preceding representative household is $\{c_a, c_c\}$, and the solution is:

$$c_a = \frac{y}{(\frac{1}{a} - 1 + p_a)}$$
$$c_c = \frac{(1-a)y}{1-a+ap_a} = y(1+\frac{1}{ap_a}) \tag{4.11}$$

If the price is given as $\{p_a, w_a, \bar{r}\}$, the production function of the agricultural sector can be unitarily simplified as:

$$y_a = A_a t_a^{\theta} l_a^{1-\theta} \quad 0 < \theta < 1. \tag{4.12}$$

Then the optimization problem of the agricultural sector can be formulated as:

$$\max p_a A_a t_a^{\theta} l_a^{1-\theta} - w_a l_a - \bar{r} k_a \tag{4.13}$$

t_a and $\bar{r}$ in each period are given, and the number of labor needed in the agricultural sector is determined from the preceding equation as:

$$l_a = \left(\frac{(1-\theta) p_a A_a t_a^{\theta}}{w_a} \right)^{1/\theta} \tag{4.14}$$

Similarly, if the price is given as $\{w_c, r_c\}$, the production function of the nonagricultural sector can be simplified as:

$$y_c = A_c k_c^{\mu} (\upsilon_g l_c)^{1-\mu} \quad 0 < \mu < 1 \tag{4.15}$$

The optimization problem of the nonagricultural sector is:

$$\max A_c k_c^{\mu} (\upsilon_g l_c)^{1-\mu} - w_c l_c - r_c k_c \tag{4.16}$$

Hence, the amount of labor needed in the nonagricultural sector can be determined as:

$$l_c = \left[\frac{(1-\mu) A_c k_c^{\mu} \upsilon_g^{1-\mu}}{w_c} \right]^{1/\mu} \tag{4.17}$$

In a general equilibrium, consumption equals output. The whole society's consumption of agricultural products equals the total output of the agricultural sector, and the whole society's consumption of nonagricultural products equals the total output of the urban economic sector, i.e.:

$$\begin{aligned} y_a &= p_a c_a \\ y_c &= c_c \end{aligned} \tag{4.18}$$

The incomes of the agricultural and nonagricultural sectors, respectively, are:

$$y_a = A_a^{1/\theta} t_a \left[\frac{(1-\theta) p_a}{w_a} \right]^{(1-\theta)/\theta} \tag{4.19}$$

$$y_c = A_c^{1/\mu} (1+\varphi) k_a \left[\frac{(1-\mu) \upsilon_g}{w_c} \right]^{(1-\mu)/\mu} \tag{4.20}$$

The urban–rural income ratio can be expressed as follows:[3]

$$\frac{y_c}{y_a} = \frac{(1+\varphi) A_c^{1/\mu} k_a w_a^{(1-\theta)/\theta} [(1-\mu)\upsilon_g]^{(1-\mu)/\mu}}{A_a^{1/\theta} t_a w_c^{(1-\mu)/\mu} [(1-\theta) p_a]^{(1-\theta)/\theta}} \tag{4.21}$$

From equation 4.21, it can be seen that the exogenous technological progress of the urban economic sector A_c, the wage level of the agricultural sector w_a, the deposits of the agriculture sector k_a, urban inclination index of fiscal expenditure υ_g, and financial development disparity index between urban and rural areas φ have a positive effect on the urban–rural income gap; i.e., the urban–rural income gap widens if the values of these variables increase. Exogenous technological progress in the agricultural sector A_a, land quantity t_a, the relative price of agricultural products versus nonagriculture products p_a, and the wage level of urban economic sector w_c are negatively correlated with the urban–rural income gap.

The intuitive meaning of these equations is more consistent with the real economic situation in China: The increase in the production technology level of the urban sector will increase the output of nonagricultural products, bringing an increase in the income of the urban economic sector. Land is one of the inputs to rural production; an increase in land area, on the one hand, will increase agricultural output. Without changing other conditions, an increase in land area, on the other hand, will certainly bring about an increase in the number of people engaged in agricultural production. With given total population, this will lead to a decrease in the number of people engaged in the nonagricultural sector, which, with a constant wage rate, will only bring about a decrease in the per capital income of the agricultural sector relative to the nonagricultural sector. The greater the relative price of agricultural versus nonagricultural products, the less the difference will be between the price of agricultural products and that of nonagricultural products, and the relative increase in the price of agricultural products inevitably brings about an increase in the income of rural residents. As for the impact of wage level of the agricultural sector and the urban sector on the urban–rural income gap, which seems at first glance to be inconsistent with people's economic intuition, it is reasonable if delved into deeply. In the case of urban–rural labor mobility, the decrease of wage level of the urban sector will lead to the decrease of income of those migrant workers from the rural areas who go to urban areas for jobs. According to statistics from the Ministry of Human Resources and Social Security of China, the number of peasant workers nationwide in 2010 was 242.23 million, accounting for 36.1% of the total number of peasants, among which the number of peasant workers going to work in the urban areas are 153.35 million, which shows that the income level of peasant workers has a direct impact on the overall income of rural residents. The increase of wage level of the agricultural sector directly increases the income of peasants, while the increase of wage level of urban economic sector will increase the wage of peasant workers, thus reducing the relative gap between urban and rural incomes.[4] Similarly, when the wage level of the agricultural sector increases, the willingness and speed of labor mobility from the rural areas to the urban ones decrease, and the labor engaging in agriculture keeps increasing. However, the production technology and the amount of land used in agricultural production do not change, which brings about a decrease in the rural production efficiency and the per capital income of peasants. The deteriorating scarcity of labor in the urban areas and the labor redistribution between the two sectors eventually widen the urban–rural income gap.

4.4 Parameter calibration

In this part, the model economy is calibrated to be consistent with the general level of long-term economic development in China since 1990. Since the model economy examines variables that are unitized in terms of population, therefore employment in the agricultural and nonagricultural sectors is measured by the distribution of the total social population between the two sectors. By referring to Gollin et al. (2002), the output elasticity of capital of the nonagricultural sector is set as 0.6, and the output elasticity of labor of the agricultural sector is set as 0.6. Based on the assumption of constant returns to scale, the land output elasticity of the agricultural sector is 0.4. According to Sun et al. (2009), the total factor productivity of the agricultural sector is set as 1.1, the total factor productivity of the nonagricultural sector is set as 1.2, and the relative price of agricultural versus nonagricultural products is set as 0.9. Then the calibration of some key parameters in the benchmark model is completed, as shown in Table 4.3.

The benchmark case is examined first, where only wage levels differ and there is no urban–rural financial market imbalance or fiscal expenditure propensity, i.e., $\phi = 0$, $\upsilon_g = 1$, and $k_a = 1$. The quantities in equation 4.21 are unitized in terms of the total population. The ratio of gross wage of primary industry workers to population is used to estimate w_a. The ratio of the gross wage of secondary and tertiary industry workers to population is used to estimate w_c. And the urban consumer price index and rural consumer price index are used to eliminate the inflation factors. Taking the period from 1996 to 2010 into account, according to the data of *China Statistical Yearbooks*, w_a equals 25.5 CNY and w_c 1346.0 CNY. According to the inventory data of the Ministry of Land and Resources in 2008, the amount of land available per capita can be calculated as 0.48 ha. In summary, the urban–rural income ratio under the benchmark situation is 3.206:1. This is basically consistent with the research results of the urban–rural income ratio since the reform and opening-up mentioned in the introduction to this chapter.

However, this chapter examines the income gap resulting from fiscal investment as well as financial market development, and in the case of complete labor market mobility, with the general equilibrium of the market, $w_a = w_c$ necessarily. w_a is assumed as 1. The extent to which these variables and parameters affect the income gap in China is examined by changing υ_g, k_a, and φ. The numerical simulation results are shown in Tables 4.4–4.6.

Table 4.3 Calibrated Values of Exogenous Variables

θ	μ	A_a	A_c	P_a
0.4	0.6	1.1	1.2	0.9

Table 4.4 Keeping ϕ and k_a Fixed and Changing υ_g

υ_g	k_a	Φ	y_c / y_a
1	1	0	2.819:1
2	1	0	4.473:1
3	1	0	5.863:1

Table 4.5 Keeping υ_g and ϕ Fixed and Changing k_a

υ_g	k_a	Φ	y_c / y_a
1	1	0	2.819:1
1	2	0	5.638:1
1	3	0	11.276:1

Table 4.6 Keeping k_a and υ_g Fixed and Changing ϕ

υ_g	k_a	Φ	y_c / y_a
1	1	0	2.819:1
1	1	1	5.638:1
1	1	2	11.276:1

The results of numerical simulation show that when the three variables υ_g, ϕ and k_a increase algebraically, ϕ has the greatest impact on the urban–rural income gap, followed by k_a and υ_g. The numerical simulation shows that the direction of the impact of the three variables on the urban–rural income gap is consistent with that analyzed by the model. The greatest impact of ϕ on the urban–rural income gap indicates, on the one hand, that the difference between urban and rural financial market development leads to the urban sector's efficient use of excess and loan capital to expand production efficiently and the obtainment of good investment opportunities, which directly leads to the income growth of the urban economic sector; on the other hand, the residents of the primary sector cannot enjoy the capital financing and reinvestment that comes with financial market development due to the lagging development of the financial market. As ϕ increases, the urban sector is encouraged to invest and increase income, and the primary sector production is suppressed. The difference in the financial markets' development can be one of the main reasons for the urban–rural income gap.

The direction and degree of the impact of the capital stock per capita in rural areas k_a, a derivative indicator of financial development difference, is consistent with ϕ. This is a bit inconsistent with the economic facts due to the model's previous assumption that the primary sector deposits in banks all the funds on hand, which are indirectly transformed into loan capital in the urban economic sector. The larger k_a is under the effect of the financial market differential index that the larger k_c is, which brings about the growth of investment, output and income in the urban economic sector. The direction of changes in k_a and its impact on the urban–rural income gap once again demonstrate the importance of creating a favorable financial market environment for peasants to increase their income.

The government investment tendency index υ_g is defined as the ratio of fiscal investment in urban areas to fiscal investment in rural areas. When the amount of urban fiscal expenditure is several times higher than the amount of rural fiscal expenditure, it necessarily leads to an increase in the income of urban residents, and the results of the numerical simulation show that when υ_g increases by one unit, the urban–rural income gap widens by the same magnitude. The impact of υ_g on the urban–rural income gap is smaller than that of the financial market development differential index ϕ, which can be mainly explained from the following three factors: First, the amount of fiscal expenditure is predictable and capped, and the government's strict annual fiscal budget system controls the amount of fiscal spending in investment in the economy, which is not as large as the magnitude of the financial market's regulatory role; under the multiplier effect, the amount of derivative deposit will be multiplied. Second, there is a certain crowding-out effect of fiscal spending on the activities of the economic sector, which brings the loss of utility. Third, the central government has been increasing fiscal investment in rural areas in recent years to accelerate the economic development there, so the value of υ_g will definitely decrease in the foreseeable future, and thus its impact on the urban–rural income gap will also tend to moderate.

4.5 Conclusion

Based on Neoclassical Growth Theory, this chapter empirically analyzed the process of Chinese economic development since the institutionalization of the reform and opening-policy using a dynamic growth model under perfectly competitive market conditions. It then calibrates the parameters to be consistent with the typical facts of Chinese economic development and calculates the value of each economic variable when the model economy reaches the steady state by combining the calibrated model with real economic data. On the basis of the parameter calibration, the two economic indexes (financial market development differential index ϕ and government investment tendency index υ_g) are numerically simulated. It is found that the dynamic growth model can better simulate the stylized fact that the fiscal investment in urban areas is higher than that in rural areas, the outflow of capital from rural areas to urban areas runs through financial institutions, and the proportion of urban residents' income out of the whole GDP gradually increases during the process of Chinese economic development. The final simulation results are very close to the real urban–rural income gap data in China.

The simulated impact of financial market development difference on the urban–rural income gap is greater than the impact of fiscal spending propensity on the urban–rural income gap. Hence, three aspects are considered to reduce the urban–rural income gap.

First, correcting the imbalance in urban and rural financial development must be seen as an important measure to narrow the urban–rural income gap. The financial development imbalance leads not only to the outflow of rural capital but also, more importantly, to the absence of an important renewable force for rural economic development. In view of the current lack of credit system in rural areas, the reform of the rural credit system should be intensified, and efforts should be made to improve the creditworthiness of the rural financial institutions, so as to provide a good financing environment for peasants' entrepreneurship and income growth. It is necessary first of all to expand the scale of rural financial development, improve the rural financial system, correct the original discriminatory treatment of financial services towards rural areas and appropriately restrict the transfer of rural financial resources to urban areas. It is also important to effectively improve the efficiency of rural financial development to transform the savings absorbed by various rural financial institutions into rural deposits and sources of funds for the rural credit market in a timely and effective manner. Certainly, it will also be of help to build a mechanism for urban finance to feed rural areas, to develop and provide financial service products and programs suitable for rural residents according to the characteristics of rural areas, and to establish and improve the channels for urban finance to flow to rural areas.

Second, government investment should be increased to support the rural areas. Financial investment in rural areas should be increased, and rural infrastructure construction, including water and electricity facilities, communication facilities and transportation, should be strengthened. The performance assessment standard in rural areas should be adjusted to encourage local governments to make full use of favorable conditions in rural areas, such as natural scenery and local typical culture to develop rural income-generating industries, thus increasing peasants' income.

Finally, the transformation of traditional agriculture should be accelerated in the process of building a new socialist countryside and taking the agricultural development path with Chinese characteristics, which is the objective needed for promoting the reform and development of the rural economy and forming a new pattern of integration of urban–rural economic and social development. It is also important to break the urban–rural dual structure to make it possible for the rural residents to compete equally with urban residents for the resources they need. Certainly, it is necessary to further promote the reform of the household registration system, so that, when rural people move to cities, they can enjoy the same treatment as urban residents in terms of employment, social security and public services, instead of becoming marginalized people in the urban areas.

Notes

1 Full text of Hu's report at 18th Party Congress: http://language.chinadaily.com.cn/news/2012-11/19/content_15941774_3.htm
2 The absolute income gap here means the per capita disposable income of urban households minus that of rural households.
3 Readers who are interested in the mathematical derivation process can contact the author.
4 For example, if the wages of the urban sector increase by CNY 2,500, the wages of migrant workers in the cities will increase by CNY 2,000. In this case, the wage increase in the urban sector is only about 50%, while the wages of migrant workers will increase by about 100%.

Bibliography

Barro, Robert J. "Government Spending in a Simple Model of Endogenous Growth." *Journal of Political Economy* no. 5 (1990): S103–S125.

Cao, Guangxi, Xia Jianwei, and Feng Yue 曹广喜, 夏建伟, 冯跃. "An Empirical Analysis of Financial Development and Urban–Rural Income Gap: Take a Sample of Jiangsu Province" 区域金融发展与城乡收入差距关系的经验分析——以江苏省为例. *Economic Geography* no. 5 (2007): 726–729.

Galor, Oded, and Joseph Zeira. "Income Distribution and Macroeconomics." *Review of Economic Studies* no. 1 (1993): 35–52.

Gollin, Dauglas, Stephen L. Parente, and Richard Rogerson. "The Role of Agriculture in Development." *The American Economic Review* no. 2 (2002): 160–164.

Greenwood, Jeremy, and Boyan Jovanovic. "Financial Development, Growth, and the Distribution of Income." *Journal of Political Economy* no. 5 (1990): 1076–1107.

Mo, Yalin, and Zhang Zhichao 莫亚琳, 张志超. "The Impact of Increased Fiscal Expenditure on Social Income Distribution in Western China: An Empirical Analysis Based on Dynamic Panel Data" 我国西部地区增加财政支出对社会收入分配的影响: 基于动态面板数据计量的实证分析. *Reform of Economic System* no. 10 (2010): 116–120.

Pradhan, Basanta K., P. K. Roy, M. R. Saluja, and Shanta Venkatram. "Rural–Urban Disparities: Income Distribution, Expenditure Patterns and Social Sector." *Economic and Political Weekly* no. 28–29 (2000): 2527–2539.

Sun, Ninghua, Du Yi, and Hong Yongmiao 孙宁华, 堵 溢, 洪永淼. "The Distortion of the Labor Market, the Efficiency Difference and the Urban–Rural Income Gap" 劳动力市场扭曲、效率差异与城乡收入差距. *Management World* no. 9 (2009): 44–52.

Wang, Ren 王韧. "The Analysis of Factors Resulting in Change of Urban–Rural Income Gap in China" 中国城乡收入差距变动的成因分析: 兼论"倒U"假说的适用性. *Statistical Research* no. 4 (2006): 14–19.

Yao, Yaojun 姚耀军. "Financial Development, Urbanization and Urban–Rural Income Gap in China" 金融发展、城市化与城乡收入差距. *China Rural Survey* no. 2 (2005): 2–8+80.

5 Informal finance, a dual-track interest rate and the effects of credit policy

The monetary and financial system in China is characterized by two stylized facts: the prospering informal finance (or private finance) and a dual-track interest rate system. These facts are interconnected and largely affect monetary policy formulation and implementation. They make the monetary policy operation in China significantly different from that in a mature market-oriented economy. Informal finance is not directly monitored by the central bank. Thus the two types of cost-of-capital give rise to the dual-track interest rate system. These two types, the market-oriented interest rate and the policy rate, are determined by the supply demand relationship of loanable funds from the informal financial system and supervision of the central bank, respectively. For this reason, this chapter tries to analyze the effectiveness of credit policy implementation by building a DSGE model consisting of informal financing channels and the dual-track interest rate system. It is found that credit expansion policy will increase the credit supply of the banking system while impeding informal financing activities; the interactions of informal financing and bank lending will weaken the regulatory effects; under the dual-track interest rate, a positive debt shock reduces enterprises' loanable funds demand from the informal financial system, thus lowering the market-oriented interest rate; debt policy exhibits both a credit supply adjustment effect and a cost-of-capital adjustment effect, thus strengthening the regulatory effectiveness of credit policy. Besides, financial deregulation policy aimed at reducing informal financing frictions can alleviate the reliance of companies on banking credit and reduce the market-oriented interest rate by increasing the loanable funds supply of informal financing channels.

5.1 New Keynesian framework with informal finance and the dual-track interest rate

Financial innovation and the supply demand relationship of the credit supply have had an increasing influence on the real economy in recent years. The financial crisis in the United States and the debt crisis in Europe have caused government intervention policies to be sought after again by the theorists. Macroeconomic theory has shifted from neoliberalism to Keynesian

DOI: 10.4324/9781003305651-5

interventionism. The RBC theory with factors of finance and credit and the New Keynesian monetary theory have become the mainstream. For a while, the preferred policy of central banks is to use quantitative tools to regulate macroeconomic operations, and it has become an urgent theoretical task to build a macroeconomic model that includes monetary and credit factors.

Credit policy accounts for an important part of the national macroregulatory system and works as a set of principles and guidelines made by the central bank. It is made to ensure the supply of credit to enterprises and the safety, liquidity and profitability of commercial banks. It helps guide and regulate the investment of bank credit funds in accordance with the national industrial policy and monetary policy. Credit policy and monetary policy constitute the main instruments supporting the central bank's macroregulations.

Before the 1980s, the main tool for monetary policy research was the IS-LM curve. Since the 1980s, economists have emphasized the microfoundation of macroeconomic models. The traditional IS-LM curve has been criticized by economists for its lack of microfoundation and the arbitrariness of parameter setting, and its unsuitability for dealing with monetary policy problems in which the interest rate is the focus. Clarida et al. (1999), Woodford (1999), McCallum and Nelsen (1999), Amano (2007) and others have applied the New Keynesian model to monetary policy research. They introduced the assumptions of monopolistic competition and nominal rigidities into the DSGE model and built the basic framework of New Keynesian theory. The New Keynesian DSGE model established a system of macroeconomic equations from the perspective of the optimization of the microeconomic agent, of which the optimal decisions of microindividuals were consistent with the prescriptiveness of various classical theories, such as price stickiness and monetary non-neutrality in the short run. Through parameter calibration and numerical simulation, the New Keynesian theory can achieve consistency between theoretical development and empirical analysis, avoiding both the Lucas critique and the dynamic inconsistency of policies. The theory is highly credible and preferable in theoretical forecasting and policy formulation.

In the New Keynesian macroeconomic model, most firms have adopted Calvo pricing, which meant that, in any period, the firm might be able to set the optimal price with a certain probability based on expected future earnings. Galí and Gertler (1999) developed a forward-looking and backward-looking hybrid pricing strategy in which firms that cannot price autonomously could adjust the price appropriately according to the previous inflation rate. Xue (2010) argued that the hybrid pricing strategy was more in line with Chinese economic reality. He pointed out that there were many frictions in the Chinese economy, such as information asymmetry, insufficient decision-making ability, price regulation, and long-term negotiation time lag, as well as the residual effects of the dual-track price system in the planned economy era.

After the financial crisis in the United States and other parts of the world, introducing financial friction into the DSGE model has drawn increasing attention from scholars. Bernanke et al. (1989) was the first to develop a general equilibrium model to study financial friction. Kiyotaki and Moore (1997) argued that there were frictions in the credit market and that the creditor was required to provide loans at a percentage of the market value of the debtor's collateral to reduce the default risk of the debtor. Iacoviello (2005) included a lending constraint on housing as collateral in the DSGE model. Liu et al. (2013) included both housing and capital goods as collateral. Both Bernanke et al. and Kiyotaki and Moore considered only credit market frictions and did not consider that the central bank could influence them with a credit policy. Probably, these scholars studied the US economy, where the Federal Reserve was less likely to intervene directly in the credit structure and credit investment of commercial banks. Nevertheless, China is another case. As the People's Bank of China (central bank)'s official website explains, "a credit policy constitutes an important part of macroeconomic policy … and a credit policy and monetary policy complement and promote each other. They are both independent and interdependent … . A monetary policy is mainly focused on regulating the total amount … while a credit policy is mainly focused on solving the structural problems of the economy."[1]

For Chinese economists, it is theoretically challenging to apply the New Keynesian DSGE model to Chinese money and credit markets. It is necessary to consider the stylized facts of the financial system and the institutional context of China. As a transitional economy, the monetary and financial system of China is characterized by two interdependent stylized facts: the prospering informal finance (or private finance) and the dual-track interest rate system.

Lian and Chen (2011) pointed out that informal finance mainly referred to the financial transaction activities in the financial system, including informal financial intermediaries and informal financial markets. These were not subject to the regulations of the People's Bank of China (PBOC). The informal financial system in this chapter has a broad sense. It refers to all financial and quasi-financial sectors that can provide loanable funds to enterprises but that are not directly influenced by credit policy, such as nonbank financial institutions including trust and investment companies, private lending etc. The financial system in China has been developed gradually on the basis of a single state-owned banking system before the reform and opening-up. Due to the rigid operation of state-owned banks and the excessive tilting of relatively scarce credit resources to state-owned enterprises (SOEs), a sizable informal financial system emerged during the evolution of China's financial system. Although Xie (2008) mentioned that the government implemented a series of commercial bank reform measures after the Asian financial crisis and significantly improved the efficiency of capital allocation in the banking system, Lu and Xiao (2008) noted that the ownership structure of commercial banks still exhibits obvious state-owned characteristics. Zhang (2000) noted that the credit discrimination faced by non-state-owned enterprises (non-SOEs) has not been fundamentally eliminated. Bai and Lian (2012) argued that the huge contrast between non-SOEs and SOEs, in terms of asset quality, debt guarantee ability, information transparency and bank–enterprise cooperation, makes it more difficult for large commercial banks to provide financial services to non-SOEs. Therefore, informal finance and formal finance (the banking system) will continue to coexist for a long time into the future. Along with the financial deregulation and the continuous innovation of financial instruments, the financing channels for enterprises are increasingly diversified. Allen et al. (2005) argued that informal finance provides most of Chinese economic growth, especially the growth of the so-called hybrid sector.[2]

The dual-track interest rate system refers to the existence of two prices for funds in the monetary and financial system of China: One is the price of funds of the banking system regulated by the central bank; the other is the market-based price of funds determined by the supply–demand relationship of loanable funds of the informal financial system. Zhang (2007) argued that the existence of a dual-track interest rate system inevitably implied the existence of other regulatory measures. The current dual-track interest rate system corresponds precisely to the existence of both informal finance and formal finance (the banking system) in the financial system of China. Although the market-oriented interest rate reform has made considerable progress, the interest rate ceiling on bank deposits has not yet been fully deregulated.[3] Yi and Wu (1999) mentioned that excessively low deposit interest rate ceilings were a major feature of financial repression. He and Wang (2011) noted that the low cost of funding sources in the banking system made the price of bank credit funds lower than the equilibrium price of funds, and the capital price distortion in the dual-track interest rate system was perpetuated.

The dual-track interest rate system and informal finance that characterize the financial system of China have a significant impact on the process of monetary policy formulation and implementation. They made the mode of monetary policy operation in China significantly different from that of developed countries. Since the credit policy of the People's Bank of China cannot directly intervene in the lending activities of the informal financial system and the resulting market-based interest rates, the transmission mechanism and regulatory effects of credit policy are thus inhibited. For example, the PBOC can regulate the credit allocation of commercial banks, but it is difficult to control the flow of funds between the informal financial system and the formal financial (banking) system. Even if the PBOC expands the scope of regulation, the market can still circumvent regulation through continuous "financial innovative tricks."

To analyze the transmission mechanism and regulatory effects of the credit policy of a transitional economy, it is innovative to introduce the stylized facts of informal finance and dual-track interest rate system into the New Keynesian analytical framework. Chen and Gong (2006) contended that a New Keynesian model that introduced price stickiness and a monopolistic competition market was more suitable to explain the cyclical fluctuations of the Chinese economy. Therefore, this chapter also adopts the New Keynesian model with price stickiness and refers to Iacoviello and Minetti (2006) and Liu et al. (2013) while setting credit frictions. It differs from the precedent of scholars in that the effects of both the dual-track interest rate and informal finance on the implementation of credit policy are considered simultaneously.

5.2 SVAR analysis of credit policy shocks

This section adopts the SVAR (structural vector autoregression) method to analyze the effects of credit policy shocks on informal financing activities, output and inflation. The macroeconomic variables selected include the financing activities of informal finance and the financing activities of formal finance, output and inflation. They are measured by incremental trust loans represented by TL_t, incremental CNY loans represented by L_t, gross industrial production represented by Y_t, and the year-on-year growth rate of the consumer price index (CPI) represented by CPI_t. The data type is monthly, the time interval is from January 2002 to December 2012, the sample size is 132, and the data source is the website of the People's Bank of China.[4] The incremental CNY loans and trust loans are compared in terms of the aggregate social financing shown as Figure 5.1.[5] It can be seen that there is a clear interactive relationship between CNY loans and trust loans, i.e., there is an opposite relationship between the financing activities of formal finance and those of informal finance.

The SVAR method is adopted to analyze the effects of credit policy shocks on informal financing activities, output and inflation. The data processing process is as follows: The producer price index (PPI) is first used to deflate the gross industrial production data and then takes the logarithm of the deflated incremental trust loans, gross industrial production and incremental CNY loans, respectively. Since these three economic variables show certain seasonal characteristics, this chapter adopts the TRAMO/SEATS method in Eviews 6.0 to adjust them seasonally. Finally, the H-P filter is used to decompose the seasonally adjusted data into trend items and periodic fluctuation items. The

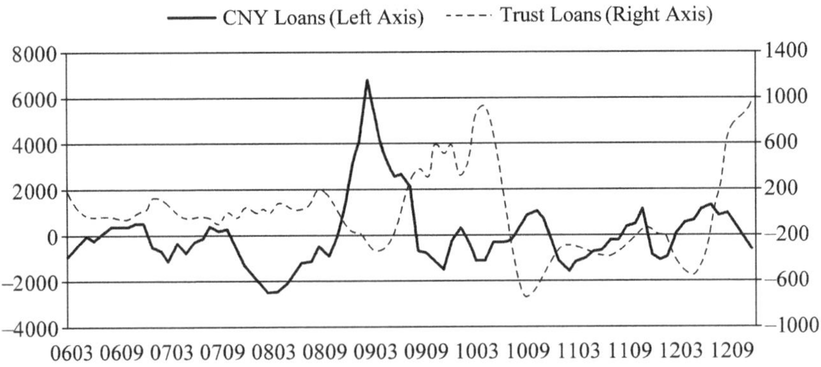

Figure 5.1 Bank Loans Versus Trust Loans.

obtained periodic fluctuation item is used to perform SVAR estimation. The SVAR model set up in this chapter is:

$$\begin{bmatrix} L_t^c \\ TL_t^c \\ Y_t^c \\ CPI_t^c \end{bmatrix} = A + C_0 \begin{bmatrix} \varepsilon_{L,t} \\ \varepsilon_{TL,t} \\ \varepsilon_{Y,t} \\ \varepsilon_{CPI,t} \end{bmatrix} + C(L) \begin{bmatrix} \varepsilon_{L,t} \\ \varepsilon_{TL,t} \\ \varepsilon_{Y,t} \\ \varepsilon_{CPI,t} \end{bmatrix}$$

where $C(L) = \sum_{i=1}^{\infty} C_i L^i$. In addition, this chapter uses the Cholesky decomposition method to impose a short-term identification constraint on the model, i.e., the short-term matrix is assumed to satisfy the following form:

$$C_0 = \begin{bmatrix} c_{11}^0 & 0 & 0 & 0 \\ c_{21}^0 & c_{22}^0 & 0 & 0 \\ c_{31}^0 & c_{32}^0 & c_{33}^0 & 0 \\ c_{41}^0 & c_{42}^0 & c_{43}^0 & c_{44}^0 \end{bmatrix}$$

It is well-known that imposing a short-run constraint on SVAR using the Cholesky decomposition method results in the situation where variables ranked later are affected by the current period and lags behind the variables ranked earlier, while the earlier variables are not affected by the current period of the later variables. We argue that credit policy shocks first affect incremental CNY loans, then indirectly trust investment and finally industrial output and CPI. This is almost irreversible. We thus rely on the difference in the speed of response to credit policy shocks. This leads to an SVAR impulse response function for the effects of credit policy shocks on output, informal financing activities and inflation, as shown in Figure 5.2. The solid lines in Figure 5.2 are the impulse response of output, informal financing activities and inflation to credit policy shocks, respectively, and the dashed lines refer to the 95% confidence interval obtained after 2000 repeated sampling with the method of Sims and Zha (1999) using Bootstrap.

It can be seen from Figure 5.2 the following data characteristics: First, credit shocks can promote an increase in output. An increase in credit expansion by banks promotes an increase in output in the current period, after which it gradually retraces, and after nine months it retraces to a trough and then starts to rebound, adjusting back to the initial steady-state level in the 14th month. Secondly, credit policy shocks affect informal financing activities, and the demand for informal finance by firms weakens when bank credit expands. When bank lending increases, trust financing is suppressed (significance level close to 5%), reaches a trough after 4 months, and then gradually rises, adjusting back to the initial steady-state level in the 14th mouth. Third, an increase in credit expansion causes inflation. The effects of credit shocks on inflation show a certain degree of persistence. The price rises in the current

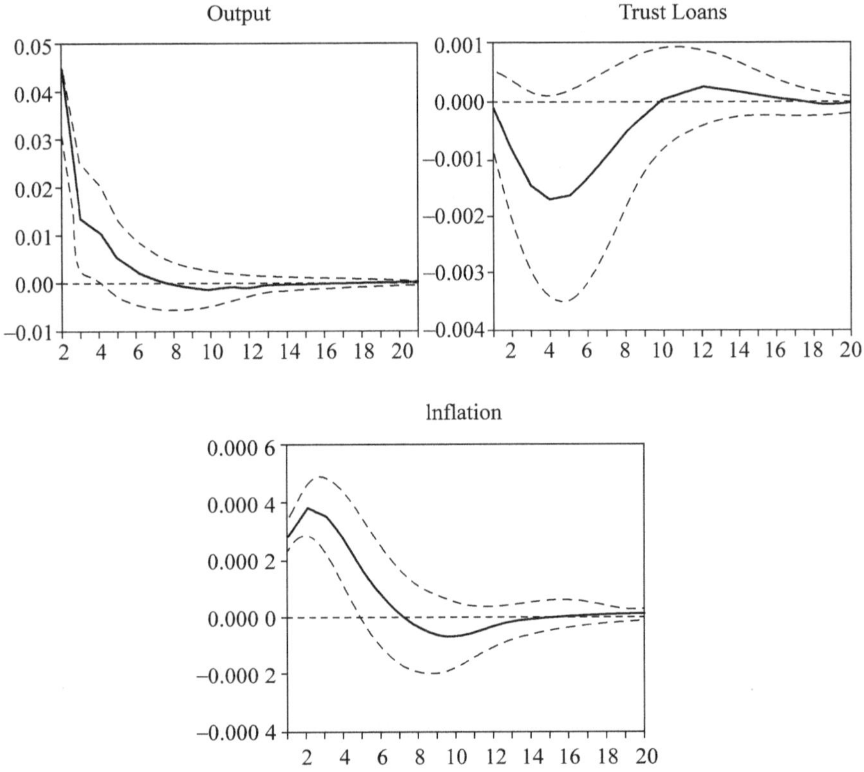

Figure 5.2 Impulse Responses of Output, Trust Loans and Inflation to Credit Expansion.

period under a positive credit shock but does not reach a peak, then peaks in the second period and gradually retraces to a trough after 9 months and starts to rebound, adjusting to the initial steady-state level in the 14th month.

In conclusion, the empirical results of the SVAR method show that credit expansion can boost output and trigger inflation. The demand by firms for informal financing like trust loans weakens when bank credit expands. It indicates that there is an opposite relationship between bank loans and informal financing, thus weakening the effects of credit shocks on aggregate social financing. A DSGE model will be built to analyze the two stylized facts of the monetary and financial system and the preceding data characteristics.

5.3 Model building

The model built is a New Keynesian type. It includes the household, intermediate goods manufacturer and monetary authority and adds the retailer to involve price stickiness by referring to Bernanke et al. (1999).

5.3.1 The household

Based on the research by Iacoviello (2005), it is assumed that the household derives utility from consumption, housing demand and leisure and that it seeks to maximize expected utility. Putting housing demand into the utility function captures the real importance of real estate consumption in the Chinese economy. Definitely, real estate is as important collateral as machines (see Liu et al., 2013). The utility function for the household sector is:

$$\max E_0 \sum_{t=0}^{\infty} \beta^t \left(\log\left(c_{H,t} - \tau c_{H,t-1}\right) + j \log h_{H,t} - \frac{1}{\eta}\left(L_t\right)^{\eta} \right)$$

where $\beta \in (0,1)$ represents the discount factor. $c_{H,t}$ represents the household consumption in period t. $h_{H,t}$ represents the amount of housing assets owned by the household in period t. L_t represents the amount of labor provided by the household to the intermediate goods manufacturer in period t. In addition, based on the usual case (e.g., Liu et al., 2013), consumption habit preference is added in setting the household utility function, and $\tau \in (0,1)$ refers to the intensity of the household's consumption habit. The household is subject to the budget constraint:

$$c_{H,t} + b_t + q_{h,t} h_{H,t} = \frac{R_{t-1} b_{t-1}}{\pi_t} + w_t L_t + q_{h,t} h_{H,t-1} + d_t^r + d_t^b$$

where b_t represents the household's real saving in period t. $q_t = \frac{Q_t}{P_t}$ represents the real house price. R_{t-1} represents the nominal deposit rate in period $t-1$. $\pi_t = P_t / P_{t-1}$ represents the inflation rate in period t. w_t represents the real wage paid by intermediate goods manufacturers. d_t^r represents the profit of retailers. d_t^b represents the spread between loans and deposits and is greater than zero under the dual-track interest rate system, equal to zero in other cases.

5.3.2 The intermediate goods manufacturer

The intermediate goods manufacturer uses capital, labor, and plant as inputs to produce intermediate goods according to the Cobb–Douglas production function, and the production function is:

$$Y_t = A_t \left(K_{t-1}\right)^{\mu} \left(h_{t-1}\right)^{\upsilon} \left(L_t\right)^{1-\mu-\upsilon}$$

where A_t represents the technological level. K_{t-1} represents the capital input accumulated in period $t-1$ for the production of intermediate goods in period t. h_{t-1} represents the plant invested in period $t-1$ for the production of period t. μ and υ represent the parameters of share of capital input and share of plant input, respectively. Using the setting of Bernanke et al. (1999), the intermediate goods manufacturer in a perfect competition position sells the produced products Y_t to the retailer at the wholesale price $P_{w,t}$, while the price of the final goods is P_t. $X_t = \frac{P_t}{P_{w,t}}$ represents the cost markup of the final goods to the intermediate goods.

According to the setting of Iacoviello (2005), it is assumed that the intermediate goods manufacturer is less patient compared to the household. That is, the discount factor of the intermediate goods manufacturer (γ) is smaller than the discount factor of the household (β). This assumption is also important in classical models, referring to Kiyotaki and Moore (1997). The expected utility function of the intermediate goods manufacturer is:

$$\max E_0 \sum_{t=0}^{\infty} \gamma^t \log c_t$$

where c_t represents the intermediate goods manufacturer's consumption in period t.

Kiyotaki and Moore (1997) argued that there were frictions in the credit market and that the creditor had to provide loans based on a certain percentage of the market value of the debtor's collateral to reduce the default risk of the debtor. Setting the intermediate goods manufacturer's lending constraint involves three cases.

Case 1: Banking system only

The only source of credit funding for the manufacturer in this case is the banking system, and by referring to Liu et al. (2013), the credit constraint imposed on the manufacturer is:

$$R_t b_t' \leq m_t E_t \left(\pi_{t+1} \left(q_{h,t+1} h_t + q_{t+1} K_t \right) \right)$$

where α_t' represents bank loans obtained by the intermediate goods manufacturer in period t. R_t represents the benchmark interest rate for loans. m_t represents the ratio of loan repayment to the sum of the value of plant and capital goods owned by the intermediate goods manufacturer, i.e., $E_t \left(\pi_{t+1} (1 - m_t) \left(q_{h,t+1} h_t + q_{t+1} K_t \right) \right)$ is the bank's loan liquidation cost. q_{t+1} represents the shadow price of capital goods K_t in period $t + 1$. $q_t = u_{K,t} / u_{c,t}$. $u_{K,t}$ represents the Lagrangian multiplier of the capital accumulation equation.[6] $u_{c,t}$ represents the marginal utility of the intermediate goods manufacturer's consumption in period t. The credit constraint can be interpreted in two ways: First, the manufacturer must use assets of a certain value as collateral to obtain loans; second, the total amount of loans available to the intermediate goods manufacturer is proportional to the value of the assets it owns; the higher the value of the assets owned, the more loans the manufacturer can obtain.

Case 2: Banking system and informal financial system coexist with only one interest rate

The sources of credit funds for the intermediate goods manufacturer in this case include the banking system and the informal financial system, and by referring to Iacoviello and Minetti (2006), the credit constraints imposed on the intermediate goods manufacturer are:

$$R_t b_t' \leq m_t \alpha_t E_t \left(\pi_{t+1} \left(q_{h,t+1} h_t + q_{t+1} K_t \right) \right)$$

$$R_t b_t'' \leq E_t \left(\left(1-\alpha_t\right) \pi_{t+1} \left(q_{h,t+1} h_t + q_{t+1} K_t \right) \left(1 - \frac{1-z_t}{q_h h + qK} \left(1-\alpha_t\right) \pi_{t+1} \left(q_{h,t+1} h_t + q_{t+1} K_t \right) \right) \right)$$

where α_t represents the ratio of banking credit to debt financing. $1-\alpha_t$ represents the ratio of informal financing loans to debt financing. b_t'' represents the informal financing funds obtained by the intermediate goods manufacturer in period t. Based on this setting, it is obtained that the liquidation cost of informal financing loans is $E_t \left(\frac{1-z_t}{q_h h + qK} \left(\pi_{t+1} \left(1-\alpha_t\right) \left(q_{h,t+1} h_t + q_{t+1} K_t \right) \right)^2 \right)$.

This cost function is a convex function, and along with increasing the scale of lending, the marginal liquidation cost keeps increasing. This setting takes into account the increase in lending frictions caused by the low degree of regulation of informal finance, the poor asset quality and transparency of financing agents and the lack of risk control ability of lenders. In this case, α_t is an endogenous variable with a first-order condition:

$$\lambda_t' m_t = \lambda_t'' E_t \left(\left(1 - \frac{2\left(1-z_t\right)}{q_h h + qK} \left(1-\alpha_t\right) \pi_{t+1} \left(q_{h,t+1} h_t + q_{t+1} K_t \right) \right) \right)$$

where λ_t' and λ_t'', respectively, represent the Lagrangian multiplier of the bank credit constraint and that of the informal finance credit constraint.

Case 3: Policy interest rate and market-oriented interest rate coexist, i.e., the dual-track interest rate system

The sources of credit funds for the intermediate goods manufacturer in this case include the banking system and the informal financial system, and the cost of funds for banking credit is the monetary policy enforcement rate of the monetary authority. The cost of funds for informal financing loans is the market-oriented interest rate determined by the supply–demand market for loanable funds. The lending constraint of informal finance imposed on the intermediate goods manufacturer is:

$$R_t' b_t'' \leq E_t \left((1-\alpha) \pi_{t+1} \left(q_{h,t+1} h_t + q_{t+1} K_t \right) \left(1 - \frac{1-z_t}{q_h h + qK} (1-\alpha) \pi_{t+1} \left(q_{h,t+1} h_t + q_{t+1} K_t \right) \right) \right)$$

R_t' represents the market-oriented interest rate that enables the supply and demand of loanable funds in the informal financial system to reach equilibrium and is an endogenous variable in this case. Its first-order condition is:

$$\frac{1}{c_t} = E_t \left(\frac{\gamma R_t}{\pi_{t+1} c_{t+1}} \right) + \lambda_t'' R_t'$$

where λ_t'' represents the Lagrangian multiplier of informal finance credit constraint.

Except for the production function constraint (technological constraint) and the credit constraint, the intermediate goods manufacturer is also subject to the following budget constraint:

$$\frac{Y_t}{X_t} + b_t' + b_t'' + q_{h,t} h_{t-1} = c_t + q_{h,t} h_t + \frac{R_{t-1} b_{t-1}'}{\pi_t} + \frac{R_{t-1}' b_{t-1}''}{\pi_t} + w_t L_t + I_t$$

where I_t represents the investment invested in capital for the production of intermediate goods in period t. Following Christiano et al. (2007) and Liu et al. (2013), the capital accumulation process with capital adjustment costs included is as follows:

$$K_t = (1-\delta_k) K_{t-1} + \left[1 - \frac{\psi}{2} \left(\frac{I_t}{I_{t-1}} - 1 \right)^2 \right] I_t$$

where δ represents the depreciation rate of capital input. ψ represents the capital adjustment factor. This capital adjustment function is a convex function. In the steady state, the current investment is equal to the depreciation of previous capital input, and the capital adjustment cost is 0.

5.3.3 The Retailer

To introduce price stickiness in the model, by referring to Bernanke et al. (1999), the retailer is involved. It is assumed that the retailer is amonopolistic with competitors continuously distributed on the interval [0,1], buys intermediate products at price P_t and decomposes them into differentiated products $Y_t(i)$, which will then be sold at price $P_t(i)$. The final products are then obtained by summing up $Y_t(i)$ as input factors according to the Dixit–Stigliz approach (1977), which is specified as follows:

$$Y_t^f = \left[\int_0^1 Y_t(i)^{(\epsilon-1)/\epsilon} \, d(i) \right]^{\epsilon/(\epsilon-1)}$$

As seen from this equation, $Y_t(i)$ represents the constant elasticity of substitution (CES). Solving the cost minimization problem of the final products can obtain the demand function $Y_t(i) = \left(P_t(i)/P_t\right)^{-\epsilon} Y_t^f$ of $Y_t(i)$, $\epsilon > 1$. $1/\epsilon$ is the price elasticity of demand of $Y_t(i)$. P_t represents the price of final goods. The specific equation is:

$$P_t = \left[\int_0^1 P_t(i)^{1-\epsilon} \, d(i) \right]^{1/(1-\epsilon)}$$

It is assumed that price stickiness exists in the economy, and Calvo (1983) argued that the probability that each retailer can adjust its own price in any period is $1-\theta$. Xue (2010) considered that the market-oriented pricing mechanism in China was still imperfect under the influence of incomplete information and government regulation and that the pricing behavior of manufacturers exhibited a dual-track system in which market pricing and planned price coexisted. Therefore, Gali and Gertler (1999) or Smets and Wouters (2003)'s forward-looking and backward-looking hybrid pricing strategy is introduced into the model. Manufacturer j, who cannot adjust prices autonomously (with a probability of θ) in the Calvo model, can make adaptive price adjustments according to the previous inflation level. The price adjustment equation is:

$$P_{t+k}(j) = P_t(j) \left(\frac{P_{t+k-1}}{P_{t-1}} \right)^{\delta_P} \qquad k = 0,1,2\ldots\ldots$$

where $\delta_P \in [0,1]$ represents the price adjustment elasticity. When $\delta_P = 1$, manufacturers adjust the price exactly according to the previous inflation level. When $\delta_P = 0$, the model equals the standard Calvo model. Manufacture i, who can autonomously adjust prices (with a probability of $1-\theta$), chooses the optimal price according to the profit maximization principle. Their expected discounted profit function affected by price adjustment is:

$$\max E_t \sum_{k=0}^{\infty} \theta^k \left\{ \Lambda_{t,t+k} \left(\frac{P_t^*}{P_{t+k}} \left(\frac{P_{t+k-1}}{P_{t-1}} \right)^{\delta_P} - \frac{1}{X_{t+k}} \right) Y_{t+k}^*(i) \right\}$$

where $\Lambda_{t,t+k} = \beta^k \left(u_{c,t+k} / u_{c,t}\right)$ represents the stochastic discount factor. The profit of the intermediate goods manufacturers is $d_t^r = Y_t\left(1 - 1/X_t\right)$. The retail goods manufacturers, who can adjust prices autonomously, maximize this equation by choosing P_t^*. The price of the final products P_t in period t is:

$$P_t = \left(\theta \left(P_{t-1} \left(\frac{P_{t-1}}{P_{t-2}} \right)^{\delta_P} \right)^{1-\epsilon} + (1-\theta)\left(P_t^*\right)^{1-\epsilon} \right)^{1/(1-\epsilon)}$$

The following Hybrid New Keynesian Phillips Curve (HNKPC) can be obtained by solving the profit maximization problem and logarithmic linearization for retail goods manufacturers:

$$\hat{\pi}_t = \frac{\beta}{1+\beta\delta_P} E_t\left(\hat{\pi}_{t+1}\right) + \frac{\delta_P}{1+\beta\delta_P}\hat{\pi}_{t-1} - \frac{(1-\theta)(1-\theta\beta)}{\theta}\frac{1}{1+\beta\delta_P}\hat{X}_t$$

where $\hat{\pi}_t$ and $\hat{X}_t$ represent, respectively, the inflation rate and the percentage of the cost markup of the final products to the intermediate products that deviates from the steady state. The steady-state value of the inflation rate is $\pi = 1$. The steady-state value of the cost markup (in the absence of price stickiness) is $X = \epsilon/(\epsilon - 1)$. ϵ represents the level of competition among retailers. The larger ϵ is, the more intense the competition is, and the smaller the cost markup is.

5.3.4 The monetary authority and government

The monetary authority and government are involved in the model. Policy shocks include credit policy shocks and financial deregulation policy shocks. The monetary authority sets the short-term nominal interest rate according to the Taylor rule; i.e., the short-term nominal interest rate is impacted by the output gap and the inflation gap. By referring to Collard and Dellas (2005) and Miao and Peng (2011), the specific form of the Taylor rule is:

$$\hat{R}_t = r_R \hat{R}_{t-1} + (1-r_R) r_\pi \hat{\pi}_t + (1-r_R) r_y \hat{Y}_t$$

The variables in this equation are their respective percentage deviations from the steady state. $\hat{\pi}_t$ and $\hat{Y}_t$ represent the inflation gap and the aggregate output gap, respectively. In addition, the monetary authority also influences economic performance by implementing the credit policy, but the credit policy only has a direct impact on the banking system's credit expansion in the form of:

$$\hat{m}_t = \rho_m \hat{m}_{t-1} + u_{m,t}$$

where $\hat{m}_t$ follows the AR(1) process and $\rho_m \in (0,1)$ represents its autocorrelation coefficient. The shock term $u_{m,t}$ follows a normal distribution with mean 0 and variance σ_m^2.

The impact of financial deregulation policies will be examined later in this chapter. Such policies are abstracted as positive shocks to variable z_t in our model; i.e., such policies reduce the lending frictions in the informal financial system in the form of:

$$\hat{z}_t = \rho_z \hat{z}_{t-1} + u_{z,t}$$

$\hat{z}_t$ follows the AR(1) process, and $\rho_z \in (0,1)$ represents its autocorrelation coefficient. The shock term $u_{z,t}$ follows a normal distribution with mean 0 and variance σ_z^2.

5.3.5 General equilibrium

In equilibrium, the commodity, credit and real estate markets must be clear simultaneously. The market clearing conditions are:

$$Y_t = c_{H,t} + c_t + I_t$$

$$b_t = b_t' + b_t''$$

$$h_{H,t} + h_t = 1$$

5.4 Parameter calibration

Fifteen parameters $(\beta, \gamma, \tau, \theta, X, \mu, v, \eta, j, \psi, \delta_k, \delta_p, r_R, r_\pi, r_y)$ will be calibrated in the model based on existing research literature.

First, the parameters related to the utility function are calibrated. The discount factor of the household is set as $\beta = 0.9925$; i.e., the annual deposit rate in the steady state is 3%; according to Zhang (2009), the average nominal loan rate between 1992 and 2008 is 8%, so the discount factor for entrepreneurs is set as $\gamma = 0.98$. Based on the estimation results of Guo and Yang (2011) using the generalized method of moment (GMM) method, the consumption habit factor τ is set as 0.58; the labor supply elasticity η is set as 1.2 by referring to the estimation of Gali et al. (2007), and it is found that the value of this parameter is reasonable through sensitivity analysis. Based on the estimation results of Yang and Chang (2012) using the Bayesian method, the housing demand coefficient j is set as 0.08.

Second, the manufacturer-related parameters are calibrated. The parameters related to the production function of the intermediate goods manufacturer are first of all calibrated based on the relevant literature. The share of labor input is set as 0.5. Chow and Li (2002) estimated the aggregate production function using Chinese data from 1952 to 1998, found that the Cobb–Douglas production function with constant returns to scale is applicable to China and that the share of labor input is estimated to be 0.45. Other scholars in China also estimated the share of labor input to be around 0.5; for example, Zhang (2002) estimated the share of labor input to be 0.501, and Wang and Fan (2000) estimated the share of labor input to be 0.5. In addition, the annual depreciation rate of capital is estimated in the literature to be between 0.04 and 0.1, and the quarterly depreciation rate of capital is set as 0.025; the elasticity of substitution ϵ of intermediate goods manufacturers determines the cost markup of final goods to intermediate goods in steady-state conditions $X = \epsilon / (\epsilon - 1)$. It is taken to be 10 by Chen et al. (2004), 3.71 by Li and Meng (2006), and 4.61 by Zhang (2009) using the GMM estimation method based on Chinese macroquarterly data. It is set as $\epsilon = 4.61$ in this chapter; i.e., the cost markup in steady state is $X = 1.277$. The capital adjustment factor ψ is set as 5 after considering the existing research, which varies widely. Christiano et al. (2007) estimated it as 15.1, while Kobayashi and Nutahara (2010) set it as 1.01. Liu et al. (2013) set it as 0.18 while considering capital as collateral and set it as 6.35 while considering both capital and land as collateral.

Finally, the parameters related to the New Keynesian Phillips curve and other parameters are calibrated. The estimation of the price stickiness factor in the Chinese economy has not yet reached any agreement. This chapter sets the price stickiness factor as $\theta = 0.75$, indicating that the time required for one price adjustment is about one year. Chen and Gong (2006) set θ as 0.6, and Zhang (2009) set θ as 0.84 based on the GMM method. In addition, the elasticity of price adjustment δ_P is set as 0.8. Due to the low frequency and minor adjustment of the interest rate instrument in the monetary policy, the autocorrelation coefficient of the interest rate of monetary policy implementation according to the Taylor rule is set as 0.9 by referring to Collard and Dellas (2005) and Miao and Peng (2011). The inflation gap coefficient r_π and output gap coefficient δ_P are set as 1.01 and 0 respectively (in the economic sense, the inflation gap coefficient should be greater than 1). The calibrated parameter values are presented in Table 5.1.

5.5 Impulse response and transmission mechanism analysis

To examine the impact of the informal financial system and the dual-track interest rate system on the effects of credit policy, impulse response to credit supply shocks of the model is simulated based on the parameter calibration results. The dynamic transmission mechanism of the model is then specifically analyzed based on the impulse response results.

5.5.1 The effects of credit policy under the impact of informal finance

The difference in impulse responses of bank loans and of informal loans to credit shocks is shown in Figure 5.3. In this model, a credit policy only has a direct effect on credit allocation in the banking system. The bank loans available

Table 5.1 Calibrated Values of Model Parameters

Parameter Calibration	*Calibrated Values*	*Notes*
β	0.9925	Household discount factor
γ	0.9800	Enterprise discount factor
τ	0.5800	Consumption inertia factor
η	1.2000	Labor supply elasticity
j	0.0800	Housing demand coefficient
Ψ	5.0000	Capital adjustment factor
Θ	0.7500	Price stickiness factor
χ	1.2770	Steady-state value of price markup
μ	0.5000	Share of labor input
ν	0.2000	Share of real estate investment
δ_k	0.0250	Capital depreciation rate
δ_p	0.8000	The probability of choosing an adaptive price according to previous inflation level by a manufacturer
r_R	0.9000	Interest rate autocorrelation coefficient
r_π	1.0100	Inflation gap coefficient
r_y	0.1000	Output gap coefficient

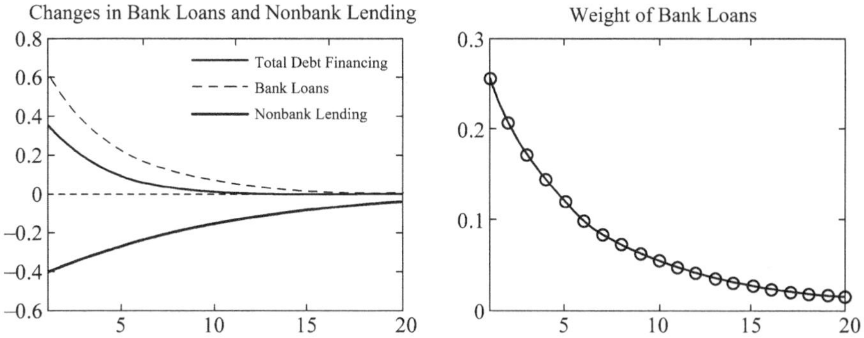

Figure 5.3 Difference of Impulse Responses of Bank Loans and Informal Loans to Credit Shocks.

to manufacturers based on the same value of tangible assets (plant and capital goods) increase with a positive credit policy shock. It can be seen from Figure 5.3 that bank loans with a positive credit shock increase significantly both in quantity (see the left side) and weight (α_t in the model, see the right side). A credit shock also indirectly affects the informal loans. In the model, informal finance complements bank loans and its relative size depends on the availability of banking credit, and the informal loans are dampened when banking credit is more readily available to manufactures and vice versa. It can be seen from Figure 5.3 that informal loans decline with a positive credit shock, both in terms of quantity (see the left side) and weight ($1-\alpha_t$, see the right side). However, aggregate debt financing for the economy as a whole (including bank loans and informal loans) still increases with a positive credit shock. Due to the opposite relationship between informal loans and bank loans, the impact of a credit policy shock on aggregate debt financing in the economy is significantly lower than its impact on banking credit. As a result, the presence of the informal financial system weakens the regulatory effects of the credit policy.

Impulse responses of the main macroeconomic variables to credit shocks with or without the informal financial system are shown in Figure 5.4, where the absence of the informal financial system is the benchmark case. It can be seen that investment, consumption and output all rise with a positive credit shock, while the high point of inflation lags the credit shocks by five quarters. Since consumption inertia and capital adjustment cost are included in the model, the impulse response of consumption and investment to credit shocks exhibits a hump-shaped pattern. That is, due to the presence of consumption inertia and capital adjustment cost, neither consumption nor investment fully responds to credit shocks in the current period. Instead, they continue to rise after the shock, reaching a peak in the fourth quarter and then gradually reverting to a steady state. By contrast, it can be found that a positive credit shock makes it easier for manufacturers to obtain bank loans and thus discourages the lending activities of the informal financial system. The decline in informal loans partially offsets the impact of the credit shocks on total debt financing in the economy and weakens the impact of the credit shocks on macroeconomic variables. In Figure 5.4, the four main macroeconomic variables (output, consumption, investment, and inflation) are less volatile in the presence of the informal financial system, so that informal finance weakens the effects of credit policy.

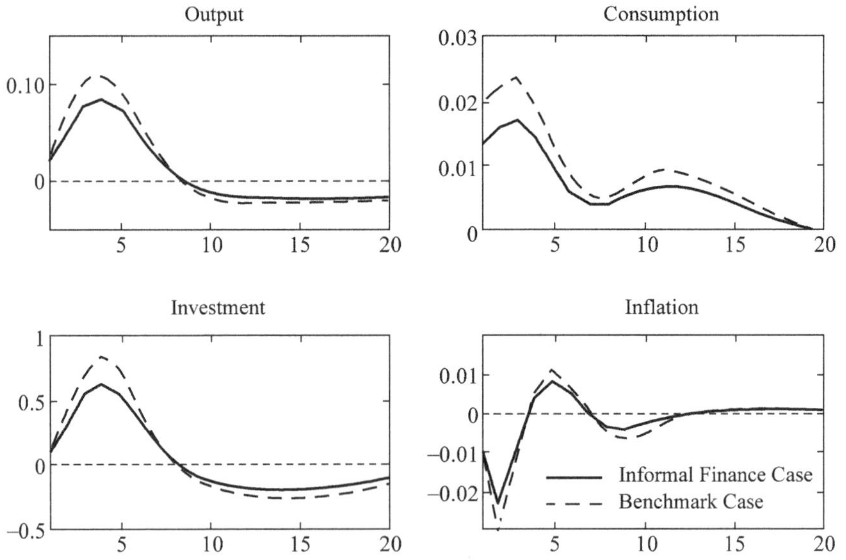

Figure 5.4 Impulse Responses of Major Macroeconomic Variables to Credit Shocks.

5.5.2 The effects of credit policy under the impact of both the dual-track interest rate and informal finance

Impulse responses to credit shocks of the monetary policy implementation rate and the market-oriented interest rate are shown in Figure 5.5. In the model, the monetary policy implementation rate is the benchmark interest rate set by the monetary authority according to the Taylor rule; the market-oriented interest rate can balance the supply and demand of loanable funds in the informal financial system. Hu (2012) noted that China's current monetary policy was still dominated by quantitative tools and that price-based tools (interest rate) were used infrequently with limited adjustment. The autocorrelation coefficient of monetary policy interest rate according to the Taylor rule is set as 0.9, and it can be seen from Figure 5.5 that the volatility of this interest rate with credit shocks is minor. Meanwhile, the market-oriented interest rate in the model is endogenously determined by the supply and demand for loanable funds in the informal financial system and is indirectly affected by credit shocks. With a positive credit shock, the credit allocation in the banking system increases, and the demand for the informal funds from manufactures decreases, so the price of funds (the market-oriented interest rate) in the informal financial system also decreases. As can be seen in Figure 5.5, the market-oriented interest rate decreases significantly in the current period with the credit shocks and then gradually increases, with volatility several times larger than that of the monetary policy rate. Thus, under the dual-track interest rate system, credit shocks have a limited impact

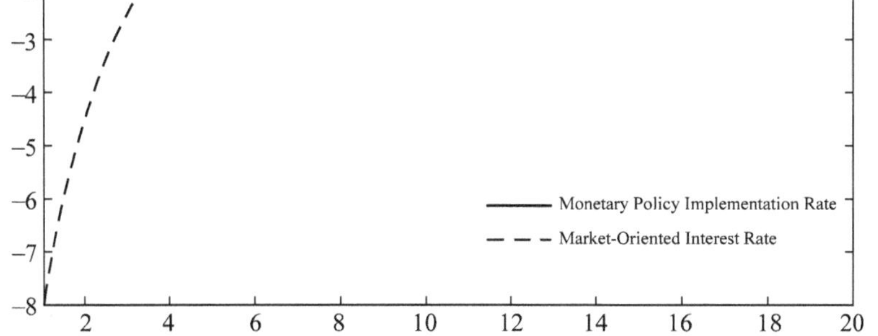

Figure 5.5 Difference of Impulse Response of the Policy Rate and the Market-Oriented Interest Rate Under the Dual-Track Interest Rate System.

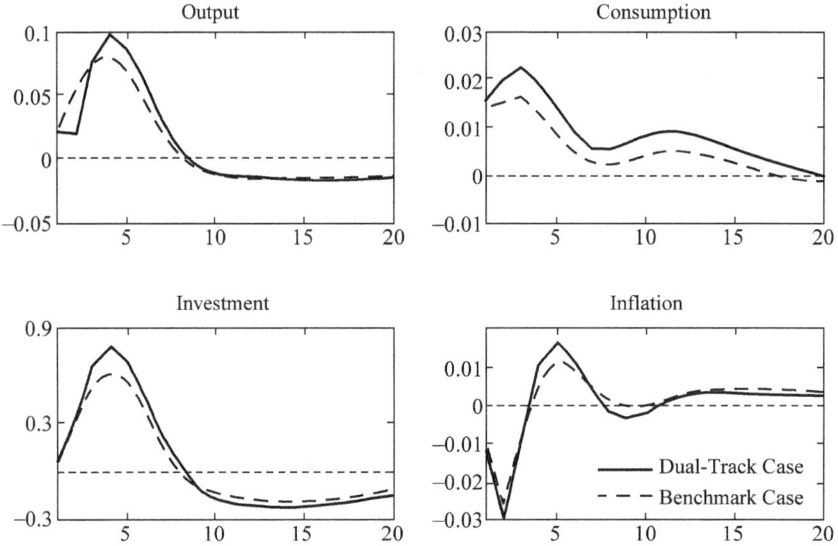

Figure 5.6 Impulse Responses of Major Macroeconomic Variables to Credit Shocks.

on the monetary policy rate but significantly impact the market-oriented interest rate.

Impulse responses of the main macroeconomic variables to credit shocks with or without the dual-track interest rate system are shown in Figure 5.6, where the reference case is that market-oriented interest rate does not exist (the interest rate is determined only by the monetary authority). A positive credit shock under the dual-track interest rate system increases the credit supply of the banking system, reduces the demand of firms for loanable funds from the informal financial system, and leads to a decrease in the market-oriented interest rate. In contrast with the reference case, under the dual-track interest rate system, a positive credit shock increases the demand for credit while reducing the cost of funds of informal financing channels, and it exhibits the dual effects of increasing credit expansion and lowering the market-oriented interest rate. The fluctuations of the four main macroeconomic variables, i.e., output, consumption, investment, and inflation, are all greater under the dual-track interest rate system than under the reference case, so the presence of the market-oriented interest rate enhances the effectiveness of credit policy.

5.5.3 The effects of the credit policy under the impact of financial deregulation

Informal finance and the dual-track interest rate system are important features of the monetary and financial system of China in the transitional period of the economy. With the further improvement of the market economy system in China, the capital market segmentation and capital price distortion will gradually disappear. In recent years, the government has introduced several policy measures conducive to alleviating the degree of financial repression, including promoting the development of nonbank financial intermediaries such as trust companies, relaxing policy restrictions on small companies and guarantee companies, and regulating and encouraging measures for private finance. All of these positively reduce the informal financial system's lending frictions. The impact of financial deregulation shocks on credit structure and the market-oriented interest rate will be analyzed next.

The difference in impulse responses of bank loans and informal loans to financial deregulation shocks is shown in Figure 5.7. In this model, financial deregulation policy is abstracted as a positive shock on the variable z_t. That is, it is believed that financial deregulation policy reduces the lending frictions of the informal financial system. From Figure 5.7, it can be seen that it is easier for firms to obtain the nonbank loans with financial deregulation shocks and that nonbank lending increases substantially in both quantity (referring to the left figure) and weight (referring to the right figure). Simultaneously, bank loans decrease and aggregate debt financing increases, suggesting that financial deregulation reduces firms' reliance on bank loans and encourages other financing sources.

The impact of financial deregulation on the market-oriented interest rate is presented in Figure 5.8. The financial deregulation shocks increase the supply of funds of the informal financial system and reduce the market-oriented interest rate, which is determined by the supply and demand of loanable funds. The financial deregulation promotes both an increase in the supply of funds and a decrease in the cost of funds for informal lending activities.

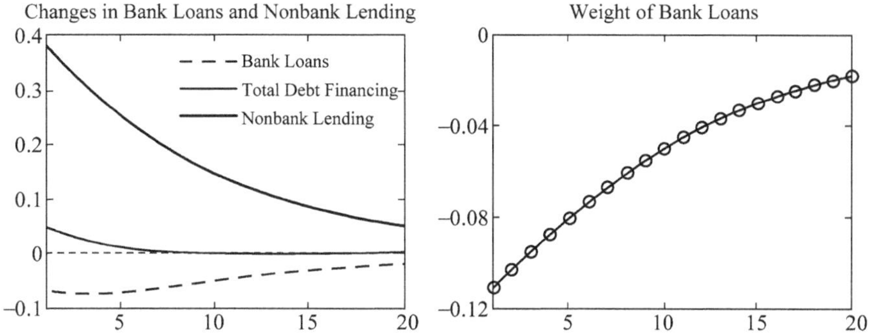

Figure 5.7 Difference of Impulse Responses of Bank Loans and Informal Loans to Financial Deregulation Shocks.

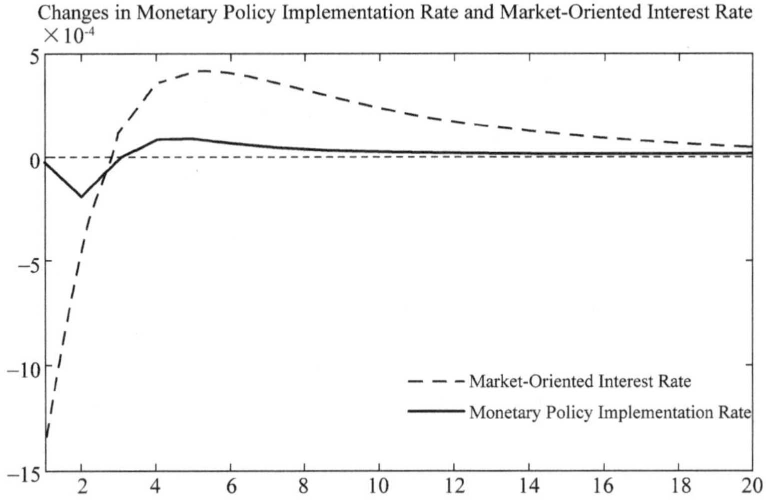

Figure 5.8 Difference of Impulse Responses of the Policy Rate and the Market-Oriented Interest Rate to Financial Deregulation Shocks.

5.6 Conclusion and policy recommendations

This chapter analyzes the transmission and regulatory effects of credit policy in the transitional economy in reference to a DSGE model consisting of informal financing channels and the dual-track interest rate system. The findings show that the credit expansion policy increases the credit supply of the banking system while impeding informal lending activities. The interactions of informal financing activities and bank lending weaken the regulatory effects. Under the dual-track interest rate system, a positive credit shock reduces enterprises' demand for loanable funds from the informal financial system, thereby lowering the market-oriented interest rate; it increases the credit supply, lowers the cost of funds for the informal financial system, and exhibits the dual effects of increasing credit supply and lowering market-oriented interest rate, enhancing the regulatory effects of credit policy. In addition, it is found that financial deregulation aimed at reducing informal financing frictions can alleviate companies' reliance on banking credit and reduce the market-oriented interest rate by increasing the loanable funds supply of informal financing channels.

Correspondingly, the following policy recommendations are put forward.

First, the diversification of corporate financing channels has made it more difficult for the central bank to carry out macroregulations through credit. Although total social financing has been treated by the central bank as an intermediate target for monetary policy, ongoing financial innovations have accelerated the flow of funds between the banking system and the informal financial system. This makes the regulatory effects of traditional credit policy much less effective.

Second, although relying much on quantitative regulation and control, the monetary policy in China still affects the market-oriented interest rate in the informal financial system through the supply and demand of funds. Under the dual-track interest rate system, the monetary policy implementation rate and the bank loan rate, distorted by a low deposit rate, can mask the real fluctuations in the cost of funds in the economy. For example, the private loan rate fluctuates much more than bank loan rates.

Third, financial deregulation and the further advancement of interest rate marketization have brought greater uncertainty to the regulatory effects of credit policy and have made its transmission mechanism very complicated. Nevertheless, it is inevitable that Chinese monetary policy will be less governmentally regulated and will rely more heavily on the market-oriented interest rate.

Bibliography

Allen, Franklin, Jun Qian, and Meijun Qian. "Law, Finance and Economic Growth in China." *Journal of Financial Economics* no. 1 (2005): 57–116.

Amano, Robert. "Inflation Persistence and Monetary Policy: A Simple Result." *Economics Letters* no. 1 (2007): 26–31.

Bai, Jun, and Lian Lishuai 白俊, 连立帅. "Differences in the Allocation of Credit Funds: Ownership Discrimination or Endowment Differences" 信贷资金配置差异: 所有制歧视抑或禀赋差异. *Management World* no. 6 (2012): 30–42+73.

Bernanke, Ben S., and Mark Gertler. "Agency Costs, Net Worth, and Business Fluctuations." *The American Economic Review* no. 1 (1989): 14–31.

Bernanke, Ben S., Mark Gertler, and Simon Gilchrist. "The Financial Accelerator in a Quantitative Business Cycle Framework." In *Handbook of Macroeconomics*, vol. 1, part C, edited by John B. Taylor and Michael Woodford, 1999: 1341–1393.

Calvo, Guillermo A. "Staggered Prices in a Utility-Maximizing Framework." *Journal of Monetary Economics* no. 3 (1983): 383–398.

Chen, Kunting, and Gong Liutang 陈昆亭, 龚六堂. "Numerical Simulation for Chinese Economy in a Sticky-Price Model" 粘滞价格模型以及对中国经济的数值模拟——对基本RBC模型的改进. *The Journal of Quantitative & Technical Economics* no. 8 (2006): 106–117.

Chen, Kunting, Gong Liutang, and Zhou Hengfu 陈昆亭, 龚六堂, 邹恒甫. "Numerical Simulation for Chinese Economy Based on the RBC Theory" 基本RBC方法模拟中国经济的数值试验. *World Economic Papers* no. 2 (2004): 41–52.

Chow, Gregory C., and Kui-Wai Li. "Chinese Economic Growth: 1952–1998." *Economic Development and Cultural Change* no. 1 (2002): 247–256.

Christiano, Lawrence J., Cosmin Ilut, Roberto Motto, and Massimo Rostagno. "Monetary Policy and Stock Market Boom-Bust Cycles." Working Paper Series 955, European Central Bank, 2007.

Clarida, Richard, Jordi Gali, and Mark Gertler. "The Science of Monetary Policy: A New Keynesian Perspective." *Journal of Economic Perspectives* no. 4 (1999): 1661–1707.

Collard, Fabrice, and Harris Dellas. "Poole in the New Keynesian Model." *European Economic Review* no. 4 (2005): 887–907.

Dixit, Avinash K., and Joseph E. Stiglitz. "Monopolistic Competition and Optimum Product Diversity." *The American Economic Review* no. 3 (1977): 297–308.

Gali, Jordi, and Mark Gertler. "Inflation Dynamics: A Structural Econometric Analysis." *Journal of Monetary Economics* no. 2 (1999): 195–222.

Gali, Jordi, J. David Lopez-Salido, and Javier Valles. "Understanding the Effects of Government Spending on Consumption." *Journal of the European Economic Association* no. 1 (2007): 227–270.

Guo, Xinqiang, and Yangkun郭新强, 杨坤. "Rigid Savings, Monetary Policy and Household Consumption Dynamics" 刚性储蓄、货币政策与居民消费动态. Working Paper, 2011.

He, Dong, and Wang Honglin 何东, 王红林. "A Dual-Track Interest-Rate System and Monetary Policy Implementation in China" 利率双轨制与中国货币政策实施. *Journal of Financial Research* no. 12 (2011): 1–18.

Hu, Zhipeng 胡志鹏. "Has Interest Rate Procedure Become Optimal for the Monetary Policy in China? Theoretical and Empirical Analysis Based on the DSGE Model." 中国货币政策的价格型调控条件是否成熟？基于动态随机一般均衡模型的理论和实践分析. *Economic Research Journal* no. 6 (2012): 60–72.

Iacoviello, Matteo, and Raoul Minetti. "International Business Cycles with Domestic and Foreign Lenders." *Journal of Monetary Economics* no. 53 (2006): 2267–2282.

Iacoviello, Matteo. "House Prices, Borrowing Constraints, and Monetary Policy in the Business Cycle." *The American Economic Review* no. 3 (2005): 739–764.

Kiyotaki, Nobuhiro, and John Moore. "Credit Cycles." *The Journal of Political Economy* no. 2 (1997): 211–248.

Kobayashi, Keiichiro, and Kengo Nutahara. "Nominal Rigidities, News-Driven Business Cycles, and Monetary Policy." *The BE Journal of Macroeconomics* no. 1 (2010): 1935–1690.

Li, Chunji, and Meng Xiaohong 李春吉, 孟晓宏. "Chinese Economic Fluctuations: An Analysis Based on the New Keynesian Monopolistic Competition Model" 中国经济波动——基于新凯恩斯主义垄断竞争模型的分析. *Economic Research Journal* no. 10 (2006): 72–82.

Lian, Yingqi, and Chen Jingting 连英祺，陈静婷. "Analysis of Impact of Informal Finance on the Effectiveness of Monetary Policy" 非正式金融对货币政策有效性的影响问题分析 *Industrial and Science Tribune* no. 5 (2011): 104–106.

Liu, Zheng, Pengfei Wang, and Tao Zha. "Land-Price Dynamics and Macroeconomic Fluctuations." *Econometrica* no. 3 (2013): 1147–1184.

Lu, Dan, and Xiao Huarong 鲁丹, 肖华荣. "Banking Market Structure, Information Production and SME Financing in China" 银行市场竞争结构、信息生产和中小企业融资. *Economic Research Journal* no. 5 (2008): 107–113.

McCallum, Bennett T., and Edward Nelson. "An Optimizing IS-LM Specification for Monetary Police and Business Cycle Analysis." *Journal of Money, Credit, and Banking* no. 3 (1999): 296–316.

Miao, Jianjun, and Peng Tao. "Business Cycles and Macroeconomic Policy in China: Evidence from an Estimated DSGE Model." Working Paper, 2011.

Smets, Frank and Raf Wouters "An Estimated Dynamic Stochastic General Equilibrium Model of the Euro Area." *Journal of the European Economic Association* no. 1 (2003): 1123–1175.

Smets, Frank, and Rafael Wouters. "Shocks and Frictions in US Business Cycles: A Bayesian DSGE Approach." *The American Economic Review* no. 3 (2007): 586–606.

Wang, Xiaolu, and Fan Gang 王小鲁，樊纲. *Sustainability of Industrial Growth in China* 我国工业增长的可持续性. Beijing: Economic Science Press, 2000.

Woodfood, Michael. "Optimal Monetary Police Inertia." NBER Working Paper 7261, 1999.
Xie, Ping 谢平. "Thirty Years' Reform of State-Owned Banks" 国有商业银行改革三十年. *Wealth Today* no. 10 (2008): 9–12.
Xue, Hexiang 薛鹤翔. "Output Persistence in China: A Dynamic Analysis Based on Sticky-Price and Sticky-Wage Models" 中国的产出持续性——基于刚性价格和刚性工资模型的动态分析. *China Economic Quarterly* no. 4 (2010): 1359–1384.
Yang, Kun, and Chang Jinxiong 杨坤，常进雄. "Property Manipulation: Controlling Demand or Adjusting Supply?" 房地产调控: 需求抑制还是供给调节？Working Paper, 2012.
Yi, Gang, and Wu Youchang 易纲, 吴有昌. *Money and Banking* 货币银行学. Shanghai: Shanghai People's Press, 1999.
Zhang, Jie 张杰. "Financial Dilemma and Financing Order of Private Economy" 民营经济的金融困境与融资次序. *Economic Research Journal* no. 4 (2000): 3–10+78.
Zhang, Jun 张军. "The Dual-Track Price System: A Miracle or a Myth?" 价格双轨制是奇迹还是神话. *The Economic Observer*. November 23, 2007.
Zhang, Jun张军. "Capital Formation, Industrialization and Economic Growth: Understanding China's Economic Reform" 资本形成、工业化与经济增长：中国的转轨特征. *Economic Research Journal* no. 6 (2002): 3–13+93.
Zhang, Wenlang. "China's Monetary Policy: Quantity Versus Price Rules." *Journal of Macroeconomics* no. 3 (2009): 473–484.

APPENDIX

The derivation is mainly divided into three steps: first, providing the solving process of the optimal first-order conditions based on the preceding model; second, providing the steady-state solution of the endogenous variables; third, providing the log-linearization equilibrium system of the model.

Case 1: Only the banking system

Step one: Optimized solution

First, the household

The objective utility function of the household is:

$$\max E_0 \sum_{t=0}^{\infty} \beta^t \left(\log\left(c_{H,t} - \tau c_{\mathrm{H},t-1}\right) + j \log h_t - \frac{1}{\eta}\left(L_{P,t}\right)^{\eta} + \chi \ln\left(\frac{M_t}{P_t}\right)\right)$$

The household is subject to the budget constraint:

$$c_{H,t} + b_t + q_{h,t} h_t + \frac{M_t - M_{t-1}}{P_t} = \frac{R_{t-1} b_{t-1}}{\grave{A}_t} + w_{P,t} \mathrm{L}_{\mathrm{P,t}} + \mathrm{q}_{\mathrm{h,t}} h_{t-1} + d_t^r$$

Solving the optimal first-order condition about $\left\{c_{H,t}, h_t, L_{P,t}, M_t\right\}$

When $\rho_t = \left(c_{H,t} - \tau c_{H,t-1}\right)^{-1}$, $E_t\left(\Lambda_{t,t+1}\dfrac{R_t}{\pi_{t+1}}\right) = 1$

where $\Lambda_{t,t+k} = \beta^k\left(u_{c,t+k} / u_{c,t}\right)$,

$$u_{c,t} = \left(c_{H,t} - \tau c_{H,t-1}\right)^{-1} - \beta\tau E_t\left(c_{H,t+1} - \tau c_{H,t}\right)^{-1} = \rho_t - \beta\tau E_t\rho_{t+1}$$

$$u_{c,t}w_{P,t} = \left(L_{P,t}\right)^{\eta-1}$$

$$u_{c,t}q_{h,t} = \frac{j}{h_t} + \beta E_t\left(u_{c,t+1}q_{h,t+1}\right)$$

$$\chi\frac{P_t}{M_t} = \left(1 - \frac{1}{R_t}\right)u_{c,t}$$

Second, the intermediate goods manufacturer

The production function of the intermediate goods manufacturer is: $Y_{P,t} = A_{P,t}\left(K_{P,t-1}\right)^{\mu_P}\left(h_{P,t-1}\right)^{\upsilon_P}\left(L_{P,t}\right)^{1-\mu_P-\upsilon_P}$.

The expected utility function of the intermediate goods manufacturer is: $\max E_0\sum_{t=0}^{\infty}\gamma^t \log c_{P,t}$.

The lending constraint faced by the intermediate goods manufacturer is:

$$R_t b'_{P,t} \le m_t E_t\left(\pi_{t+1}\left(q_{h,t+1}h_{P,t} + q_{P,t+1}K_{P,t}\right)\right)$$

The budget constraint faced by the intermediate goods manufacturer is:

$$\frac{Y_{P,t}}{X_{P,t}} + b'_{P,t} + q_{h,t}h_{P,t-1} = c_{P,t} + q_{h,t}h_{P,t} + \frac{R_{t-1}b'_{P,t-1}}{\grave{A}_t} + w_{P,t}L_{P,t} + I_{P,t}$$

The capital accumulation equation including capital adjustment cost is:

$$K_{P,t} = (1-\delta_P)K_{P,t-1} + \left[1 - \frac{\psi_P}{2}\left(\frac{I_{P,t}}{I_{P,t-1}} - 1\right)^2\right]I_{P,t}$$

The Lagrangian equation is:

$$\Lambda = \log\left(\frac{Y_{P,t}}{X_{P,t}} + b'_{P,t} + b''_{P,t} + q_{h,t}h_{P,t-1} - q_{h,t}h_{P,t}\right.$$
$$\left. - \frac{R_{t-1}b'_{P,t-1}}{\pi_t} - \frac{R_{t-1}b''_{P,t-1}}{\pi_t} - w_{P,t}L_{P,t} - I_{P,t}\right)$$
$$+ \gamma\log\left(\frac{Y_{P,t+1}}{X_{P,t+1}} + b'_{P,t+1} + b''_{P,t+1} + q_{h,t+1}h_{P,t} - q_{h,t+1}h_{P,t+1}\right.$$
$$\left. - \frac{R_t b'_{P,t}}{\pi_{t+1}} - \frac{R_t b''_{P,t}}{\pi_{t+1}} - w_{P,t+1}L_{P,t+1} - I_{P,t+1}\right)$$
$$- \lambda'_{P,t}\left(R_t b'_{P,t} - m_t\alpha_t\pi_{t+1}\left(q_{h,t+1}h_{P,t} + q_{P,t+1}K_{P,t}\right)\right) - u_{P,t}$$
$$\left(K_{P,t} - (1-\delta_P)K_{P,t-1} - \left[1 - \frac{\psi_P}{2}\left(\frac{I_{P,t}}{I_{P,t-1}} - 1\right)^2\right]I_{P,t}\right)$$
$$- \gamma u_{P,t+1}\left(K_{P,t+1} - (1-\delta_P)K_{P,t} - \left[1 - \frac{\psi_P}{2}\left(\frac{I_{P,t+1}}{I_{P,t}} - 1\right)^2\right]I_{P,t+1}\right) + \ldots$$

Solving the optimization problem of the intermediate goods manufacturer, the six first-order conditions about consumption, capital accumulation, capital efficiency, plant demand and labor demand are:

$$\frac{1}{c_{P,t}} = E_t\left(\frac{\gamma R_t}{\pi_{t+1}c_{P,t+1}}\right) + \lambda'_{P,t}R_t$$

$$\frac{q_{h,t}}{c_{P,t}} = \gamma E_t\left(\frac{1}{c_{P,t+1}}\left(\frac{\upsilon_P Y_{P,t+1}}{X_{P,t+1}h_{P,t}} + q_{h,t+1}\right)\right) + \lambda'_{P,t}m_t q_{h,t+1}\pi_{t+1}$$

$$w_{P,t} = \frac{(1-\mu_P-\upsilon_P)Y_{P,t}}{X_{P,t}L_{P,t}}$$

$$q_{P,t} = \frac{u_{P,t}}{u_{c,t}}$$

$$\frac{q_{P,t}}{c_{P,t}} = \gamma E_t\left(\frac{1}{c_{P,t+1}}\left(\frac{\mu_P Y_{P,t+1}}{X_{P,t+1}K_{P,t}} + (1-\delta_P)q_{P,t+1}\right)\right) + \lambda'_{P,t}q_{P,t+1}\pi_{t+1}$$

$$1 = q_{P,t}\left[1 - \frac{\psi_P}{2}\left(\frac{I_{P,t}}{I_{P,t-1}} - 1\right)^2 - \psi_P\left(\frac{I_{P,t}}{I_{P,t-1}} - 1\right)\frac{I_{P,t}}{I_{P,t-1}}\right] + \gamma\psi_P E_t\left[\frac{c_{P,t}}{c_{P,t+1}} q_{P,t+1}\left(\frac{I_{P,t}}{I_{P,t-1}} - 1\right)\left(\frac{I_{P,t}}{I_{P,t-1}}\right)^2\right]$$

Third, the retailer

The profit function of the retailer is

$$\max E_t \sum_{k=0}^{\infty} \theta^k \left\{\Lambda_{t,t+k}\left(\frac{P_t^*}{P_{t+k}}\left(\frac{P_{t+k-1}}{P_{t-1}}\right)^{\delta_P} - \frac{1}{X_{t+k}}\right) Y_{t+k}^*(i)\right\}$$

Solving the first-order condition about the optimal price P_t^*, the following can be obtained:

$$E_t \sum_{k=0}^{\infty} \theta^k \Lambda_{t,t+k}\left(\frac{P_t^*}{P_{t+k}}\left(\frac{P_{t+k-1}}{P_{t-1}}\right)^{\delta_P} - \frac{X}{X_{t+k}}\right) Y_{t+k}^*(i)$$

The profit obtained by the retailer is:

$$d_t^r = Y_t\left(\frac{P_t - P_t^w}{P_t}\right)$$

Fourth, the Taylor rule and the credit policy

The Taylor rule is:

$$\hat{R}_t = r_R \hat{R}_{t-1} + (1 - r_R) r_\pi \hat{\pi}_t + (1 - r_R) r_y \hat{Y}_t$$

The credit policy is:

$$\hat{m}_t = \rho_m \hat{m}_{t-1} + u_{m,t}$$

where $\hat{m}_t$ follows the AR(1) process and its autocorrelation coefficient is $\rho_m \in (0,1)$, and the shock term $u_{m,t}$ obeys a normal distribution with the mean value of 0 and the variance of σ_m^2.

Fifth, general equilibrium conditions

In terms of the goods market, the market clearing condition is:

$$Y_t = c_{H,t} + c_{P,t} + I_{P,t}$$

In terms of credit market, the market clearing condition is:

$$b_t = b_t'$$

In terms of housing market, the market clearing condition is:

$$h + h_t = 1$$

Step two: Steady-state solution

$$\pi = 1$$

$$R = 1/\beta$$

$$\frac{1}{\rho} = (1-\tau)c_H$$

$$u_c = (1-\beta\tau)\rho$$

$$\left(\frac{(1-\beta\tau)}{(1-\tau)\zeta_8}\frac{(1-\mu_P-\upsilon_P)}{X_P}\right)^{1/\eta} = L_P$$

$$\lambda_P' = \frac{\beta-\gamma}{c_P}$$

$$X_P = \frac{\epsilon}{\epsilon-1}$$

$$w_P L_P = \frac{(1-\mu_P-\upsilon_P)Y}{X_P}$$

$$q_h = \frac{j(1-\tau)}{(1-\beta)(1-\beta\tau)}\frac{c_H}{h} = \zeta_1\frac{c_H}{h}$$

$$q_P = 1$$

$$K_P = \frac{\gamma\mu_P}{1-\gamma(1-\delta_P)-(\beta-\gamma)m}\frac{1}{X_P}Y = \zeta_5 Y$$

$$q_h = \frac{\gamma\upsilon_P}{1-\gamma-(\beta-\gamma)m}\frac{1}{X_P}\frac{Y}{h_P} = \zeta_3\frac{Y}{h_P}$$

$$b'_P = \beta m(\zeta_3 + \zeta_5)Y$$

$$d^r = \left(1 - \frac{1}{X_P}\right)Y$$

$$c_H = \left(1 + \left(\frac{1}{\beta} - 1\right)\zeta_7 - \frac{(\mu_P + \upsilon_P)}{X_P}\right)Y = \zeta_8 Y$$

$$c_P = \left(\frac{\mu_P + \upsilon_P}{X_P} - (1 - {}^{2})m(\zeta_3 + \zeta_5) - \delta_P \zeta_5\right)Y = \zeta_{10} Y$$

$$h_P = \frac{\zeta_3}{\zeta_1 \zeta_8} h$$

$$h = \frac{\zeta_1 \zeta_8}{\zeta_1 \zeta_8 + \zeta_3}$$

Step three: Log-linearization

$$\hat{c}_{H,t} - \tau \hat{c}_{H,t-1} + (1-\tau)\hat{\rho}_t = 0$$

$$(1 - \beta\tau)\hat{u}_{c,t} = \hat{\rho}_t - \beta\tau\hat{\rho}_{t+1}$$

$$\hat{u}_{c,t+1} - \hat{u}_{c,t} + \hat{R}_t - \hat{\pi}_{t+1} = 0$$

$$\frac{1}{\eta}\frac{(1-\beta\tau)}{(1-\tau)\zeta_8}\frac{(1-\mu_P-\upsilon_P)}{X_P}\left(\hat{u}_{c,t} + \hat{Y}_{P,t} - \hat{X}_{P,t}\right) = L_P^{\eta}\hat{L}_{P,t}$$

$$\frac{1-\beta\tau}{1-\tau}\left(\hat{u}_{c,t} + \hat{q}_{h,t}\right) + \frac{j}{\zeta_1}\hat{h}_t = \frac{\beta(1-\beta\tau)}{1-\tau}\left(\hat{u}_{c,t+1} + \hat{q}_{h,t+1}\right)$$

$$\beta\left(\hat{c}_{P,t} + \hat{R}_t\right) - \gamma\left(\hat{\pi}_{t+1} + \hat{c}_{P,t+1}\right) + (\beta - \gamma)\hat{\lambda}'_{P,t} = 0$$

$$\hat{q}_{P,t} = (1-\gamma)\psi_P\left(\hat{I}_{P,t} - \hat{I}_{P,t-1}\right)$$

$$(\zeta_3 + \zeta_5)\left(\hat{R}_t + \hat{b}'_{P,t} - \hat{m}_t - \hat{\pi}_{t+1}\right) = \zeta_3\left(\hat{q}_{h,t+1} + \hat{h}_{P,t}\right) + \zeta_5\left(\hat{q}_{P,t+1} + \hat{K}_{P,t}\right)$$

$$(\beta - \gamma)\Big[m\alpha\left(\hat{\lambda}'_{P,t} + \hat{m}_t + \hat{\alpha}_t + \hat{q}_{P,t+1} + \hat{\pi}_{t+1}\right) + (1-\alpha)\omega\left(\hat{q}_{P,t+1} + \hat{\pi}_{t+1} + \hat{\lambda}''_{P,t}\right)$$
$$-\alpha\omega\hat{\alpha}_t - (1-\alpha)(1-\omega)\hat{\chi}_t\Big]$$

$$\left(\hat{q}_{P,t}-\hat{c}_{P,t}\right)=\frac{\gamma\mu_P}{X_P\zeta_5}\left(\hat{Y}_{P,t+1}-\hat{X}_{P,t+1}-\hat{K}_{P,t}-\hat{c}_{P,t+1}\right)+\gamma\left(1-\delta_P\right)\left(\hat{q}_{P,t+1}-\hat{c}_{P,t+1}\right)$$
$$+(\beta-\gamma)m\left(\hat{\lambda}'_{P,t}+\hat{m}_t+\hat{q}_{P,t+1}+\hat{\pi}_{t+1}\right)$$

$$\left(\hat{q}_{h,t}-\hat{c}_{P,t}\right)=\frac{\gamma\upsilon_P}{X_P\zeta_3}\left(\hat{Y}_{P,t+1}-\hat{X}_{P,t+1}-\hat{h}_{P,t}-\hat{c}_{P,t+1}\right)+\gamma\left(\hat{q}_{h,t+1}-\hat{c}_{P,t+1}\right)$$
$$+(\beta-\gamma)m\left(\hat{\lambda}'_{P,t}+\hat{m}_t+\hat{q}_{h,t+1}+\hat{\pi}_{t+1}\right)$$

$$\hat{b}_t=\hat{b}'_{P,t}$$

$$\left(1-\frac{1}{X_P}\right)\hat{d}_t^r=\hat{Y}_t-\frac{1}{X_P}\left(\hat{Y}_{P,t}-\hat{X}_{P,t}\right)$$

$$\zeta_8\hat{c}_{H,t}+\zeta_7\hat{b}_t+\zeta_1\zeta_8\left(\hat{h}_t-\hat{h}_{t-1}\right)$$
$$=\frac{1}{\beta}\zeta_7\left(\hat{R}_{t-1}+\hat{b}_{t-1}-\hat{\pi}_t\right)+\frac{\left(1-\mu_P-\upsilon_P\right)}{X_P}\left(\hat{Y}_{P,t}-\hat{X}_{P,t}\right)$$
$$+\left(1-\frac{1}{X_P}\right)\hat{d}_t^r$$

$$\frac{\left(\mu_P+\upsilon_P\right)}{X_P}\left(\hat{Y}_{P,t}-\hat{X}_{P,t}\right)+\beta m\left(\zeta_3+\zeta_5\right)\hat{b}'_{P,t}=\zeta_{10}\hat{c}_{P,t}+\zeta_3\left(\hat{h}_{P,t}-\hat{h}_{P,t-1}\right)$$
$$+m\left(\zeta_3+\zeta_5\right)\left(\hat{R}_{t-1}+\hat{b}'_{P,t-1}-\hat{\pi}_t\right)$$
$$+\zeta_5\delta_P\hat{I}_{P,t}$$

$$\frac{\zeta_1\zeta_8}{\zeta_1\zeta_8+\zeta_3}\hat{h}_t+\frac{\zeta_3}{\zeta_1\zeta_8+\zeta_3}\hat{h}_{P,t}=0$$

$$\hat{Y}_{P,t}=\hat{A}_{P,t}+\mu_P\hat{K}_{P,t-1}+\upsilon_P\hat{h}_{P,t-1}+\left(1-\mu_P-\upsilon_P\right)\hat{L}_{P,t}$$

$$\hat{K}_{P,t}=\left(1-\delta_P\right)\hat{K}_{P,t-1}+\delta_P\hat{I}_{P,t}$$

Case 2: The banking system and informal finance system coexist

Step one: Optimized solution

First, the household

The objective utility function of the household is:

$$\max E_0\sum_{t=0}^{\infty}\beta^t\left(\log\left(c_{H,t}-\tau c_{H,t-1}\right)+j\log h_t-\frac{1}{\eta}\left(L_{P,t}\right)\eta+\chi\ln\left(\frac{M_t}{P_t}\right)\right)$$

The budget constraint faced by the household is:

$$c_{H,t}+b_t+q_{h,t}h_t+\frac{M_t-M_{t-1}}{P_t}=\frac{R_{t-1}b_{t-1}}{\pi_t}+w_{P,t}L_{P,t}+q_{h,t}h_{t-1}+d_t^r$$

Solving the optimal first-order condition about $\{c_{H,t}, h_t, L_{P,t}, M_t\}$:

When $\rho_t=\left(c_{H,t}-\tau c_{H,t-1}\right)^{-1}$, $E_t\left(\Lambda_{t,t+1}\frac{R_t}{\pi_{t+1}}\right)=1$

where

$$\Lambda_{t,t+k}=\beta^k\left(u_{c,t+k}/u_{c,t}\right), u_{c,t}=\left(c_{H,t}-\tau c_{H,t-1}\right)^{-1}$$
$$-\beta\tau E_t\left(c_{H,t+1}-\tau c_{H,t}\right)^{-1}=\rho_t-\beta\tau E_t\rho_{t+1}$$

$$u_{c,t}w_{P,t}=\left(L_{P,t}\right)^{\eta-1}$$

$$u_{c,t}q_{h,t}=\frac{j}{h_t}+\beta E_t\left(u_{c,t+1}q_{h,t+1}\right)$$

$$\chi\frac{P_t}{M_t}=\left(1-\frac{1}{R_t}\right)u_{c,t}$$

Second, the intermediate goods manufacturer

The production function of the intermediate goods manufacturer is:

$$Y_{P,t}=A_{P,t}\left(K_{P,t-1}\right)^{\mu_P}\left(h_{P,t-1}\right)^{\upsilon_P}\left(L_{P,t}\right)^{1-\mu_P-\upsilon_P}$$

The expected utility function of the intermediate goods manufacturer is:

$$\max E_0\sum_{t=0}^{\infty}\gamma\log c_{P,t}$$

The lending constraint faced by the intermediate goods manufacturer is:

$$R_t b'_{P,t}\le m_t\alpha_t E_t\left(\pi_{t+1}\left(q_{h,t+1}h_{P,t}+q_{P,t+1}K_{P,t}\right)\right)$$

$$R_t b''_{P,t} \leq E_t\left((1-\alpha_t)\pi_{t+1}\left(q_{h,t+1}h_{P,t}+q_{P,t+1}K_{P,t}\right)\right.$$
$$\left.\left(1-\frac{1-z}{qh+q_P K}(1-\alpha_t)\pi_{t+1}\left(q_{h,t+1}h_{P,t}+q_{P,t+1}K_{P,t}\right)\right)\right)$$

The budget constraint faced by the intermediate goods manufacturer is:

$$\frac{Y_{P,t}}{X_{P,t}}+b'_{P,t}+b''_{P,t}+q_{h,t}h_{P,t-1}=c_{P,t}+q_{h,t}h_{P,t}+\frac{R_{t-1}b'_{P,t-1}}{\pi_t}$$
$$+\frac{R_{t-1}b''_{P,t-1}}{\pi_t}+w_{P,t}L_{P,t}+I_{P,t}$$

The capital accumulation equation including capital adjustment cost is:

$$K_{P,t}=(1-\delta_P)K_{P,t-1}+\left[1-\frac{\psi_P}{2}\left(\frac{I_{P,t}}{I_{P,t-1}}-1\right)^2\right]I_{P,t}$$

The Lagrangian equation is:

$$\Lambda=\log\left(\frac{Y_{P,t}}{X_{P,t}}+b'_{P,t}+b''_{P,t}+q_{h,t}h_{P,t-1}-q_{h,t}h_{P,t}-\frac{R_{t-1}b'_{P,t-1}}{\pi_t}\right.$$
$$\left.-\frac{R_{t-1}b''_{P,t-1}}{\pi_t}-w_{P,t}L_{P,t}-I_{P,t}\right)$$
$$+\gamma\log\left(\frac{Y_{P,t+1}}{X_{P,t+1}}+b'_{P,t+1}+b''_{P,t+1}+q_{h,t+1}h_{P,t}-q_{h,t+1}h_{P,t+1}\right.$$
$$\left.-\frac{R_t b'_{P,t}}{\pi_{t+1}}-\frac{R_t b''_{P,t}}{\pi_{t+1}}-w_{P,t+1}L_{P,t+1}-I_{P,t+1}\right)$$
$$-\lambda'_{P,t}\left(R_t b'_{P,t}-m_t\alpha_t\pi_{t+1}\left(q_{h,t+1}h_{P,t}+q_{P,t+1}K_{P,t}\right)\right)-\lambda''_{P,t}$$
$$\left(R_t b''_{P,t}-(1-\alpha_t)\pi_{t+1}\left(q_{h,t+1}h_{P,t}+q_{P,t+1}K_{P,t}\right)\right.$$
$$\left.\left(1-\frac{1-z}{qh+q_P K}(1-\alpha_t)\pi_{t+1}\left(q_{h,t+1}h_{P,t}+q_{P,t+1}K_{P,t}\right)\right)\right)$$
$$-u_{P,t}\left(K_{P,t}-(1-\delta_P)K_{P,t-1}-\left[1-\frac{\psi_P}{2}\left(\frac{I_{P,t}}{I_{P,t-1}}-1\right)^2\right]I_{P,t}\right)$$
$$-\gamma u_{P,t+1}=\left(K_{P,t+1}-(1-\delta_P)K_{P,t}-\left[1-\frac{\psi_P}{2}\left(\frac{I_{P,t+1}}{I_{P,t}}-1\right)^2\right]I_{P,t+1}\right)$$
$$+\ldots$$

Solving the optimization problem of the intermediate goods manufacturer, the first-order conditions about consumption, capital accumulation, capital efficiency, plant demand and labor demand are:

$$\frac{1}{c_{P,t}} = E_t\left(\frac{\gamma R_t}{\pi_{t+1} c_{P,t+1}}\right) + \lambda'_{P,t} R_t$$

$$\frac{1}{c_{P,t}} = E_t\left(\frac{\gamma R_t}{\pi_{t+1} c_{P,t+1}}\right) + \lambda'_{P,t} R_t$$

$$\frac{q_{h,t}}{c_{P,t}} = \gamma E_t\left(\frac{1}{c_{P,t+1}}\left(\frac{\upsilon_P Y_{P,t+1}}{X_{P,t+1} h_{P,t}} + q_{h,t+1}\right)\right) + \lambda'_{P,t} m_t \alpha_t q_{h,t+1} \pi_{t+1} + \lambda''_{P,t}$$
$$(1-\alpha_t) q_{h,t+1} \pi_{t+1} - \lambda''_{P,t} \frac{2(1-z)}{q_h h_P + q_P K_P} q_{h,t+1} \left((1-\alpha_t)\pi_{t+1}\right)^2$$
$$\left(q_{h,t+1} h_{P,t} + q_{P,t+1} K_{P,t}\right)$$

$$w_{P,t} = \frac{(1-\mu_P - \upsilon_P) Y_{P,t}}{X_{P,t} L_{P,t}}$$

$$q_{P,t} = \frac{u_{P,t}}{u_{c,t}}$$

$$\frac{q_{P,t}}{c_{P,t}} = \gamma E_t\left(\frac{1}{c_{P,t+1}}\left(\frac{\mu_P Y_{P,t+1}}{X_{P,t+1} K_{P,t}} + (1-\delta_P) q_{P,t+1}\right)\right) + \lambda''_{P,t} m_t \alpha_t q_{P,t+1} \pi_{t+1} + \lambda''_{P,t}$$
$$(1-\alpha_t) q_{P,t+1} \pi_{t+1} - \lambda''_{P,t} \frac{2(1-z)}{q_h h_P + q_P K_P} q_{P,t+1}$$
$$\left((1-\alpha_t)\pi_{t+1}\right)^2 \left(q_{h,t+1} h_{P,t} + q_{P,t+1} K_{P,t}\right)$$

$$1 = q_{P,t}\left[1 - \frac{\psi_P}{2}\left(\frac{I_{P,t}}{I_{P,t-1}} - 1\right)^2 - \psi_P\left(\frac{I_{P,t}}{I_{P,t-1}} - 1\right)\frac{I_{P,t}}{I_{P,t-1}}\right]$$
$$+ \gamma \psi_P E_t\left[\frac{c_{P,t}}{c_{P,t+1}} q_{P,t+1}\left(\frac{I_{P,t}}{I_{P,t-1}} - 1\right)\left(\frac{I_{P,t}}{I_{P,t-1}}\right)^2\right]$$

$$\lambda'_{P,t} m_t = \lambda''_{P,t} E_t\left(1 - \frac{2(1-z)}{q_h h_P + q_P K_P}(1-\alpha_t)\pi_{t+1}\left(q_{h,t+1} h_{P,t} + q_{P,t+1} K_{P,t}\right)\right)$$

Third, the retailer

The profit function of the retailer is:

$$\max E_t \sum_{k=0}^{\infty} \theta^k \left\{ \Lambda_{t,t+k} \left(\frac{P_t^*}{P_{t+k}} \left(\frac{P_{t+k-1}}{P_{t-1}} \right)^{\delta_P} - \frac{1}{X_{t+k}} \right) Y_{t+k}^*(i) \right\}.$$

Solving the first-order condition about the optimal price P_t^*, the following can be obtained:

$$E_t \sum_{k=0}^{\infty} \theta^k \Lambda_{t,t+k} \left(\frac{P_t^*}{P_{t+k}} \left(\frac{P_{t+k-1}}{P_{t-1}} \right)^{\delta_P} - \frac{X}{X_{t+k}} \right) Y_{t+k}^*(i)$$

The profit obtained by the retailer is:

$$d_t^r = Y_t \left(\frac{P_t - P_t^w}{P_t} \right)$$

Fourth, the Taylor rule and the credit policy

The Taylor rule is:

$$\hat{R}_t = r_R \hat{R}_{t-1} + (1 - r_R) r_\pi \hat{\pi}_t + (1 - r_R) r_y \hat{Y}_t$$

The credit policy is:

$$\hat{m}_t = \rho_m \hat{m}_{t-1} + u_{m,t}$$

where $\hat{m}_t$ follows the AR(1) process, and its autocorrelation coefficient is $\rho_m \in (0,1)$; the shock term $u_{m,t}$ obeys a normal distribution with the mean value of 0 and the variance of σ_m^2.

Fifth, general equilibrium conditions

In terms of the goods market, the market clearing condition is:

$$Y_t = c_{H,t} + c_{P,t} + I_{P,t}$$

In terms of the credit market, the market clearing condition is:

$$b_t = b'_{P,t} + b''_{P,t}$$

In terms of housing market, the market clearing condition is:

$$h + h_P = 1$$

Step two: Steady-state solution

$$\pi = 1$$

$$R = \frac{1}{\beta}$$

$$\frac{1}{\rho} = (1-\tau)c_H$$

$$u_c = (1-\beta\tau)\rho$$

$$\left(\frac{(1-\beta\tau)}{(1-\tau)\zeta_8}\frac{(1-\mu_P-\upsilon_P)}{X_P}\right)^{1/\eta} = L_P$$

$$w_P L_P = \frac{(1-\mu_P-\upsilon_P)Y}{X_P}$$

$$q_h = \frac{j(1-\tau)}{(1-\beta)(1-\beta\tau)}\frac{c_H}{h} = \zeta_1\frac{c_H}{h}$$

$$\lambda_P' = \frac{\beta-\gamma}{c_P}$$

$$\lambda_P'' = \frac{\beta-\gamma}{c_P}$$

$$\alpha = 1 - \frac{1-m}{2(1-z)}$$

$$q_P = 1$$

$$K_P = \frac{\gamma\mu_P}{1-\gamma(1-\delta_P)-(\beta-\gamma)(m\alpha+\omega(1-\alpha))}\frac{1}{X_P}Y = \zeta_5 Y$$

$$\omega = 1-2(1-z)(1-\alpha)$$

$$q_h = \frac{\gamma \upsilon_P}{1-\gamma-(\beta-\gamma)\left(m\alpha+\omega(1-\alpha)\right)} \frac{1}{X_P} \frac{Y}{h_P} = \zeta_3 \frac{Y}{h_P}$$

$$b_S = \beta m(\zeta_2 + \zeta_4)Y$$

$$b'_P = \beta m\alpha(\zeta_3 + \zeta_5)Y$$

$$b''_P = \beta(1-\alpha)\left(1-(1-z)(1-\alpha)\right)(\zeta_3 + \zeta_5)Y = \zeta_6 Y$$

$$b = \left(\beta m\alpha(\zeta_3 + \zeta_5) + \zeta_6\right)Y = \zeta_7 Y$$

$$d^r = \left(1 - \frac{1}{X_P}\right)Y$$

$$c_H = \left(1 + \left(\frac{1}{\beta} - 1\right)\zeta_7 - \frac{(\mu_P + \upsilon_P)}{X_P}\right)Y = \zeta_8 Y$$

$$c_P = \left(\frac{\mu_P + \upsilon_P}{X_P} - (1-\beta)m\alpha(\zeta_3 + \zeta_5) - \left(\frac{1}{\beta} - 1\right)\zeta_6 - \delta_P \zeta_5\right)Y = \zeta_{10} Y$$

$$h_P = \frac{\zeta_3}{\zeta_1 \zeta_8} h$$

$$h = \frac{\zeta_1 \zeta_8}{\zeta_1 \zeta_8 + \zeta_3}$$

Step three: Log-linearization

$$\hat{c}_{H,t} - \tau \hat{c}_{H,t-1} + (1-\tau)\hat{\rho}_t = 0$$

$$(1-\beta\tau)\hat{u}_{c,t} = \hat{\rho}_t - \beta\tau\hat{\rho}_{t+1}$$

$$\hat{u}_{c,t+1} - \hat{u}_{c,t} + \hat{R}_t - \hat{\pi}_{t+1} = 0$$

$$\frac{1}{\eta} \frac{(1-\beta\tau)}{(1-\tau)\zeta_8} \frac{(1-\mu_P - \upsilon_P)}{X_P} \left(\hat{u}_{c,t} + \hat{Y}_{P,t} - \hat{X}_{P,t}\right) = L_P^{\eta} \hat{L}_{P,t}$$

$$\frac{1-\beta\tau}{1-\tau}\left(\hat{u}_{c,t}+\hat{q}_{h,t}\right)+\frac{j}{\zeta_1}\hat{h}_t=\frac{\beta(1-\beta\tau)}{1-\tau}\left(\hat{u}_{c,t+1}+\hat{q}_{h,t+1}\right)$$

$$\beta\left(\hat{c}_{P,t}+\hat{R}_t\right)-\gamma\left(\hat{\pi}_{t+1}+\hat{c}_{P,t+1}\right)+(\beta-\gamma)\hat{\lambda}'_{P,t}=0$$

$$\beta\left(\hat{c}_{P,t}+\hat{R}_t\right)-\gamma\left(\hat{\pi}_{t+1}+\hat{c}_{P,t+1}\right)+(\beta-\gamma)\hat{\lambda}''_{P,t}=0$$

$$m\left(\hat{\lambda}'_{P,t}+\hat{m}_t\right)+(1-\omega)\left(\hat{\lambda}''_{P,t}+\hat{\pi}_{t+1}+\frac{\zeta_3}{\zeta_3+\zeta_5}\left(\hat{q}_{h,t+1}+\hat{h}_{P,t}\right)\right.$$
$$\left.+\frac{\zeta_5}{\zeta_3+\zeta_5}\left(\hat{q}_{P,t+1}+\hat{K}_{P,t}\right)\right)=\hat{\lambda}''_{P,t}+2\alpha(1-z)\hat{\alpha}_t$$

$$\hat{q}_{P,t}=(1-\gamma)\psi_P\left(\hat{I}_{P,t}-\hat{I}_{P,t-1}\right)$$

$$(\zeta_3+\zeta_5)\left(\hat{R}_t+\hat{b}'_{P,t}-\hat{m}_t-\hat{\pi}_{t+1}-\hat{\alpha}_t\right)=\zeta_3\left(\hat{q}_{h,t+1}+\hat{h}_{P,t}\right)+\zeta_5\left(\hat{q}_{P,t+1}+\hat{K}_{P,t}\right)$$

$$\chi_t=(1-\alpha_t)\pi_{t+1}\left(q_{h,t+1}h_{P,t}+q_{P,t+1}K_{P,t}\right)$$

$$\hat{\chi}_t=\hat{\pi}_{t+1}+\frac{\zeta_3}{\zeta_3+\zeta_5}\left(\hat{q}_{h,t+1}+\hat{h}_{P,t}\right)+\frac{\zeta_5}{\zeta_3+\zeta_5}\left(\hat{q}_{P,t+1}+\hat{K}_{P,t}\right)-\frac{\alpha}{1-\alpha}\hat{\alpha}_t$$

$$\zeta_6\left(\hat{R}_t+\hat{b}''_{P,t}\right)=\beta(1-\alpha)(\zeta_3+\zeta_5)\omega\hat{\chi}_t$$

$$(\beta-\gamma)\left[m\alpha\left(\hat{\lambda}'_{P,t}+\hat{m}_t+\hat{\alpha}_t+\hat{q}_{P,t+1}+\hat{\pi}_{t+1}\right)+(1-\alpha)\omega\left(\hat{q}_{P,t+1}+\hat{\pi}_{t+1}+\hat{\lambda}''_{P,t}\right)\right.$$
$$\left.-\alpha\omega\hat{\alpha}_t-(1-\alpha)(1-\omega)\hat{\chi}_t\right]$$

$$\omega=1-2(1-z)(1-\alpha)$$

$$\left(\hat{q}_{P,t}-\hat{c}_{P,t}\right)=\frac{\gamma\mu_P}{X_P\zeta_5}\left(\hat{Y}_{P,t+1}-\hat{X}_{P,t+1}-\hat{K}_{P,t}-\hat{c}_{P,t+1}\right)+\gamma(1-\delta_P)$$
$$\left(\hat{q}_{P,t+1}-\hat{c}_{P,t+1}\right)+(\beta-\gamma)\left[m\alpha\left(\hat{\lambda}'_{P,t}+\hat{m}_t+\hat{\alpha}_t+\hat{q}_{P,t+1}+\hat{\pi}_{t+1}\right)+\right.$$
$$\left.(1-\alpha)\omega\left(\hat{q}_{P,t+1}+\hat{\pi}_{t+1}+\hat{\lambda}''_{P,t}\right)-\alpha\omega\hat{\alpha}_t-(1-\alpha)(1-\omega)\hat{\chi}_t\right]$$

$$
\begin{aligned}
\left(\hat{q}_{h,t}-\hat{c}_{P,t}\right)= & \frac{\gamma v_P}{X_P\zeta_3}\left(\hat{Y}_{P,t+1}-\hat{X}_{P,t+1}-\hat{h}_{P,t}-\hat{c}_{P,t+1}\right)+\gamma\left(\hat{q}_{h,t+1}-\hat{c}_{P,t+1}\right)\\
&+(\beta-\gamma)\Big[m\alpha\left(\hat{\lambda}'_{P,t}+\hat{m}_t+\hat{\alpha}_t+\hat{q}_{h,t+1}+\hat{\pi}_{t+1}\right)\\
&+(1-\alpha)\,\omega\left(\hat{q}_{h,t+1}+\hat{\pi}_{t+1}+\hat{\lambda}''_{P,t}\right)-\alpha\omega\hat{\alpha}_t-(1-\alpha)(1-\omega)\hat{\chi}_t\Big]
\end{aligned}
$$

$$
\zeta_7\hat{b}_t=\beta m\alpha(\zeta_3+\zeta_5)\hat{b}'_{P,t}+\zeta_6\hat{b}''_{P,t}
$$

$$
\left(1-\frac{1}{X_P}\right)\hat{d}^r_t=\hat{Y}_t-\frac{1}{X_P}\left(\hat{Y}_{P,t}-\hat{X}_{P,t}\right)
$$

$$
\begin{aligned}
&\zeta_8\hat{c}_{H,t}+\zeta_7\hat{b}_t+\zeta_1\zeta_8\left(\hat{h}_t-\hat{h}_{t-1}\right)\\
&\quad=\frac{1}{\beta}\zeta_7\left(\hat{R}_{t-1}+\hat{b}_{t-1}-\hat{\pi}_t\right)+\frac{(1-\mu_P-v_P)}{X_P}\left(\hat{Y}_{P,t}-\hat{X}_{P,t}\right)\\
&\quad\quad+\left(1-\frac{1}{X_P}\right)\hat{d}^r_t
\end{aligned}
$$

$$
\begin{aligned}
\frac{(\mu_P+v_P)}{X_P}\left(\hat{Y}_{P,t}-\hat{X}_{P,t}\right)+\beta m\alpha(\zeta_3+\zeta_5)\hat{b}'_{P,t}+\zeta_6\hat{b}''_{P,t}=\zeta_{10}\hat{c}_{P,t}\\
+\zeta_3\left(\hat{h}_{P,t}-\hat{h}_{P,t-1}\right)+m\alpha(\zeta_3+\zeta_5)\left(\hat{R}_{t-1}+\hat{b}'_{P,t-1}-\hat{\pi}_t\right)\\
+\frac{\zeta_6}{\beta}\left(\hat{R}_{t-1}+\hat{b}''_{P,t-1}-\hat{\pi}_t\right)+\zeta_5\delta_P\hat{I}_{P,t}
\end{aligned}
$$

$$
\frac{\zeta_1\zeta_8}{\zeta_1\zeta_8+\zeta_3}\hat{h}_t+\frac{\zeta_3}{\zeta_1\zeta_8+\zeta_3}\hat{h}_{P,t}=0
$$

$$
\hat{Y}_{P,t}=\hat{A}_{P,t}+\mu_P\hat{K}_{P,t-1}+v_P\hat{h}_{P,t-1}+(1-\mu_P-v_P)\hat{L}_{P,t}
$$

$$
\hat{K}_{P,t}=(1-\delta_P)\hat{K}_{P,t-1}+\delta_P\hat{I}_{P,t}
$$

Case 3: Policy rate and market-oriented interest rate coexist

Step one: Optimized solution

First, the household

The objective utility function of the household is:

$$
\max E_0\sum_{t=0}^{\infty}\beta^t\left(\log\left(c_{H,t}-\tau c_{H,t-1}\right)+j\log h_t-\frac{1}{\eta}\left(L_{P,t}\right)^{\eta}+\chi\ln\left(\frac{M_t}{P_t}\right)\right)
$$

The budget constraint faced by the household is:

$$c_{H,t} + b_t + q_{h,t}h_t + \frac{M_t - M_{t-1}}{P_t} = \frac{R_{t-1}b_{t-1}}{\pi_t} + w_{P,t}L_{P,t} + q_{h,t}h_{t-1} + d_t^r + d_t^b$$

Solving the optimal first-order condition about

$$\{c_{H,t}, h_t, L_{P,t}, M_t\}$$

when $\rho_t = \left(c_{H,t} - \tau c_{H,t-1}\right)^{-1}$, $E_t\left(\Lambda_{t,t+1}\frac{R_t}{\pi_{t+1}}\right) = 1$

where

$$\Lambda_{t,t+k} = \beta^k\left(u_{c,t+k} / u_{c,t}\right), u_{c,t} = \left(c_{H,t} - \tau c_{H,t-1}\right)^{-1} - \beta\tau E_t\left(c_{H,t+1} - \tau c_{H,t}\right)^{-1} = \rho_t - \beta\tau E_t\rho_{t+1}$$

$$u_{c,t}w_{P,t} = \left(L_{P,t}\right)^{\eta-1}$$

$$u_{c,t}q_{h,t} = \frac{j}{h_t} + \beta E_t\left(u_{c,t+1}q_{h,t+1}\right)$$

$$\chi\frac{P_t}{M_t} = \left(1 - \frac{1}{R_t}\right)u_{c,t}$$

Second, the intermediate goods manufacturer

The production function of the intermediate goods manufacturer is:

$$Y_{P,t} = A_{P,t}\left(K_{P,t-1}\right)^{\mu_P}\left(h_{P,t-1}\right)^{\upsilon_P}\left(L_{P,t}\right)^{1-\mu_P-\upsilon_P}$$

The expected utility function of the intermediate goods manufacturer is:

$$\max E_0\sum_{t=0}^{\infty}\gamma^t \log c_{P,t}$$

The lending constraints faced by the intermediate goods manufacturer are:

$$R_t b'_{P,t} \le m_t \alpha E_t\left(\pi_{t+1}\left(q_{h,t+1}h_{P,t} + q_{P,t+1}K_{P,t}\right)\right)$$

$$R_t'b_{P,t}'' \leq E_t\left(\left(1-\alpha\right)\pi_{t+1}\left(q_{h,t+1}h_{P,t}+q_{P,t+1}K_{P,t}\right)\right.$$
$$\left.1-\frac{1-z}{qh+q_PK}\left(1-\alpha\right)\pi_{t+1}\left(q_{h,t+1}h_{P,t}+q_{P,t+1}K_{P,t}\right)\right)$$

The budget constraint faced by the intermediate goods manufacturer is:

$$\frac{Y_{P,t}}{X_{P,t}}+b_{P,t}'+b_{P,t}''+q_{h,t}h_{P,t-1}$$
$$=c_{P,t}+q_{h,t}h_{P,t}+\frac{R_{t-1}b_{P,t-1}'}{\pi_t}+\frac{R_{t-1}'b_{P,t-1}''}{\pi_t}+w_{P,t}L_{P,t}+I_{P,t}$$

The capital accumulation equation including capital adjustment cost is:

$$K_{P,t}=\left(1-\delta_P\right)K_{P,t-1}+\left[1-\frac{\psi_P}{2}\left(\frac{I_{P,t}}{I_{P,t-1}}-1\right)^2\right]I_{P,t}$$

The Lagrangian equation is:

$$\Lambda = log\left(\frac{Y_{P,t}}{X_{P,t}}+b_{P,t}'+b_{P,t}''+q_{h,t}h_{P,t-1}-q_{h,t}h_{P,t}\right.$$
$$\left.-\frac{R_{t-1}b_{P,t-1}'}{\pi_t}-\frac{R_{t-1}b_{P,t-1}''}{\pi_t}-w_{P,t}L_{P,t}-I_{P,t}\right)$$
$$+\gamma log\left(\frac{Y_{P,t+1}}{X_{P,t+1}}+b_{P,t+1}'+b_{P,t+1}''+q_{h,t+1}h_{P,t}-q_{h,t+1}h_{P,t+1}\right.$$
$$\left.-\frac{R_tb_{P,t}'}{\pi_{t+1}}-\frac{R_tb_{P,t}''}{\pi_{t+1}}-w_{P,t+1}L_{P,t+1}-I_{P,t+1}\right)$$
$$-\lambda_{P,t}'\left(R_tb_{P,t}'-m_t\alpha_t\pi_{t+1}\left(q_{h,t+1}h_{P,t}+q_{P,t+1}K_{P,t}\right)\right)-\lambda_{P,t}''$$
$$\left(R_tb_{P,t}''-\left(1-\alpha_t\right)\pi_{t+1}\left(q_{h,t+1}h_{P,t}+q_{P,t+1}K_{P,t}\right)\right.$$
$$\left.\left(1-\frac{1-z}{qh+q_PK}\left(1-\alpha_t\right)\pi_{t+1}\left(q_{h,t+1}h_{P,t}+q_{P,t+1}K_{P,t}\right)\right)\right)$$
$$-u_{P,t}\left(K_{P,t}-\left(1-\delta_P\right)K_{P,t-1}-\left[1-\frac{\psi_P}{2}\left(\frac{I_{P,t}}{I_{P,t-1}}-1\right)^2\right]I_{P,t}\right)$$
$$-\gamma u_{P,t+1}\left(K_{P,t+1}-\left(1-\delta_P\right)K_{P,t}-\left[1-\frac{\psi_P}{2}\left(\frac{I_{P,t+1}}{I_{P,t}}-1\right)^2\right]I_{P,t+1}\right)$$
$$+\ldots$$

Solving the optimization problem of the intermediate goods manufacturer, the first-order conditions about consumption, capital accumulation, capital efficiency, plant demand and labor demand are:

$$\frac{1}{c_{P,t}} = E_t\left(\frac{\gamma R_t}{\pi_{t+1} c_{P,t+1}}\right) + \lambda'_{P,t} R_t$$

$$\frac{1}{c_{P,t}} = E_t\left(\frac{\gamma R_t}{\pi_{t+1} c_{P,t+1}}\right) + \lambda''_{P,t} R'_t$$

$$\begin{aligned}\frac{q_{h,t}}{c_{P,t}} = {} & \gamma E_t\left(\frac{1}{c_{P,t+1}}\left(\frac{\upsilon_P Y_{P,t+1}}{X_{P,t+1} h_{P,t}} + q_{h,t+1}\right)\right) \\ & + \lambda'_{P,t} m_t \alpha q_{h,t+1} \pi_{t+1} + \lambda''_{P,t}(1-\alpha) q_{h,t+1} \pi_{t+1} \\ & - \lambda''_{P,t} \frac{2(1-z)}{q_h h_P + q_P K_P} q_{h,t+1}\left((1-\alpha)\pi_{t+1}\right)^2 \left(q_{h,t+1} h_{P,t} + q_{P,t+1} K_{P,t}\right)\end{aligned}$$

$$w_{P,t} = \frac{(1-\mu_P - \upsilon_P) Y_{P,t}}{X_{P,t} L_{P,t}}$$

$$q_{P,t} = \frac{u_{P,t}}{u_{c,t}}$$

$$\begin{aligned}\frac{q_{P,t}}{c_{P,t}} = {} & \gamma E_t\left(\frac{1}{c_{P,t+1}}\left(\frac{\mu_P Y_{P,t+1}}{X_{P,t+1} K_{P,t}} + (1-\delta_P) q_{P,t+1}\right)\right) \\ & + \lambda'_{P,t} m_t \alpha q_{P,t+1} \pi_{t+1} + \lambda''_{P,t}(1-\alpha) q_{P,t+1} \pi_{t+1} \\ & - \lambda''_{P,t} \frac{2(1-z)}{q_h h_P + q_P K_P} q_{P,t+1}\left((1-\alpha)\pi_{t+1}\right)^2 \left(q_{h,t+1} h_{P,t} + q_{P,t+1} K_{P,t}\right)\end{aligned}$$

$$\begin{aligned}1 = {} & q_{P,t}\left[1 - \frac{\psi_P}{2}\left(\frac{I_{P,t}}{I_{P,t-1}} - 1\right)^2 - \psi_P\left(\frac{I_{P,t}}{I_{P,t-1}} - 1\right)\frac{I_{P,t}}{I_{P,t-1}}\right] \\ & + \gamma \psi_P E_t\left[\frac{c_{P,t}}{c_{P,t+1}} q_{P,t+1}\left(\frac{I_{P,t}}{I_{P,t-1}} - 1\right)\left(\frac{I_{P,t}}{I_{P,t-1}}\right)^2\right]\end{aligned}$$

$$\lambda'_{P,t} m_t = \lambda''_{P,t} E_t\left(1 - \frac{2(1-z)(1-\alpha)}{q_h h_P + q_P K_P} \pi_{t+1}\left(q_{h,t+1} h_{P,t} + q_{P,t+1} K_{P,t}\right)\right)$$

$$d_t^b = \frac{\left(R'_{t-1} - R_{t-1}\right) b''_{P,t-1}}{\pi_t}$$

Third, the retailer

The profit function of the retailer is:

$$\max E_t \sum_{k=0}^{\infty} \theta^k \left\{ \Lambda_{t,t+k} \left(\frac{P_t^*}{P_{t+k}} \left(\frac{P_{t+k-1}}{P_{t-1}} \right)^{\delta_P} - \frac{1}{X_{t+k}} \right) Y_{t+k}^*(i) \right\}$$

Solving the first-order condition about the optimal price P_t^*, the following can be obtained:

$$E_t \sum_{k=0}^{\infty} \theta^k \Lambda_{t,t+k} \left(\frac{P_t^*}{P_{t+k}} \left(\frac{P_{t+k-1}}{P_{t-1}} \right)^{\delta_P} - \frac{X}{X_{t+k}} \right) Y_{t+k}^*(i)$$

The profit obtained by the retailer is:

$$d_t^r = Y_t \left(\frac{P_t - P_t^w}{P_t} \right)$$

Fourth, the Taylor rule and the credit policy

The Taylor rule is:

$$\hat{R}_t = r_R \hat{R}_{t-1} + (1 - r_R) r_\pi \hat{\pi}_t + (1 - r_R) r_y \hat{Y}_t$$

The credit policy is:

$$\hat{m}_t = \rho_m \hat{m}_{t-1} + u_{m,t}$$

where $\hat{m}_t$ follows the AR(1) process and its autocorrelation coefficient is $\rho_m \in (0,1)$, and the shock term $u_{m,t}$ obeys a normal distribution with the mean value of 0 and the variance of σ_m^2.

Fifth, general equilibrium conditions

In terms of the goods market, the market clearing condition is:

$$Y_t = c_{H,t} + c_{P,t} + I_{P,t}$$

In terms of the credit market, the market clearing condition is:

$$b_t = b_t^{'} + b_t^{''}$$

In terms of the housing market, the market clearing condition is:

$$h + h_P = 1$$

Step two: Steady-state value

$$R = \frac{1}{\beta}$$

$$\frac{1}{\rho} = (1-\tau)c_H$$

$$u_c = (1-\beta\tau)\rho$$

$$\left(\frac{(1-\beta\tau)}{(1-\tau)\zeta_8}\frac{(1-\mu_P-\upsilon_P)}{X_P}\right)^{1/\eta} = L_P$$

$$w_P L_P = \frac{(1-\mu_P-\upsilon_P)Y}{X_P}$$

$$q_h = \frac{j(1-\tau)}{(1-\beta)(1-\beta\tau)}\frac{c_H}{h} = \zeta_1\frac{c_H}{h}$$

$$\lambda_P^{'} = \frac{\beta-\gamma}{c_P}$$

$$\lambda_P^{''} = \frac{\beta'-\gamma}{c_P}$$

$$\beta' = \frac{(\beta-\gamma)m}{\omega} + \gamma$$

$$R' = \frac{1}{\beta'} = \frac{\omega}{(\beta-\gamma)m + \gamma\omega}$$

$$\lambda_P'' = \frac{(\beta-\gamma)m}{\omega c_P}$$

$$\alpha = 1 - \frac{1-m}{2(1-z)}$$

$$q_P = 1$$

$$K_P = \frac{\gamma\mu_P}{1-\gamma(1-\delta_P)-(\beta-\gamma)m}\frac{1}{X_P}Y = \zeta_5 Y$$

$$\omega = 1-2(1-z)(1-\alpha)$$

$$q_h = \frac{\gamma\upsilon_P}{1-\gamma-(\beta-\gamma)m}\frac{1}{X_P}\frac{Y}{h_P} = \zeta_3\frac{Y}{h_P}$$

$$b_P' = \beta m\alpha(\zeta_3+\zeta_5)Y$$

$$b_P'' = \left(\frac{(\beta-\gamma)m}{\omega}+\gamma\right)(1-\alpha)(1-(1-z)(1-\alpha))(\zeta_3+\zeta_5)Y = \zeta_6 Y$$

$$b_t = b_{P,t}' + b_{P,t}''$$

$$b = (\beta m\alpha(\zeta_3+\zeta_5)+\zeta_6)Y = \zeta_7 Y$$

$$d^b = \left(\frac{\omega}{(\beta-\gamma)m+\omega\gamma}-\frac{1}{\beta}\right)\zeta_6 Y$$

$$d^r = \left(1-\frac{1}{X_P}\right)Y$$

$$c_H = \left(1+\left(\frac{1}{\beta}-1\right)\zeta_7-\frac{(\mu_P+\upsilon_P)}{X_P}+\left(\frac{\omega}{(\beta-\gamma)m+\omega\gamma}-\frac{1}{\beta}\right)\zeta_6\right)Y = \zeta_8 Y$$

$$c_P = \left(\frac{\mu_P+\upsilon_P}{X_P}-(1-\beta)m\alpha(\zeta_3+\zeta_5)-\left(\frac{\omega}{(\beta-\gamma)m+\omega\gamma}-1\right)\zeta_6-\delta_P\zeta_5\right)Y$$
$$= \zeta_{10} Y$$

$$h_P = \frac{\zeta_3}{\zeta_1\zeta_8} h$$

$$h = \frac{\zeta_1\zeta_8}{\zeta_1\zeta_8 + \zeta_3}$$

Step three: Log-linearization

$$\hat{c}_{H,t} - \tau\hat{c}_{H,t-1} + (1-\tau)\hat{\rho}_t = 0$$

$$(1-\beta\tau)\hat{u}_{c,t} = \hat{\rho}_t - \beta\tau\hat{\rho}_{t+1}$$

$$\hat{u}_{c,t+1} - \hat{u}_{c,t} + \hat{R}_t - \hat{\pi}_{t+1} = 0$$

$$\frac{1}{\eta}\frac{(1-\beta\tau)}{(1-\tau)\zeta_8}\frac{(1-\mu_P-\upsilon_P)}{X_P}\left(\hat{u}_{c,t} + \hat{Y}_{P,t} - \hat{X}_{P,t}\right) = L_P^{\eta}\hat{L}_{P,t}$$

$$\frac{1-\beta\tau}{1-\tau}\left(\hat{u}_{c,t} + \hat{q}_{h,t}\right) + \frac{j}{\zeta_1}\hat{h}_t = \frac{\beta(1-\beta\tau)}{1-\tau}\left(\hat{u}_{c,t+1} + \hat{q}_{h,t+1}\right)$$

$$\beta\left(\hat{c}_{P,t} + \hat{R}_t\right) - \gamma\left(\hat{\pi}_{t+1} + \hat{c}_{P,t+1}\right) + (\beta-\gamma)\hat{\lambda}'_{P,t} = 0$$

$$((\beta-\gamma)m + \omega\gamma)\left(\hat{c}_{P,t} + \hat{R}'_t\right) - \omega\gamma\left(\hat{\pi}_{t+1} + \hat{c}_{P,t+1}\right) + (\beta-\gamma)m\hat{\lambda}''_{P,t} = 0$$

$$\hat{\lambda}''_{P,t} = \omega\left(\hat{\lambda}'_{P,t} + \hat{m}_t\right) + (1-\omega)\left(\hat{\chi}_t + \hat{\lambda}''_{P,t}\right)$$

$$\hat{q}_{P,t} = (1-\gamma)\,\psi_P\left(\hat{I}_{P,t} - \hat{I}_{P,t-1}\right)$$

$$(\zeta_3 + \zeta_5)\left(\hat{R}_t + \hat{b}'_{P,t} - \hat{m}_t - \hat{\pi}_{t+1}\right) = \zeta_3\left(\hat{q}_{h,t+1} + \hat{h}_{P,t}\right) + \zeta_5\left(\hat{q}_{P,t+1} + \hat{K}_{P,t}\right)$$

$$\chi_t = (1-\alpha)\,\pi_{t+1}\left(q_{h,t+1}h_{P,t} + q_{P,t+1}K_{P,t}\right)$$

$$\hat{\chi}_t = \hat{\pi}_{t+1} + \frac{\zeta_3}{\zeta_3+\zeta_5}\left(\hat{q}_{h,t+1} + \hat{h}_{P,t}\right) + \frac{\zeta_5}{\zeta_3+\zeta_5}\left(\hat{q}_{P,t+1} + \hat{K}_{P,t}\right)$$

$$\zeta_6\left(\hat{R}'_t + \hat{b}''_{P,t}\right) = ((\beta-\gamma)m + \gamma\omega)(1-\alpha)(\zeta_3+\zeta_5)\hat{\chi}_t$$

$$\omega = 1 - 2(1-z)(1-\alpha)$$

$$\begin{aligned}(\hat{q}_{P,t} - \hat{c}_{P,t}) = {} & \frac{\gamma\mu_P}{X_P\zeta_5}\left(\hat{Y}_{P,t+1} - \hat{X}_{P,t+1} - \hat{K}_{P,t} - \hat{c}_{P,t+1}\right) + \gamma(1-\delta_P)\left(\hat{q}_{P,t+1} - \hat{c}_{P,t+1}\right) \\ & + (\beta-\gamma)m\Big[\alpha\left(\hat{\lambda}'_{P,t} + \hat{m}_t + \hat{q}_{P,t+1} + \hat{\pi}_{t+1}\right) \\ & + (1-\alpha)\left(\hat{q}_{P,t+1} + \hat{\pi}_{t+1} + \hat{\lambda}''_{P,t}\right) - \frac{(1-\alpha)(1-\omega)}{\omega}\hat{\chi}_t\Big]\end{aligned}$$

$$\begin{aligned}(\hat{q}_{h,t} - \hat{c}_{P,t}) = {} & \frac{\gamma\upsilon_P}{X_P\zeta_3}\left(\hat{Y}_{P,t+1} - \hat{X}_{P,t+1} - \hat{h}_{P,t} - \hat{c}_{P,t+1}\right) + \gamma\left(\hat{q}_{h,t+1} - \hat{c}_{P,t+1}\right) \\ & + (\beta-\gamma)m\Big[\alpha\left(\hat{\lambda}'_{P,t} + \hat{m}_t + \hat{q}_{h,t+1} + \hat{\pi}_{t+1}\right) \\ & + (1-\alpha)\left(\hat{q}_{h,t+1} + \hat{\pi}_{t+1} + \hat{\lambda}''_{P,t}\right) - \frac{(1-\alpha)(1-\omega)}{\omega}\hat{\chi}_t\Big]\end{aligned}$$

$$\zeta_7\hat{b}_t = \beta m\alpha(\zeta_3 + \zeta_5)\hat{b}'_{P,t} + \zeta_6\hat{b}''_{P,t}$$

$$\left(1 - \frac{1}{X_P}\right)\hat{d}_t^r = \hat{Y}_{P,t} - \frac{1}{X_P}\left(\hat{Y}_{P,t} - \hat{X}_{P,t}\right)$$

$$d_t^b = \frac{(R'_{t-1} - R_{t-1})b''_{P,t-1}}{\pi_t}$$

$$\begin{aligned}&\left(\frac{\omega}{(\beta-\gamma)m + \omega\gamma} - \frac{1}{\beta}\right)\hat{d}_t^b \\ &\quad = \frac{\omega}{(\beta-\gamma)m + \omega\gamma}\left(\hat{R}'_{t-1} + \hat{b}''_{P,t-1} - \hat{\pi}_t\right) - \frac{1}{\beta}\left(\hat{R}_{t-1} + \hat{b}''_{P,t-1} - \hat{\pi}_t\right)\end{aligned}$$

$$\begin{aligned}&\zeta_8\hat{c}_{H,t} + \zeta_7\hat{b}_t + \zeta_1\zeta_8\left(\hat{h}_t - \hat{h}_{t-1}\right) \\ &\quad = \frac{1}{\beta}\zeta_7\left(\hat{R}_{t-1} + \hat{b}_{t-1} - \hat{\pi}_t\right) + \frac{(1-\mu_P-\upsilon_P)}{X_P}\left(\hat{Y}_{P,t} - \hat{X}_{P,t}\right) \\ &\quad + \left(1 - \frac{1}{X_P}\right)\hat{d}_t^r + \left(\frac{\omega}{(\beta-\gamma)m + \omega\gamma} - \frac{1}{\beta}\right)\hat{d}_t^b\end{aligned}$$

$$\frac{(\mu_P + \upsilon_P)}{X_P}\left(\hat{Y}_{P,t} - \hat{X}_{P,t}\right) + \beta m\alpha(\zeta_3 + \zeta_5)\hat{b}'_{P,t} + \zeta_6\hat{b}''_{P,t}$$

$$= \zeta_{10}\hat{c}_{P,t} + \zeta_3\left(\hat{h}_{P,t} - \hat{h}_{P,t-1}\right) + m\alpha(\zeta_3 + \zeta_5)\left(\hat{R}_{t-1} + \hat{b}'_{P,t-1} - \hat{\pi}_t\right)$$

$$+ \frac{\zeta_6\omega}{(\beta - \gamma)m + \gamma\omega}\left(\hat{R}'_{t-1} + \hat{b}''_{P,t-1} - \hat{\pi}_t\right) + \zeta_5\delta_P\hat{I}_{P,t}$$

$$\frac{\zeta_1\zeta_8}{\zeta_1\zeta_8 + \zeta_3}\hat{h}_t + \frac{\zeta_3}{\zeta_1\zeta_8 + \zeta_3}\hat{h}_{P,t} = 0$$

$$\hat{Y}_{P,t} = \hat{A}_{P,t} + \mu_P\hat{K}_{P,t-1} + \upsilon_P\hat{h}_{P,t-1} + (1 - \mu_P - \upsilon_P)\hat{L}_{P,t}$$

$$\hat{K}_{P,t} = (1 - \delta_P)\hat{K}_{P,t-1} + \delta_P\hat{I}_{P,t}$$

Notes

1 An Introduction to the credit policy: www.pbc.gov.cn/jinrongshichangsi/147160/147289/147304/2899801/index.html Monetary policy focuses on the regulation of aggregate money, while a credit policy focuses on the regulation of the ratio, structure and duration of bank credit funds invested.

2 The "hybrid sector" defined by Allen et al. (2005) included all non-state-owned, nonlisted enterprises. It included but was not limited to private enterprises and privately run enterprises.

3 In October 2004, the People's Bank of China (central bank) removed regulations over the lower bound on deposit rates and the upper bound on loan rates. The upper bound on deposit rates was raised in 2012, and the lower bound of 30% off loans was removed in 2013.

4 Selecting incremental trust loans as the proxy variable for informal financing involves the following reasons: First, trust financing accounts for a relatively high proportion of informal financing. According to data released by the China Trustee Association, as of the end of 2012, the scale of trust assets has reached CNY 7.5 trillion, of which financing trust assets are CNY 3.7 trillion, accounting for about 50%. Secondly, the financing of trust companies is very similar to bank loans, which is usually called "trust loans." Compared with commercial banks, trust companies are subject to looser supervision and are especially less affected by credit line control and credit management.

5 All data are fluctuations after seasonal adjustment and H-P filter.

6 The capital accumulation equation that includes the capital adjustment cost is

$$K_t = (1 - \delta_k)K_{t-1} + \left[1 - \frac{\psi}{2}\left(\frac{I_t}{I_{t-1}} - 1\right)^2\right]I_t$$

6 Habit formation in consumption, monetary policy and Chinese economic fluctuations

In this chapter, a macroeconomic fluctuation model with monetary policy is used to analyze the impact of financial innovation and monetary policy on the real economy. Before the pension insurance system, social security system and various insurance undertakings in China are truly perfected, it will be hard to change the consumption habits rooted in traditional cultural customs and institutional arrangements. Therefore, habit formation is introduced into the money-in-the-utility (MIU) model. Based on calibration analysis and empirical evidences, the author argues that household consumption in China shows strong habit formation. The MIU model with habit formation well simulates the real economy. It can explain about 98% of real fluctuations in output and perform better than the basic real business cycle (RBC) model in explaining fluctuations in consumption. Furthermore, monetary shocks can explain 11.36% and 10.27% of fluctuations in the nominal interest rate and the inflation rate, respectively. The initial impact of monetary shocks is less than that of technology shocks and lasts a shorter time.

6.1 The MIU model with habit formation in consumption

The impact of financial innovation and monetary policy on the real economy has become more and more prominent. The formation mechanism of crisis and the economic cycle theory considering financial and monetary factors have become mainstream in the field of macroeconomic theory research. In the postcrisis era, the preferred policy of central banks in various countries is to use quantitative tools to regulate macroeconomic operations. It is an urgent theoretical task to build a macroeconomic fluctuation model including monetary policy.

It is observed that, along with the cyclical booms and recessions of the Chinese economy, monetary policy in China has been adjusting between expansion and contraction. According to the data from 1978 to 2005, the volatility of money supply (M0, M1 and M2) in the Chinese economy is greater than the volatility of output and is positively correlated with output. Among them, broad money supply (M2) and cash in circulation (M0) have a

DOI: 10.4324/9781003305651-6

more positive correlation with output, while narrow money supply (M1) has a less positive correlation with output. The stylized facts of Chinese economic fluctuations are largely associated and consistent with fluctuations of monetary policy. It is quite necessary to study the relationship between monetary shocks and economic cycle fluctuations.

Since the 1960s, it is realized that money has had a value of its own. After a long period of attempts and efforts, economists introduced monetary factors into the DSGE model, including mainly the following three models.

First, in the MIU model, Sidrauski (1967) proposed that holding money can increase the utility level of the economic agent, so the money balance can be directly put into the utility function of the agent in the model. Sidrauski originally argued that the number of goods consumed and the amount of money held determined the utility level of the economic agent, which was later extended by economists to include the leisure time possessed by the economic agent. The marginal utility brought by increasing the money balance includes two parts: (1) the convenience of the transaction; (2) the real amount of money in the present period can increase available resources in the future. As there is a certain substitute relation between consumption and money, there is a trade-off between the two. When an economic actor holds too great a money balance, the consumption level will decline. In order to maximize utility, an economic actor must choose between the amount of consumption and the real amount of holding money.

Second is the cash-in-advance (CIA) model. According to Clower (1967), this model assumes that there is some form of transaction cost and that some transactions must use money. It assumes that the acquisition of consumer goods is a form of service that needs to be provided by both time and money or that goods acquired through barter have a time cost, so money is needed as a medium of exchange (Kiyotaki and Wright, 1989). The CIA model proposed by Clower (1967) is essentially the same as Sidrauski's MIU model in the light of demonstrating the superneutrality of money.

Third, the overlapping-generation (OLG) model assumes that money is a special medium capable of transferring the resources of different periods (Samuelson, 1958).

Chinese scholars have two obviously different analysis perspectives on the relationship between monetary policy and economic fluctuations and have correspondingly reached two different conclusions: First, from the perspective of analyzing the transmission mechanism of monetary policy in China, the research concludes that the impact of monetary policy on the economy is neutral and ineffective. For example, Ai and Fan (2002) found that the increase in the degree of economic monetization, the acceleration of financial modernization and the rising savings rate all led to the decline in the velocity of money in China, thus limiting the role of monetary policy. Pei and Xiong (2003) believed that the expanded money supply in monetary policies was often occupied by the stock market and banking industry and could not be fully utilized in production, circulation, consumption of the real economy to promote economic growth, thus greatly reducing the effectiveness of the monetary policies of China.

The other is an econometric empirical study. The research findings suggest that there is a close relationship between economic fluctuations and money supply; that is, money is non-neutral in the short term. Zhao et al. (2002) built a vector autoregression (VAR) model to analyze the impact of money supply on economic fluctuations. The main variables in the model included real gross domestic product (GDP), broad money holding index, consumer price index and real interest rate. It was found that in the short run, the change of the broad money index played an important role in Chinese economic growth, but in the long run, it only affected the price level. By building a VAR model, Xie (2004) concluded that monetary supply policy would affect economic growth rate in the short run, while monetary supply had no effect on output in the long run. Ran et al. (2008) mainly discussed the factors that affected the economic cycle fluctuations by introducing the factor supply and monetary factors in the adding elements into the analysis framework. They believed that the relationship between money supply and economic fluctuations is mutual; that is to say, the money supply has an important influence on economic cyclical fluctuations, and, in turn, economic changes can also produce an effect on money. This indicated that the money supply in China is not neutral. Zhang (2010) built a structural vector autoregression model through the method of an endogenous breakpoint test in the presence of interference coefficients. Using counterfactual contrast experiments, he further found that monetary policy played an increasingly important role in regulating and controlling economic cycle fluctuations in China and that there is still room for improvement. Based on the quarterly data from 1993 to 2008, Yang and Li (2011) found in a new Keynesian model with price stickiness that monetary policy was effective for the real economy, though the effect was limited.

This chapter attempts to build an MIU with consumption habit formation, obtain the arithmetic solution of the model by means of linearization, and then determine the parameters by using the calibration method. The modeled economy is then compared with the real economy to analyze its interpretation of the economic reality. At the same time, the impact of technology shocks and monetary shocks on economic fluctuations is compared through impulse response analysis.

The reasons why consumption habit formation should be introduced into the MIU model when studying monetary economics in China include the following: First of all, it is inevitable and necessary to consider the consumption habits of Chinese residents. After the financial crisis in the United States and the world, the Chinese economy on the demand side is mainly driven by domestic demand, and consumption is the core of domestic demand. Second, until the endowment insurance policy, social security administration and various insurance undertakings for residents in China are truly perfected, it will be difficult to change consumption habits rooted in traditional cultural customs and institutional arrangements. Consumption habit becomes the main factor influencing residents' intertemporal choice. Third, a large number of empirical studies show that Chinese residents' consumption is characterized by habit formation. For example, Lei (2003) showed that, in terms of the consumption function of rural residents and that of urban residents, the coefficient of the previous period's living consumption expenditure is both relatively large and that the two are very close to 1. It meant that the intensity of consumption habits of Chinese residents is very high and that the consumption habit has a significant impact on current consumption. Hang (2010) showed that in the long run, every 1% increase in the parameter of habit formation would reduce the average propensity to consume by about 0.17%. By introducing habit formation into the model, habit formation affects the consumption level of residents and then indirectly affects the money demand, economic fluctuations in China and the way and degree that monetary shocks and technology shock the economy.

6.2 Data sources and stylized facts

The data selected in this chapter are the real data of GDP, consumption, investment, capital and the annual data of employment from 1978 to 2010. The original data of variables are all from the *China Statistical Yearbooks.* Except for employment, the other variables are nominal variables. Therefore, it is necessary to process these original data and convert them into real data based on 1978. The data of money supply (M0, M1 and M2) were calculated as follows: The data of M2 from 1978 to 1989 refers to the data collected by Zuo (1999); other data were collected from the CEInet statistics database. The nominal money supply is converted into real money supply based on 1978 using the GDP deflator index. According to the data of GDP, capital stock, consumption, investment and money supply in China from 1978 to 2010, there are large fluctuations in various economic variables in China. After logarithmic processing of these data, H-P filter processing is carried out by using the Eviews 6.0 software, and the fluctuations of variables can be obtained as shown from Figures 6.1–6.8, which can intuitively reflect the fluctuations in the process of Chinese economic growth.

It can be seen from these eight variables' H-P filter that since the reform and opening-up, these economic indexes have shown several large fluctuations that have also shown great consistency. The components of total demand and output all show strong procyclicality. In particular, the fluctuations of capital, consumption and investment are highly consistent with output fluctuations, but labor input fluctuations represented by the employment are not highly consistent with output fluctuations, showing noncyclicality. The fluctuations of money supply M0, M1 and M2 are consistent and show strong cyclicality. That is, the fluctuations of money supply present periodic characteristics. However, compared with the real GDP, the fluctuation range is larger, and the fluctuation frequency is higher.

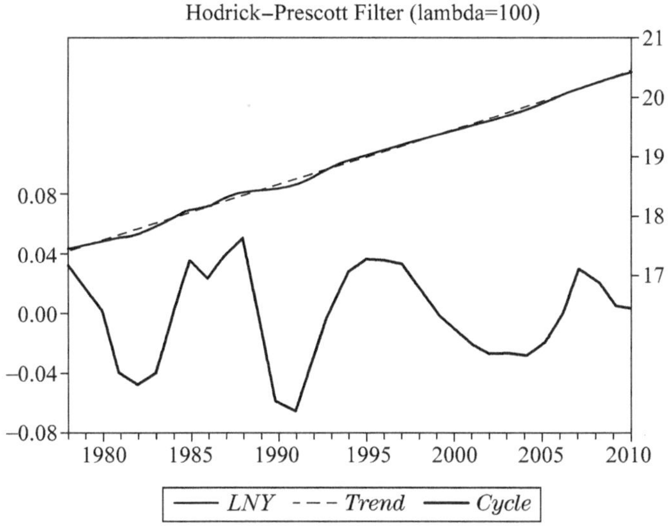

Figure 6.1 Output Fluctuations from 1978 to 2010.

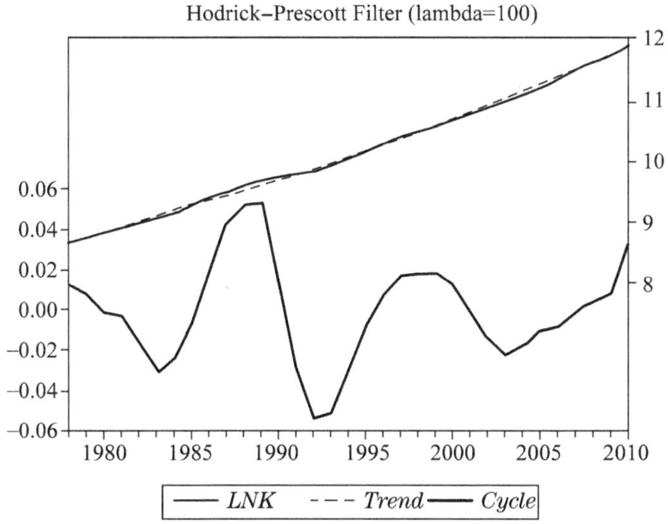

Figure 6.2 Capital Fluctuations from 1978 to 2010.

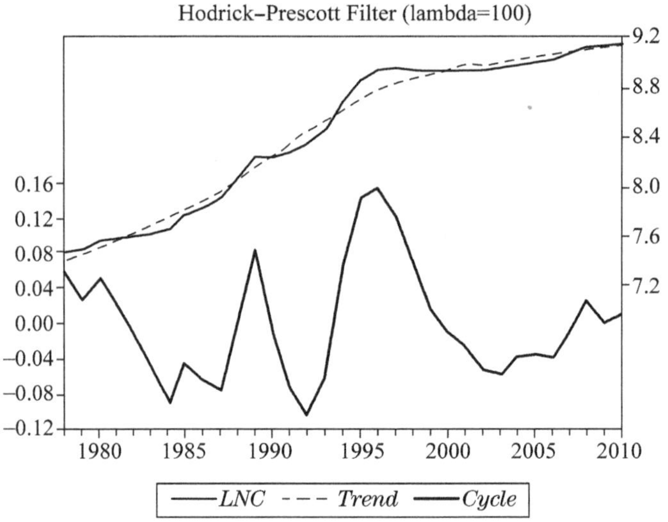

Figure 6.3 Consumption Fluctuations from 1978 to 2010.

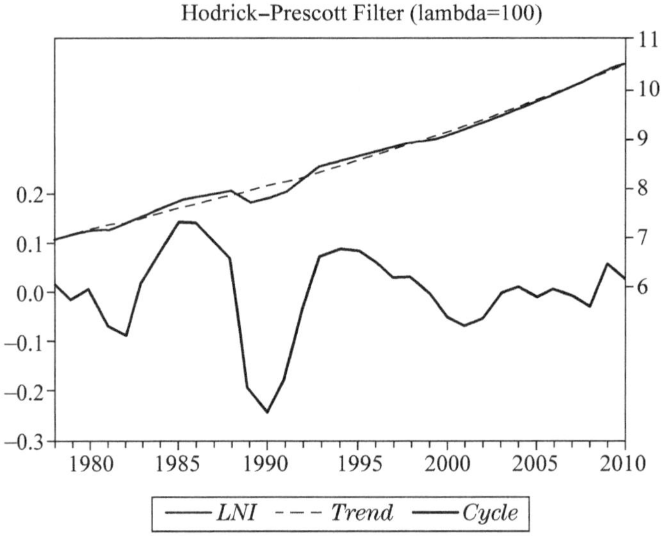

Figure 6.4 Investment Fluctuations from 1978 to 2010.

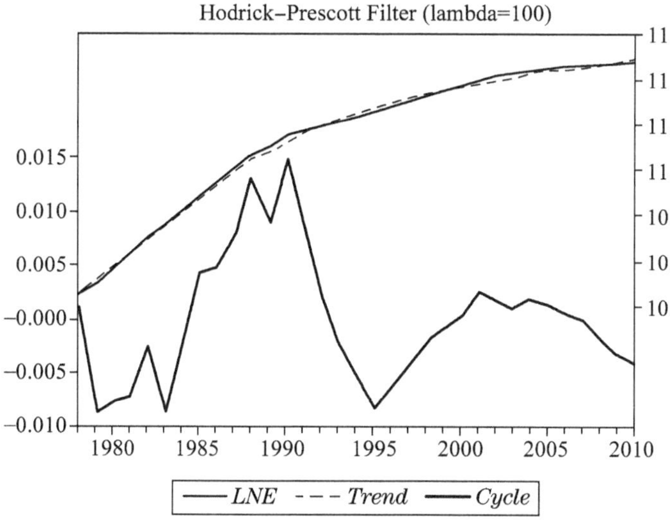

Figure 6.5 Employment Fluctuations from 1978 to 2010.

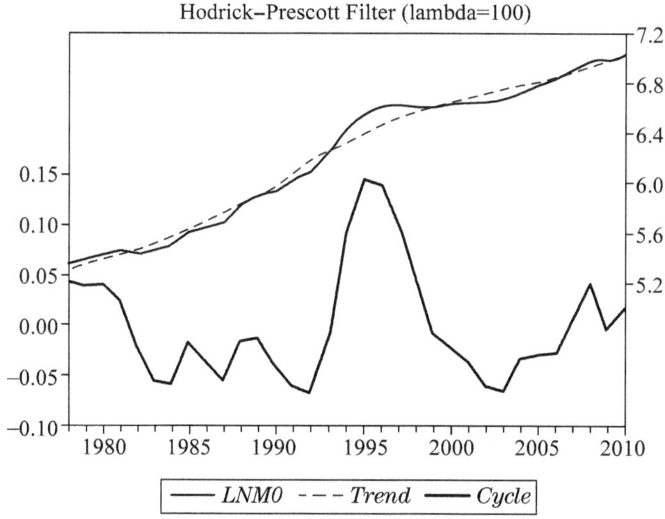

Figure 6.6 Real M0 Fluctuations from 1978 to 2010.

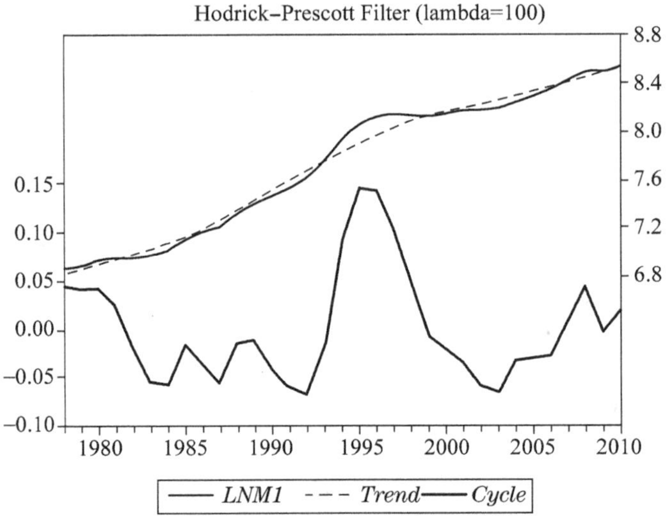

Figure 6.7 Real M1 Fluctuations from 1978 to 2010.

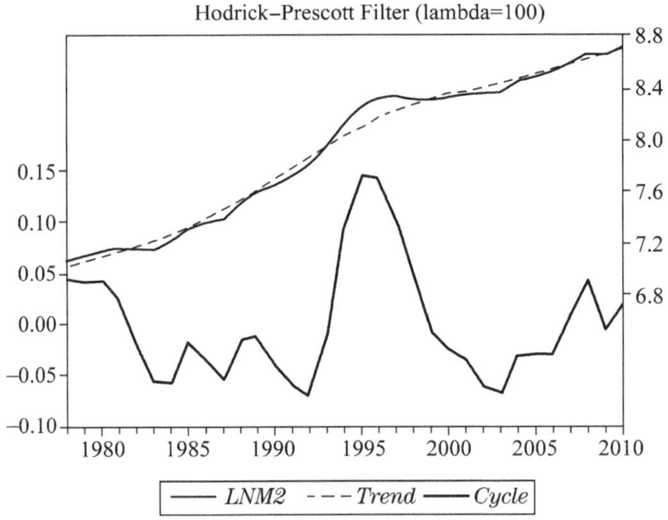

Figure 6.8 Real M2 Fluctuations from 1978 to 2010.

6.3 Model building and parameter calibration

Suppose that the representative households in an economy are homogeneous: They have the same preferences and can live infinitely, and the utility comes from consumption, leisure and money holdings. The form of the utility function is:

$$U = E_t \sum_{t=0}^{\infty} \beta^t [u(C_t, L_t, m_t)] \tag{6.1}$$

where $u(C_t, L_t, m_t) = a\ln(C_t - bC_{t-1}) + (1-a)\ln m_t + \phi\ln(1-L_t)$, C_t represents consumption in period t, and the formative parameter of consumption customs b is usually between 0 and 1, which determines the formation degree of consumption customs. Introducing consumption customs into the utility function indicates that the utility of consumers of the t period not only depends on the current consumption but also is related to the consumption in the previous period. $m_t = \frac{M_t}{P_t}$ represents the real money balance. $M_t > 0$ represents the nominal money balance. P_t represents the price level. L_t represents the labor hours of the family in period t. The total time endowment for each period is normalized to 1. Thus, the $1 - L_t$ represents the leisure time for the family.

The budget constraint confronting consumers is:

$$C_t + I_t + b_t + m_t \le Y_t + \frac{1+i_{t-1}}{1+\pi_t} b_{t-1} + \frac{m_{t-1}}{1+\pi_t} + t_t \tag{6.2}$$

where $b_t = \frac{B_t}{P_t}$ represents the actual value of holding government-issued bonds, i_t represents the nominal interest rate, $t_t = \frac{T_t}{P_t}$ represents the actual value of the government transfer payment, and π_t represents the inflation rate.

Assume that the production function is a Cobb–Douglas form with constant returns to scale:

$$Y_t = A_t K_t^{\alpha} L_t^{1-\alpha} \tag{6.3}$$

where A_t represents the exogenous technological variable, K_t represents the real capital input, α represents the output elasticity of capita, $1-\alpha$ is the output elasticity of labor. The capital stock evolves according to $K_{t+1} = I_t + (1-\delta)K_t$, of which δ represents the depreciation rate of capital, $0 < \delta < 1$.

The technology evolves according to $\ln A_t = (1-\rho_A)\ln \bar{A} + \rho_A \ln A_{t-1} + \varepsilon_t^A$, $\varepsilon_t^A \sim i.i.d.N(0, \sigma_A^2)$, where $\bar{A}$ represents the steady-state value of technology shock A_t. ρ_A represents the autoregressive coefficient of technology, $-1 < \rho_A < 1$. ε_t^A represents the white noise disturbance term of technology, and its standard deviation is σ_A, indicating the impact of exogenous random shock on technology.

The resulting equation of the real money balance is $m_t = \frac{1+\theta_t}{1+\pi_t} m_{t-1}$, and θ_t represents the nominal capital stock growth rate. Define the deviation of money growth rate from its average growth rate as $u_t = \theta_t - \bar{\theta}$, where $\bar{\theta}$ represents the average of θ_t, $\bar{\theta} > 0$, and the resulting equation of money growth rate deviation is $u_t = \rho_u u_{t-1} + \varepsilon_t^u$, $\varepsilon_t^u \sim i.i.d. N(0, \sigma_u^2)$, of which $0 \le \rho_u \le 1$ measures the persistence of monetary shocks. ε_t^u represents the white noise disturbance term of monetary growth rate deviation, and its standard deviation is σ_u.

Based on the assumptions of this model, the programming problems faced by the representative household are as follows:

$$\begin{aligned}
&\underset{(C_t, L_t, m_t)}{MAX}\ E_t\{\sum_{t=0}^{\infty} \beta^t [a \ln(C_t - bC_{t-1}) + (1-a)\ln m_t + \phi \ln(1-L_t)]\} \\
&\text{s.t.: } C_t + K_{t+1} + b_t + m_t = (1-\delta)K_t + A_t K_t^{\alpha} L_t^{1-\alpha} + \frac{1+i_{t-1}}{1+\pi_t} b_{t-1} + \frac{m_{t-1}}{1+\pi_t} + t_t \\
&\qquad \ln A_t = (1-\rho_A)\ln \bar{A} + \rho_A \ln A_{t-1} + \varepsilon_t^A, \quad \varepsilon_t^A \sim iidN(0, \sigma_A^2) \\
&\qquad u_t = \rho_u u_{t-1} + \varepsilon_t^u, \quad \varepsilon_t^u \sim iidN(0, \sigma_u^2) \\
&\qquad m_t = \frac{1+\theta_t}{1+\pi_t} m_{t-1} \\
&\qquad K_0 \text{ given}
\end{aligned} \tag{6.4}$$

Equilibrium is defined as clearing in all markets over all periods with respect to consumption, capital, labor input, real bonds, holding money and a series of price systems including real factor price, nominal interest rate and inflation rate.

Since it is assumed that all households are homogeneous, the bond stock must be zero at equilibrium; i. e., $\bar{b} = 0$. Therefore, bonds and transfer payments are not considered here. It is convenient to use value function to express the decision-making problems faced by the households. The value function of the representative household's decision problems is:[1]

$$V_t = \max_{(C_t, K_t, m_t, L_t, b_t)} \{u(C_t - bC_{t-1}, m_t, 1-L_t) + \beta E_t V_{t+1}\}$$

For the sake of derivation, when $C_t' = C_t - bC_{t-1}$, this value function can be expressed as:

$$V_t = \max_{(C_t, K_t, m_t, L_t, b_t)} \{u(C_t', m_t, 1-L_t) + \beta E_t V_{t+1}\} \tag{6.5}$$

At this point, the constraint condition remains unchanged:

$$C_t + K_{t+1} + b_t + m_t \le (1-\delta)K_t + A_t K_t^{\alpha} L_t^{1-\alpha} + \frac{1+i_{t-1}}{1+\pi_t} b_{t-1} + \frac{m_{t-1}}{1+\pi_t} + t_t \tag{6.6}$$

Take derivatives for each state variable in the preceding equation to obtain the corresponding first-order necessary conditions:

$$\frac{a(1-\alpha)}{C_t - bC_{t-1}} \cdot \frac{Y_t}{L_t} - \frac{\phi}{1-L_t} - a(1-\alpha)\beta b E_t\left(\frac{1}{C_{t+1} - bC_t} \cdot \frac{Y_t}{L_t}\right) = 0 \tag{6.7}$$

$$\frac{a}{C_t - bC_{t-1}} = a\beta E_t\left[\frac{1}{C_{t+1} - bC_t} \cdot \left(\alpha \frac{Y_{t+1}}{K_{t+1}} + 1 - \delta + b\right)\right] \tag{6.8}$$

$$R_t = f_K(K_t, L_t, A_t) + 1 - \delta = \alpha \frac{Y_t}{K_t} + (1-\delta) \tag{6.9}$$

$$\frac{u_m}{u_c} = \frac{(1-a)(C_t - bC_{t-1})}{am_t} = \frac{i_t}{1 + i_t + b(1+\pi_{t+1})} \tag{6.10}$$

The existence of the set of equations should follow the following boundary conditions: First, the initial capital input K_0 is given. Second, the transversality conditions of an economy are:

$$\lim_{i\to\infty} \beta^i E_t\left(\frac{a}{C_i - bC_{i-1}} K_{i+1}\right) = 0 \tag{6.11}$$

$$\lim_{i\to\infty} \beta^i E_t\left(\frac{a}{C_i - bC_{i-1}} m_i\right) = 0 \tag{6.12}$$

$$\lim_{i\to\infty} \beta^i E_t\left(\frac{a}{C_i - bC_{i-1}} b_i\right) = 0 \tag{6.13}$$

The transversality condition means that the marginal utility discounted by the consumer is equal to zero at infinity and that, in the steady state, the labor supply of consumers is a constant.

The economic system equilibrium is defined as follows: Given preferences, technologies and resource constraints in the economy, households achieve expected utility maximization, firms achieves expected profit maximization, and the market is cleared under the given state variables and exogenous shock variables. This is a dynamic stochastic programming problem whose equilibrium solutions can be expressed as a strategy profile: k_t, c_t, m_t, a_t, u_t, y_t, l_t, r_t, π_t and i_t.

Since there are no analytical solutions to nonlinear differential equations, the numerical solution is used as an alternative in this chapter through log-linearization and numerical equivalent substitution. After log-linearization, the following can be obtained:

$$\overline{Y}\cdot\hat{y}_t=\overline{C}\cdot\hat{c}_t+\overline{K}\cdot\hat{k}_{t+1}-(1-\delta)\overline{K}\cdot\hat{k}_t \tag{6.14}$$

$$y_t\approx a_t+\alpha\hat{k}_t+(1-\alpha)\hat{l}_t \tag{6.15}$$

$$\overline{R}\hat{r}_t=\alpha\frac{\overline{Y}}{\overline{K}}\left(\hat{y}_t-\hat{k}_t\right) \tag{6.16}$$

$$\hat{i}_t=\hat{r}_t+\hat{\pi}_t \tag{6.17}$$

$$\begin{aligned}&E_t\{J(1-\beta b)-\phi\overline{C}^2\overline{L}(1-b)^2+J(1-\beta b)\cdot\hat{y}_t\\&-[\overline{L}\frac{J}{1-\overline{L}}(1-\beta b)+\phi\overline{C}^2\overline{L}(1-b)^2]\cdot\hat{l}_t+[\frac{J}{1-b}-\phi\overline{C}^2\overline{L}(1-b)]\cdot\hat{c}_{t+1}\\&-[b\frac{J}{1-b}(1+\beta)+\phi\overline{C}^2\overline{L}(1-b)^2]\cdot\hat{c}_t+[b^2\beta\frac{J}{1-b}-\phi\overline{C}^2\overline{L}(b^2-b)]\cdot\hat{c}_{t-1}\}=0\end{aligned} \tag{6.18}$$

$$E_t[\hat{c}_{t+1}-(1+b)\hat{c}_t-b\hat{c}_{t-1}-(1-b\beta-b+b^2\beta)\hat{r}_{t+1}]=0 \tag{6.19}$$

$$(1+\overline{\pi})\hat{m}_t=\overline{\pi}u_t+(1+\overline{\pi})\hat{m}_{t-1}-\overline{\pi}\hat{\pi}_t \tag{6.20}$$

$$\begin{aligned}&\frac{a\overline{m}\overline{i}}{1-a}-\overline{C}(1+\overline{i}-b\overline{i}-b^2+b\overline{\pi}-b^2\overline{\pi})-\overline{C}(1+\overline{i}+b+b\overline{\pi})\cdot\hat{c}_t\\&+b\overline{C}(1+\overline{i}+b+b\overline{\pi})\cdot\hat{c}_{t-1}-\overline{i}\overline{C}(1-b)\cdot\hat{i}-b\overline{C}\overline{\pi}(1-b)\cdot\hat{\pi}_{t+1}+\frac{a\overline{m}\overline{i}}{1-a}\cdot\hat{m}_t=0\end{aligned} \tag{6.21}$$

$$a_t=\rho_A a_{t-1}+\varepsilon_t^A \tag{6.22}$$

and the resulting equation of the money growth rate is $u_t=\rho_u u_{t-1}+\varepsilon_t^u$.

After log-linearization, ten equations and ten variables are obtained, as shown from equations 6.14–6.22 plus 6.3. And the endogenous state variables are k_t, c_t and m_t, the exogenous state variables are a_t and u_t, and the endogenous control variables are y_t, l_t, r_t, π_t and i_t. Therefore, the economic system described by the economic programming problems can be approximately represented by the preceding ten stochastic linear equations.

The following parameters are assigned according to the historical data of China:

First, output elasticity, technology shocks and monetary shocks: To measure the output elasticity of capital and labor and the regression coefficients of technology and monetary shocks, it is necessary to first estimate the production function. Assume that the production function is the Cobb–Douglas form with constant returns to scale:

$$Y_t=e^{a_t+\mu T}K_t^{\alpha}L_t^{1-\alpha}$$

where T represents the time trend variable, $T = 1, 2, \ldots$, μ represents the parameter value of the variable T. In order to eliminate the linear correlation between regression variables, the intensive form of output and capital is adopted to transform the production function.

In the selection of capital stock data, this chapter uses the basic capital accumulation equation $K_{t+1} = I_t + (1-\delta)K_t$.

Real investment is obtained by using the price index of investment in fixed assets to calculate the nominal investment. This chapter agrees with Zhang, Wu and Zhang (2004) and Shan (2008) and takes gross fixed capital formation as the investment data of the year. Referring to the research by Zhang and Zhang (2003) and Guo and Jia (2004), the fixed asset investment price index from 1978 to 2002 was obtained. Based on the fixed asset price index provided by National Bureau of Statistics (2011), the time series of the fixed asset investment price index from 1978 to 2010 is constructed. As for the capital stock of the base period 1978, based on a great extent of existing literature, this chapter adopts the research by Huang, Ren and Liu (2002); that is, the capital stock of 1978 is set at CNY 582.166 billion. The annual depreciation rate is typically regarded as 0.1, and the capital stock in the past years is calculated through the perpetual inventory method. Based on these data, the production function is as follows:

$$\begin{aligned} &\ln\frac{Y}{L} = 3.337 + 0.46\ln\frac{K}{L} + 0.04T \\ &\qquad\quad (8.86)\quad (8.30)\qquad\quad (9.04) \\ &R^2 = 0.998,\quad S.E. = 0.036,\quad F = 7355.31 \end{aligned}$$

Under the parameter estimates of this measurement model are t-test values, and the goodness of fit reaches 99.8%. Both the parameters and the model pass the test. The measurement results show that the output elasticity of capital is 0.46, so the output elasticity of labor is $1 - 0.46 = 0.54$.

According to this equation, the time series of the Solow residual A_t can be further obtained:

$$\ln A = \ln\frac{Y}{L} - 0.46\cdot\ln\frac{K}{L} - 0.04\cdot T$$

This is the time series data of technology shock A. According to this series data, the technology shock model can be obtained by econometric regression:

$$\begin{aligned} &\ln A = 0.706 + 0.788\ln A(-1) \\ &\qquad\quad (1.92)\quad (7.11) \end{aligned}$$

The first-order autoregressive coefficient of technology shocks (ρ_A) is 0.788. The standard deviation σ_A is 2.34%. $\bar{A}$ represents the technical level of equilibrium with only level effect and without volatility effect, so it is set as 1.

For the parameters related to monetary shocks, first of all, the growth rate data of nominal money supply variables (M0, M1, M2) are log-linearized, and then H-P filtering is carried out to obtain three deviation fluctuation sequences of nominal money growth rate as $M0cycle$, $M1cycle$ and $M2cycle$. Then, according to the assumption of the variation equation of the deviation variable of monetary growth rate u_t in the preceding model, namely

$$u_t = \rho_u u_{t-1} + \varepsilon_t^u, \text{where } \varepsilon_t^u \sim i.i.d.N\left(0, \sigma_u^2\right)$$

First-order autoregressions were performed for the time series $M0cycle$, $M1cycle$ and $M2cycle$, respectively, and three regression results were obtained:

$$\begin{array}{c} M0cycle = 0.798 M0cycle(-1) \\ (7.512) \\ s.e. = 0.034 \end{array} \qquad \begin{array}{c} M1cycle = 0.798 M1cycle(-1) \\ (7.513) \\ s.e. = 0.034 \end{array}$$

$$\begin{array}{c} M2cycle = 0.798 M2cycle(-1) \\ (7.513) \\ s.e. = 0.034 \end{array}$$

Based on these three regression results, the autocorrelation coefficient ρ_u of the money growth rate with monetary shocks is 0.789, and the standard deviation is 3.4%.

Second, the depreciation rate (δ): Internationally, the seasonal depreciation rate is generally taken as 0.025, and the annual depreciation rate is 0.1. We assume that the annual limit of the fixed assets of China is 10 years. Hence, the value of depreciation rate is 0.1.

Third, return on capital ($\bar{R}$): According to the equation for the return on capital, $R = (\sum_{t=1978}^{2010} \frac{(1-\alpha)Y_t}{K_t})/33 + 1 - \delta$, the estimated value of R is about 1.166.

Fourth, consumption habit formation degree (b): Christiano and Eichenbaum (2005) set the value of parameter b as 0.65, which indicates the persistence degree of customs. Chinese scholars Hang Bin (2010) obtained a series of estimated values of custom-forming parameters when studying the reasons for the continuous decline of average consumption propensity of urban residents, and the average value of b was 0.265. In this chapter, to ensure that equations 4.21, $\frac{\bar{Y}}{\bar{K}} = \frac{1}{\alpha}(\frac{1}{\beta} - b - 1 + \delta)$, and 4.23, $\bar{C} = [\frac{1}{\alpha}(\frac{1}{\beta} - b - 1 + \delta) - \delta]\bar{K}$, are positive in equilibrium, b is set as 0.1.[2]

Fifth, subjective discount rate (β): According to equilibrium conditions of first-order conditions, $\bar{R} = \frac{1}{\beta} - b$, $\beta = 0.79$.

Six, labor supply ($\bar{L}$): Among the available statistics in China, only employment data can be used to measure labor input in the production function. Therefore,

Table 6.1 Values of Benchmark Model Parameters

β	B	δ	a	ϕ
0.79	0.1	0.1	0.95	2.569
ρ_A	σ_A	ρ_u	σ_u	α
0.788	0.0234	0.798	0.034	0.46

Table 6.2 Steady-State Values Based on the Benchmark Parameter Values

$\overline{R}$	$\overline{Y}$	$\overline{C}$	$\overline{K}$	$\overline{m}$	$\overline{i}$	$\overline{L}$	$\overline{\pi}$
1.166	0.882	0.729	1.525	0.131	0.399	0.553	0.2

the labor input index uses employment each year. According to Huang (2005), the series of the proportion of the employed population is relatively stable, and the fluctuation range of this value is small. Since the average of the series of the proportion of the employed population from 1978 to 2010 is 0.553, the labor supply is normalized as 1. Therefore, the value of labor supply $\overline{L}$ is 0.553.

Seventh, value of average inflation rate ($\overline{\pi}$): We agree with Cooley and Hansen (1995). Since the average annual growth rate of the nominal money stock M0, M1 and M2 of China is 0.19, 0.2 and 0.22, respectively, and the average is 0.2, the average of the annual data on the inflation rate $\overline{\pi}$ is 0.2.

Eighth, value of the weight of consumption (a) *and value of the weight of leisure* (ϕ): For the weight of consumption a, the value selected in this chapter is consistent with the estimated value reported by Chari, Kehoe and McGrattan (2002), that is, a is set as 0.95.

By using the equilibrium results of first-order conditions and the equilibrium values of other parameters and related variables, the weight of leisure ϕ can be calculated as 2.569.

In summary, the calibrated model parameters are shown in Table 6.1.

According to the parameter values in the table, the value of the equilibrium labor supply $\overline{L}$ and the preceding equilibrium equations, the equilibrium values of all variables can be obtained as in Table 6.2.

6.4 Empirical results analysis

According to the equilibrium relationships among macroeconomic variables, the MATLAB software is adopted to obtain all economic variables' standard deviations in the equilibrium condition and their correlation coefficients with output; see Table 6.3. Comparing the results obtained by the model with the data of real economic variables will tell whether the MIU model involving consumption custom formation can reflect the real economic fluctuations well.

Table 6.3 Cyclical Characteristics of Simulated Economy

Parameters	*Real Economy*		*Simulated Economy*		*Kydland–Prescott Ratio*
	Standard Deviation (%)	*Corresponding Correlation Coefficient with Output*	*Standard Deviation (%)*	*Corresponding Correlation Coefficient with Output*	
Output	3.10	1.00	3.05	1.00	0.98
Consumption	6.17	0.48	4.71	0.28	0.76
Capital	2.50	0.44	6.85	0.29	2.74
Labor	0.58	–0.14	5.96	0.32	10.2
Nominal Rate	22.19	0.37	11.99	0.71	0.54
Aggregate Money	5.61	0.57	2.70	0.33	0.48
Inflation Rate	29.87	0.16	11.87	0.78	0.40

The real economic data and simulated economic data in Table 6.3 are detrended with the H-P filter. Kydland–Prescott ratio is obtained by dividing the standard deviation of the model's economic variables by that of the corresponding variables of the real economy. It indicates the effects of the model's interpretation of the real economy. Generally speaking, the closer the ratio is to 1, the better the interpretation effects are.

In terms of output fluctuations, the standard deviation of the real economy is 0.031, and that of the simulated economy is 0.0305. The model can explain 98% of periodic characteristics of output fluctuations. The fluctuations of output in two cases are very similar.

In terms of consumption fluctuations, the standard deviation of real economy is 0.0617, and that of the simulated economy is 0.0471. The model can explain 76% of real fluctuations. The corresponding correlation coefficient with output in the case of simulated economy is 0.28, and in the case of the real economy it is 0.48; both show procyclicality.

In terms of capital fluctuations, the standard deviation of the real economy is 0.025, while that of simulated economy is 0.0685. The model can explain 274% of real fluctuations. The reason why they differ greatly may be that there are many accounting methods for capital in China and that the statistical accounting data used in this chapter may not be accurate enough. However, the coincident correlation coefficient with output in the model economy is close to that in the real economy with a difference of only 0.15, both showing procyclicality.

In terms of the labor fluctuations, the standard deviation of the real economy is 0.0596, and that of the simulated economy is 0.00058. The fluctuations of the simulated economy are much larger than that of the real economy. Moreover, the corresponding correlation coefficient with output in the simulated economy is 0.32, showing weak procyclicality, while the correlation coefficient with output in the real economy is −0.14, showing countercyclicality.

There are five reasons for these results. First, the statistical method of China's employment has changed since 1990. Before 1990, the employment data were obtained through the "three in one" statistical method;[3] after 1990, the employment data are obtained through the census data, resulting in a great difference in the statistical results.[4] Second, from the perspective of the statistical object of labor, the National Bureau of Statistics ignores the hidden unemployment problem in rural areas. Rural employment in China presents obvious characteristics of seasonal unemployment. Third, internationally, the labor input adopts the labor hours of workers, and the change of labor hours are much more flexible than the change of the population of workers. Fourth, compared with developed countries, labor volatility in the Chinese real economy is relatively small because the financial system in China is not developed enough, and it is difficult to realize the intertemporal substitution of capital. Finally, as the utility function in the model introduces the monetary factor, the labor in the simulated economy in this chapter is more sensitive to the monetary shocks and shows larger variance compared with other RBC models. All these explain why the labor fluctuations of the simulated economy are significantly greater than that of the real economy.

In terms of the nominal interest rate fluctuations, the standard deviation of the real economy is 0.2219, and that of the simulated economy is 0.1199. The model can explain about 54% of real fluctuations. The correlation coefficient with output in the simulated economy is 0.71, and that of the real economy is 0. 37, showing procyclicality.

In terms of aggregate money fluctuations, the standard variation of the real economy is 0.0561, while that of the simulated economy is 0.027. The model can solve about 48% of real fluctuations. In the model economy, the corresponding correlation coefficient with output is 0.33, and in the real economy it is 0.57, both showing procyclicality.

In terms of inflation rate fluctuations, the standard deviation of the real economy is 0.2987, and that of the model is 0.1187. The model can explain about 40% of real fluctuations. In the model economy, the correlation coefficient with output is 0.78, and in the real economy 0.16, both showing procyclicality.

The simulated economy well explains output and consumption fluctuations, which indicates that the formative factor of consumption customs can be involved in the model to explain the changes of household consumption. It also indicates that in the case of introducing the monetary factor into the utility function, the money supply not only has an impact on economic fluctuations but also indirectly affects the changes of other macroeconomic variables by affecting the market interest rate. Therefore, the effects of consumption customs and monetary shocks on the growth and fluctuations of the Chinese economy should not be ignored.

Based on the economic data of the model obtained after the calibration, the variance of each economic variable can be obtained; that is, the ratio of the

Table 6.4 Variance Decomposition of Variables

Parameters	*Proportion of Technology Shock(%)*	*Proportion of Monetary Shock(%)*
Output	90.03	9.97
Consumption	94.56	5.44
Capital	98.82	1.18
Labor	93.78	6.22
Nominal Interest Rate	88.64	11.36
Real Interest Rate	94.92	5.08
Aggregate Money	0.55	99.45
Inflation Rate	89.73	10.27
Technology Shock	100	0
Monetary Shock	0	100

impact of technology shocks and that of monetary shocks can be obtained; see Table 6.4.

Except for the two types of shocks, all variables—in the variance decomposition, even the minimum ratio of technology shocks reaches 88.64%—reach above 90%. This shows that the impact of technology shocks plays an important role in economic fluctuations. But the impact of monetary shocks is also important. On the one hand, it accounts for 11.36% of the nominal interest rate and 10.27% of the inflation rate, which is consistent with the real economic situation. Monetary policy causes changes in the market interest rate by adjusting the amount of the money supply's impact on the financial market and changing the ratio of money supply and demand. On the other hand, it also affects the variables of consumption and labor to a certain extent. From this aspect, it can be seen that the model economy is very consistent with the economic reality and that the predictability of the model is good.

According to the economic data of the model obtained after parameter calibration, the impulse responses of different variables to shocks can be established; see Figures 6.9 and 6.10.

In the model, both technology and money are exogenous shock variables, but the impulse response caused by them differs greatly.

First of all, from the overall point of view, the initial effect of technology shocks is greater than that of monetary shocks. This is understandable because technology can be quickly translated into real productivity, which can have a significant impact on the economy and is ultimately reflected in output fluctuations. And the decline of monetary shocks is slow and does not obviously impact the economy in the initial stage.

Second, in terms of duration, the impact of technology shocks can last for a long time. After 20 years, technology shocks still have a certain impact, while the impact of monetary shocks is not as long. However, considering

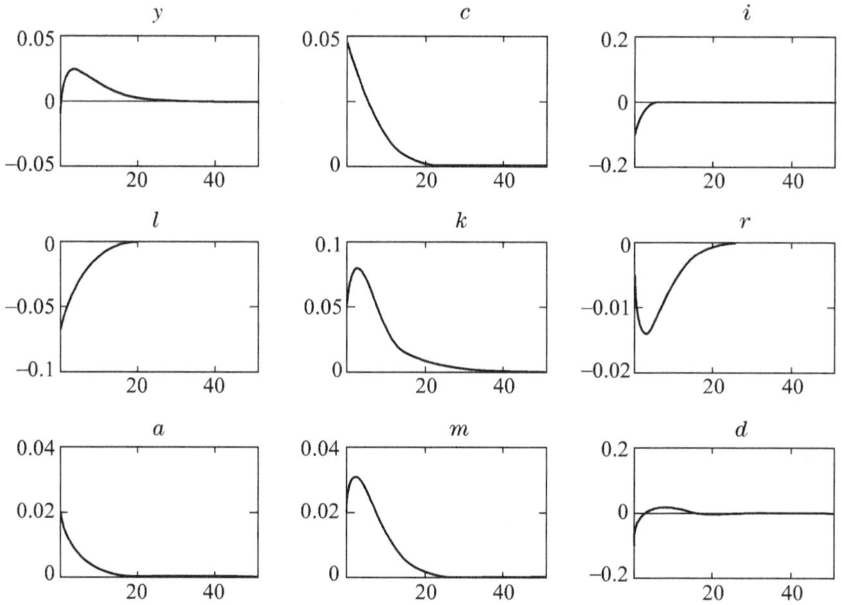

Figure 6.9 Impulse Responses to Technology Shocks.[a]

[a] Here the variable *d* represents inflation rate. It is a temporary modification for the sake of the fluent operation of the software MATLAB.

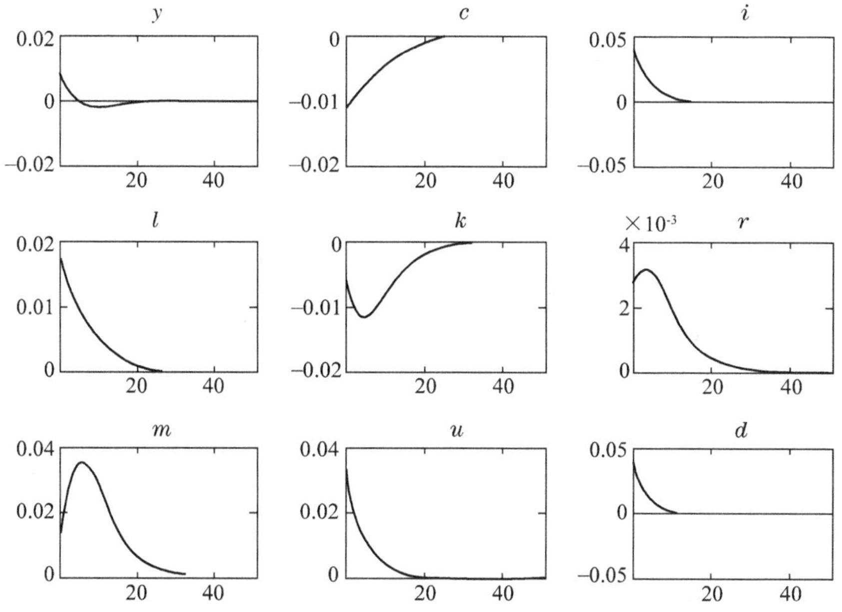

Figure 6.10 Impulse Responses to Monetary Shocks.

that in the same period of time, the magnitude and frequency of monetary fluctuations are much larger than those of technological fluctuations, it is necessary to consider the effects of the money supply in researching on the economic growth and fluctuations of China.

6.5 Conclusion

In this chapter, the MIU model involving habit formation is built under the DSGE framework, and the monetary factor is included in the investigation of economic growth and fluctuations. While using econometric methods to determine the impact factors of monetary policy, the consumption habit factor is determined through several simulation tests. Computer technology is adopted to simulate the model economic data, by comparing the model economic data with the real economic data, so as to analyze the fitting effects of the model economy.

The empirical findings show that the MIU model with habit formation in consumption well simulates the real economy and can explain 98% of real fluctuations in output. Compared with the basic RBC model without habit formation, this model performs well in explaining fluctuations in consumption, from the original 24% to 76%. This suggests that household consumption in China presents obvious characteristics of habit formation. The current level of consumption is affected by the previous consumption level, and the consumption levels of successive periods are closely correlated. Moreover, from the variance decomposition results of variables, monetary shocks also help explain the fluctuations of the nominal interest rate, the inflation rate and so on.

In addition, in terms of correlation coefficients of model economic variables with the corresponding real output, there is a high consistency between model economic variables and real ones. Except labor, the correlation coefficient of consumption, capital, interest rate, monetary balance, and inflation rate with real output, respectively, are all procyclical, which also illustrates the role of monetary factors in economic fluctuations and growth and the applicability of the model.

Finally, the impulse response analysis of the exogenous random variables shows that the initial impact of monetary shocks is less than that of technology shocks. In addition, the duration of monetary shocks is relatively short. However, considering that the frequency and intensity of monetary policy changes in the real economy are greater than that of technological factors, the implementation of a stable monetary policy should become a basic principle for the monetary authority to follow. Scientific and reasonable monetary policy can create a good financial market environment for economic development, provide sustained and strong policy support for economic development, and reduce adverse fluctuations in the process of economic growth. On the contrary, unreasonable monetary policy is not conducive to stable economic growth, and it even increases the range of economic fluctuations. The impulse response analysis in this chapter also indicates that the policy must take into account the sustained influence of such policies and minimize the adverse monetary shocks on the economy.

Notes

1 The value function V_t is a function of the variables including C_t, m_t, L_t, K_t and b_t.
2 In fact, the average level of consumption habit formation degree in China is relatively low. To make the equilibrium solution of variables meaningful and the subjective discount rate not too low, and it is appropriate to set β as 0.1 after many simulation tests.
3 The number of employed persons by industry is determined by using three different statistical methods.
4 Yue Ximing, "Problems of Current Employment Statistics in China," *Economic Research Journal* no. 3 (2005): 46–56.

Bibliography

Ai, Hongde, and Fan Nan 艾洪德, 范南. "An Empirical Analysis of the Velocity of Money in China" 中国货币流通速度影响因素的经验分析. *The Journal of World Economy* no. 8 (2002): 53–59+80.

Chari, Varadarajan, Patrick Kehoe, and Ellen McGrattan. "Can Sticky Price Models Generate Volatile and Persistent Real Exchange Rate?" *Review of Economics Studies* no.69 (2002): 533–563.

Chari, Varadarajan, Patrick Kehoe, and Ellen McGrattan. "Sticky Price Models of the Business Cycle: Can the Contract Multiplier Solve the Persistence Problem?" *Econometrica* no. 5 (2000): 1151–1179.

Christiano, Lawrence J., and Martin Eichenbaum. "Nominal Regidities and the Dynamic Effects of a Shock to Monetary Policy." *Journal of Political Economy* no.1 (2005): 1–45.

Clower, Robert W. "A Reconsideration of the Microfoundations of Monetary Theory." *Western Economic Journal* no. 1 (1967): 1–9.

Cooley, Thomas F., and Gary D. Hansen. "Money and the Business Cycle." In *Frontiers of Business Cycle Research*, edited by T. F. Cooley. Princeton University Press, 1995: 175–216.

Guo, Qingwang, and Jia Junxue 郭庆旺, 贾俊雪. "Estimating Potential Output and the Output Gap in China" 中国潜在产出与产出缺口的估算. *Economic Research Journal* no. 5 (2004): 31–39.

Hang, Bin 杭斌. "Why Is Chinese Urban Residents' APC Keep Decreasing?" 城镇居民的平均消费倾向为何持续下降——基于消费习惯形成的实证分析. *The Journal of Quantitative & Technical Economics* no. 6 (2010): 126–138.

Huang, Yongfeng, Ren Ruoen, and Liu Xiaoshegn 黄勇峰, 任若恩, 刘晓生. "Capital Stock Estimates in Chinese Manufacturing by Perpetual Inventory Method" 中国制造业资本存量永续盘存法估计. *China Economic Quarterly* no. 2 (2002): 377–396.

Huang, Zelin 黄赜琳. "A Study on Business Cycle and the Effects of Fiscal Policy in China: An Empirical Study on a RBC Model with Three Sections" 中国经济周期特征与财政政策效应——一个基于三部门RBC模型的实证分析. *Economic Research Journal* no. 6 (2005): 27–39.

Kiyotaki, Nobuhiro, and Randall Wright. "On Money as a Medium of Exchange." *Journal of Political Economy* no. 4 (1989): 927–954.

Lei, Qinli 雷钦礼. "Incremental Utility Function: Restructuring Household Consumption Theory" 增量效用函数：家庭消费理论的重新构建. *Statistical Research* no. 12 (2003): 7–12.

National Bureau of Statistics 国家统计局. *China Statistical Yearbook 2011*《中国统计年鉴2011》. Beijing: China Statistics Press, 2011.

Pei, Ping, and Xiong Peng 裴平, 熊鹏. "The 'Leaking' Effect in Transmission of the Monetary Policy in China" 中国货币政策传导过程中的"渗漏"效应. *Economic Research Journal* no. 8 (2003): 21–27+91.

Ran, Guanghe, Cao Yuequn, and Zhong Dehua 冉光和, 曹跃群, 钟德华. "Factor Input, Money Supply and Chinese Economic Fluctuations" 要素投入、货币供应与中国经济波动. *Management World* no. 2 (2008): 170–171.

Samuelson, Paul A. "An Exact Comsumption-Loan Model of Interest with the Social Contrivance of Money." *Journal of Political Economy* no. 6 (1958): 467–482.

Shan, Haojie 单豪杰. "Resestimating the Capital Stock of China: 1952–2006" 中国资本存量K的再估算: 1952–2006年. *The Journal of Quantitative & Technical Economics* no. 10 (2008): 17–31.

Sidrasuki, Miguel. "Rational Choice and Patterns of Growth in a Monetary Economy." *American Economic Review* no. 2 (1967): 534–544.

Wang, Xianyong, and Han Xu 王宪勇, 韩煦. "Technology Shocks, Monetary Shocks and Chinese Economic Fluctuations" 技市冲击、货币冲击与中国经济波动——一个基于RBC模型的数值模拟. *Journal of Dongbei University of Finance and Economics* no. 2 (2009): 3–7.

Xie, Ping 谢平. "An Analysis of the Monetary Policy in China: 1998–2002" 中国货币政策分析: 1998–2002. *Journal of Financial Research* no. 8 (2004): 1–20.

Yang, Liu, and Li Li 杨柳, 李力. "Monetary Shocks and Chinese Economic Fluctuations: A Quantitative Analysis Based on a DSGE Model" 货币冲击与中国经济波动——基于 DSGE模型的数量分析. *Modern Economic Science* no. 5 (2011): 1–9+124.

Yue, Ximing 岳希明. "Problems of Current Employment Statistics in China" 我国现行劳动统计的问题. *Economic Research Journal* no. 3 (2005): 46–56.

Zhang, Chengsi 张成思. "Random Shocks, Monetary Policy and Business Cycle Volatility" 随机冲击、货币政策与经济周期波动. *Journal of Renmin University of China* no. 6 (2010): 31–39.

Zhang, Jun, and Zhang Yuan 张军, 章元. "Recalculating the Capital of China" 对中国资本存量K的再估计. *Economic Research Journal* no. 7 (2003): 35–43+90.

Zhang, Jun, Wu Guiying, and Zhang Jipeng 张军, 吴桂英, 张吉鹏. "The Estimation of China's Provincial Capital Stock: 1952–2000" 中国省际物质资本存量估算: 1952–2000. *Economic Research Journal* no. 10 (2004): 35–44.

Zhao, Xindong, Chen Fei, and Gao Tiemei 赵昕东, 陈飞, 高铁梅. "An Empirical Analysis of the Effect of Monetary-Policy Institutional Variables in China" 中国货币政策工具变量效应的实证分析. *The Journal of Quantitative & Technical Economics* no. 7 (2002): 103–106.

Zuo, Xiaoshun 左孝顺. "The Changes in the Velocity of Money: An Example from China" 货币流通速度的变化: 中国的例证, 1978–1997. *Journal of Financial Research* no. 6 (1999): 39–45.

7 Money supply and Chinese economic fluctuations

The data properties of the Chinese monetary economy indicate that there are similarities between the fluctuations of money supply and macroeconomic variables. The econometric test shows that there is Granger causality between these variables. Therefore, this chapter adopts the vector autoregression (VAR) model to construct the money supply equation on output and introduces this equation into the cash-in-advance (CIA) model as money supply shocks. It thus incorporates monetary factors into the real business cycle (RBC) model. We solve the differential equation system by the log-linearization method. After that, we get the numerical form of the differential equation system by calibrating the parameters and computing the steady-state values of variables. We get the data of the model economy by simulating the dynamic stochastic equations. Comparing the model economy to the real economy, it is found that the model economy can explain the fluctuations in the real economy very well. It explains 80.5% of fluctuations in output. Moreover, through impulse response and variance decomposition analysis, it can be seen that, though the monetary policy in China has some impact on real variables, it has greater impact on nominal variables. Money tends to be neutral.

7.1 Monetary policy and economic fluctuations

Based on the data of Chinese monetary economy, it is clear that rapid economic development accompanied by large fluctuations is one of the notable features of the Chinese economy since the reform and opening-up. Accompanying the rapid growth and large fluctuations is the rapid growth and violent fluctuations of the money supply. The fluctuation trends of the Chinese economy and money supply are very similar, as shown in Figure 7.1. Specifically, before 1992, the frequency and range of the two fluctuations were high; after 1992, the fluctuation range was much flatter and the fluctuations irregular. This fact demonstrates that the relationship between Chinese money supply and economic growth and fluctuations is worth studying.

Since the 1960s, it has been realized that money has had its own value. After a long period of experiment and research, economists have introduced monetary factors into the DSGE model, including mainly three models: First

DOI: 10.4324/9781003305651-7

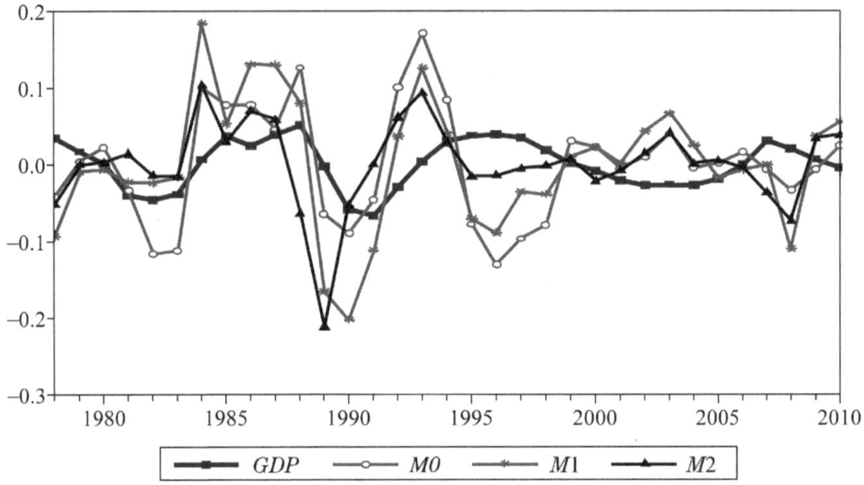

Figure 7.1 Output and Money Supply Fluctuations from 1978 to 2010.

is the money-in-the-utility (MIU) model. Sidrauski (1967) proposed that holding money can increase the utility level of an economic person, so the money balance can be directly put into the utility function of the agent in the model. Sidrauski originally held that the amount of consumer goods and the amount of holding money determine the utility level of the economic agent. Later, economists extended it to include the leisure time owned by the economic agent. The marginal utility brought about by increasing the holding money includes two parts: One is the convenience of transactions; the other is that the real amount of money in the current period can increase available resources in the future. Since there is a certain substitution relationship between consumption and money, when the economic agent holds too much money, it will lead to a decline in the level of consumption. To achieve the goal of maximizing utility, the economic agent must choose between the amount of consumption and the real amount of holding money. Second is the cash-in-advance (CIA) model. Clower (1967) assumed that there was a certain form of transaction cost, and certain transactions must use money. Or, according to Kiyotaki and Wright (1989), the acquisition of consumer goods required time and money, or in the case that goods obtained through barter had a time cost, so money was needed as a medium of exchange. Third is the overlapping-generation (OLG) model. Based on Samuelson (1958), in the model, money is a special carrier that could transfer resources between different periods.

The real business cycle (RBC) theory first used the DSGE method to analyze economic fluctuations. Kydland and Prescott (1982) and Long and Plosser (1983) have pioneered RBC theories. Lucas and Stokey (1987) added the CIA constraint to the RBC model—"the cash-in-advance constraint."

That is, transactions could only be carried out if you held cash or promised to pay cash in the next period and assuming that the role of the government was to supply money and that the growth of money supply is affected by random shocks. They finally proved the existence of general equilibrium under these conditions. Cooley and Hansen (1989) studied the RBC model with invisible labor and the CIA constraint.

Chinese scholars have done certain research on the relationship between monetary policy and economic fluctuations. Chen and Gong (2006) introduced sticky prices through the monopolistic intermediate goods manufacture under the framework of the basic RBC model. They constructed a money supply mechanism based on the Taylor rule to build a dynamic/periodic model for researching money. They found that the simulated economy that implemented monetary policy in accordance with the Taylor rule could better simulate the real economy than a simple RBC model. Lu and Shu (2002) used Granger causality and a two-step OLS method to analyze the relationship between money and output in China from 1978 to 2000. They found that in the short term, money had an impact on real output but that, in the long run, money is neutral. Liu and Zhang (2003) studied the Granger causality between the growth rate of money supply and that of output from January 1990 to February 2001. They found that the real relationship between money and output relied on the economic cycle. Only when the real demand in the economy was strong and the real supply capacity increased would money have a substantial impact on output.

Most Chinese research still supports the view that, in the short run, money is non-neutral and in the long run neutral. Based on the existing research at home and abroad, this chapter attempts to build the RBC model with divisible labor that introduces money supply shocks based on the CIA method. The numerical solution of the model is obtained through log-linearization, and then calibration is used to determine the model parameters. By comparing the simulated economy and the real economy, this chapter illustrates the extent to which the model explains economic reality. In addition, this chapter also compares the impact of technology shocks and monetary shocks on economic fluctuations through impulse response analysis.

Typically, modern macroeconomic research first examines the stylized facts of macroeconomics, secondly builds a theoretical model that can illustrate these facts as much as possible, and then calibrates the parameters to nudge the model closer to the real economy. It aims to propose policy recommendations accordingly.

7.2 Stylized facts of Chinese monetary economy

7.2.1 Stylized facts of Chinese macroeconomic fluctuations

From the H-P filter shown in Figure 7.1, it can be seen that since the reform and opening-up, output and money supply have experienced several large fluctuations that exhibit high consistency. This chapter also calculates the standard deviation of various economic indexes $\sigma_{\hat{X}_t}$ and the correlation coefficient of the time difference between the volatility of macroeconomic indexes $\hat{X}_t$ and the volatility of real output$\hat{Y}_t$, as shown in Table 7.1. This will help us accurately observe the stylized facts of economic fluctuations and have a deep sense of the internal relationship between the fluctuations of various macroeconomic indexes.

Through analyzing Figure 7.1 and Table 7.1, it can be seen that Chinese macroeconomic fluctuations have the following characteristics.

First, the economic fluctuations remain relatively large, whether it is judged from the intuitive analysis of the H-P filter of macroeconomic indexes or from the calculation results of the standard deviation. The standard deviation of output that deviates from the long-term trend reaches 3.14%. In comparison, from the end of World War II to the 1990s in the United States, the standard deviation of real GDP that deviates from the long-term trend was only 1.66%, far below Chinese economic volatility.[1]

The standard deviation of consumption, government expenditure, and investment remains higher than that of the output volatility. Investment is the highest, which is 2.774 times the standard deviation of output. Consumption is basically the same as output, only 1.123 times the standard deviation of output. It can also be seen from Table 7.1 that the standard deviation of capital stock is 0.824 times the standard deviation of output, which is in line with the economic intuition.

Second, the business cycles remain variable. Taking 1992 as the boundary year, the standard deviations from 1978 to 1992 and from 1993 to the present are respectively calculated. It is found that the latter's fluctuations are smaller, which can also be seen from Figure 7.1. The economic cycle is four to five years on average before 1992, but it becomes about ten years after 1992. This may be related to the better use of macroeconomic policies after 1992, and it may also reflect that the Chinese economic transition has gradually entered a normal track.

Third, economic volatility is irregular. First of all, from the perspective of volatility, before 1992, the absolute value of Chinese economic volatility deviated from the long-term trend, reaching up to 6.727%, but after 1992, the value is only 3.77%, a very large decline. From the perspective of the fluctuation cycle, before 1992, the Chinese economic cycle averages four to- five years, and after that it is nearly ten years, and the gap is also very large. This also explains the irregularity of economic volatility.

From Table 7.1, it can be seen that output itself has a positive dependence within two periods, especially the impact on the previous and subsequent periods, exceeding 0.7; in the corresponding period, consumption and output are the highest related. The sign of the correlation coefficient of each time difference between consumption and output is consistent with the sign of the correlation coefficient of the time difference of output itself. It can be seen that consumption is a highly procyclical index. The correlation between

Table 7.1 Standard Deviation of Macroeconomic Indexes Fluctuations and Correlation Coefficient of Time Difference Between the Fluctuations of Macroeconomic Indexes and Output Fluctuations

$\hat{X}_t$	$\sigma_{\hat{X}_t}$	$\frac{\sigma_{\hat{X}_t}}{\sigma_{\hat{Y}_t}}$	*Correlation Relationship of Time Difference Between Volatility of Macroeconomic Indexes $\hat{X}_t$ and Output Volatility $\hat{Y}_t$*										
			−5	*−4*	*−3*	*−2*	*−1*	*0*	*+1*	*+2*	*+3*	*+4*	*+5*
$\hat{Y}_t$	0.031	1.000	−0.735	−0.618	−0.287	0.211	0.733	**1.000**	0.709	0.152	−0.275	−0.590	−0.722
$\hat{C}_t$	0.035	1.123	−0.693	−0.557	−0.156	0.325	0.760	**0.835**	0.417	−0.042	−0.250	−0.457	−0.564
$\hat{G}_t$	0.056	1.795	−0.270	−0.093	0.358	**0.646**	**0.638**	0.238	−0.340	−0.616	−0.552	−0.179	0.242
$\hat{I}_t$	0.087	2.774	−0.656	−0.363	0.069	0.604	**0.908**	0.766	0.252	−0.258	−0.536	−0.631	−0.499
$\hat{K}_t$	0.026	0.824	−0.393	−0.723	−0.804	−0.598	−0.118	0.445	**0.832**	0.847	0.523	0.075	−0.361

government expenditure lagging by two periods and one period and output is relatively high, exceeding 0.6. This indicates that government expenditure tends to change often ahead of output, appearing to be countercyclical. This confirms that government expenditure is a macroeconomic regulation and control tool. The correlation between output lagging investment by one period remains greatest, indicating that investment requires a period to bring output. The correlation between capital stock volatility and output volatility indicates that capital takes longer to be effective than investment and that the period for large-scale equipment to function is longer.

7.2.2 *Stylized facts of the money supply in China*[2]

Money supply is usually measured by three types of indexes: M_0, narrow money M_1 and broad money M_2.[3] Money supply (M_0, M_1, M_2) is adjusted with the consumer price index (CPI) to eliminate the price impact, and then the logarithm of them is obtained. H-P filtering is performed to obtain the volatility and the corresponding standard deviation of the volatility of each money supply index from the long-term trend, as shown in Figure 7.1.

After H-P filter analysis, the money supply in China can be divided into three stages in terms of volatility. The first stage ranges from 1978 to 1983 with relatively small volatility; the second stage ranges from 1984 to 1995 with pretty large volatility in high frequency; the third stage ranges from 1995 to the present with larger volatility than that of the first stage but weaker than the second stage.

The specific volatility of money supply is shown in Table 7.2. It indicates that the money supply volatility presents the following characteristics: First, the volatility is large. The maximum volatility of M_0, M_1 and M_2, respectively, reaches 17.088%, −20.370% and −21.268%; even in the stage from 1984 to 1995, the real standard deviation of volatility of M_1 reaches 13.046%. Compared with the 3.1% standard deviation of the volatility of output, it is relatively large. Second, the volatility is irregular. The difference of money supply volatility in different stages is demonstrated, through either the intuitive analysis

Table 7.2 Maximum Fluctuation Range and Standard Deviation of Money Supply Fluctuations

Stage / *Index*	*Year 1978–1983*		*Year 1984–1995*		*1995–Now*	
	Maximum Fluctuation Range	*Standard Deviation of Volatility*	*Maximum Fluctuation Range*	*Standard Deviation of Volatility*	*Maximum Fluctuation Range*	*Standard Deviation of Volatility*
M_0	−11.685%	5.804%	17.088%	8.410%	−13.118%	5.073%
M_1	−9.452%	3.253%	−20.370%	13.046%	−11.136%	5.135%
M_2	−5.219%	2.299%	−21.268%	9.186%	−7.342%	2.868%

of the H-P filter or the quantitative analysis of the standard deviation. This shows that the volatility of money supply remains irregular.

7.2.3 The relationship between money supply and macroeconomic fluctuations

The standard deviation and the correlation coefficient of time difference between the money supply index and output are calibrated, as shown in Table 7.3.

The data in Table 7.3 shows that the standard deviation of the money supply indexes is much higher than the output volatility. The standard deviation of M_1 is the largest, 2.693 times the standard deviation of output. The volatility of M_1, as shown in Figure 7.1, is also significantly greater than that of output.

Through the correlation coefficient of –time difference between the volatility of money supply and the output volatility, it can be seen that the output volatility in the lagging periods is negatively correlated with the money supply volatility, while the money supply volatility in the lagging periods shows a positive correlation with output volatility. This reflects that the monetary policy represented by the money supply has a countercyclical effect on economic fluctuations. The difference of the relationship between three money supply indexes and the output remains. The volatility of M_0 andM_1 lagging one period has the largest positive correlation with output volatility, which are 0.357 and 0.589, respectively. But the volatility of M_2 lagging two periods has the largest positive correlation with output volatility, which is 0.654.

The Granger causality between the volatility of money supply and output volatility will be examined. To avoid a spurious correlation, we first perform a stationary test on the time series of the volatility of money supply and the time series of output volatility. The test results show that the series of money supply volatility $\hat{X}_t$ and output volatility $\hat{Y}_t$ are both stationary time series with a confidence coefficient of 1%. Therefore, the Granger causality test of money supply and output can be directly done. The test results show that under the 10% confidence level, Y_t is the Granger cause of M_0, but M_0 is not the Granger cause of Y_t, and M_1, M_2 and Y_t are the Granger causality of one another.[4] This shows that there is a Granger causality between money supply and output.

By referring to the analysis of the stylized facts of real economic indexes and monetary indexes, it is clear that money in China is not completely neutral and that there is a causal connection between it and actual economic indexes. Based on this, monetary factors are introduced into the theoretical model to be built so that the model can better explain the real economy and analyze the monetary policy in reality.

7.3 The CIA model with money supply shocks

Before building this theoretical model, it is necessary to set several assumptions contained in the model: First, the utility function of the economic agent

Table 7.3 Standard Deviation of Money Supply Fluctuations and Correlation Coefficient of Time Difference Between the Fluctuations of Macroeconomic Indexes and Output Fluctuations

$\hat{X}_t$	$\sigma_{\hat{X}_t}$	$\frac{\sigma_{\hat{X}_t}}{\sigma_{\hat{Y}_t}}$	*Correlation Relationship of Time Difference Between Volatility of Money Supply Index $\hat{X}_t$ and Output Volatility $\hat{Y}_t$*										
			−5	*−4*	*−3*	*−2*	*−1*	*0*	*+1*	*+2*	*+3*	*+4*	*+5*
$\hat{M}_{0t}$	0.074	2.360	−0.204	−0.068	0.024	0.175	**0.357**	0.209	−0.352	−0.612	−0.418	0.029	0.396
$\hat{M}_{1t}$	0.085	**2.693**	−0.343	−0.199	0.028	0.363	**0.598**	0.358	−0.196	−0.461	−0.414	−0.161	0.160
$\hat{M}_{2t}$	0.056	1.792	−0.238	0.071	0.397	**0.654**	0.617	0.076	−0.482	−0.524	−0.399	−0.165	0.231

is of constant relative risk aversion (CRRA) type; second, the production function is a Cobb–Douglas form with constant returns to scale; third, technology is regarded as an exogenous random shock and obeys the first-order autoregressive AR(1) process; fourth, the growth rate of nominal money stock is regarded as an exogenous random shock and also obeys the first-order autoregressive AR(1) process; fifth, money has the special property of facilitating transactions, and, based on Cooley and Hansen (1989), consumer goods are cash goods and must use money, investment and leisure as credit goods; sixth, according to Svensson (1985), the commodity market in the model is set to open first, which means that the economic agent can only use cash held before the market opens to purchase consumer goods; seventh, the growth rate of money is equal to the inflation rate when the model is in a steady state, that is, the model is money neutral at this time; eighth, the model is assumed to be two-sector closed economy, and there is a general equilibrium with market clearing.

Assuming that the economic agents in the economy are homogeneous, are subject to the same consumption constraint and have the same utility function, so a single economic agent can represent the entire economy. Here, the typical representative agent is used to represent the economy as a whole, and its utility function is:

$$E_{\mathrm{t}}\sum_{t=0}^{\infty}\beta^{t}U\left(c_t,1-n_t\right) \tag{7.1}$$

$$U\left(c_t,1-n_t\right)=\frac{c_t^{1-\Phi}-1}{1-\Phi}+\psi\ln\left(1-n_t\right)$$

where β^t represents the subjective discount rate in the period t, $\beta\in(0,1)$. c_t represents the consumption of the representative agent in the period t; n_t represents the labor time of the representative agent in the period t; Φ is the relative risk aversion coefficient, $\Phi>0$. In particular, when $\Phi=1$, the first term $\frac{C_t^{1-\Phi}-1}{1-\Phi}$ of the CRRA utility function becomes a logarithm $\ln C_t$; ψ is the relative weight of consumption and leisure, $\psi\in(0,1)$, which reflects the preference for consumption or leisure in the utility function of the representative agent.

In this model, the representative agent supplies labor and leases capital to the firm. At the beginning of each period, the representative agent holds a nominal money balance M_{t-1} and receives a lump sum transfer T_{t} from the government (the government function in this model is limited to this). Assuming that the nominal money supply growth rate in period t is θ_{t} and that all the representative agents have known θ_t from the beginning of period t, and we can get $M_t=(1+\theta_t)M_{t-1}$. From the perspective of the aggregate money in the whole society, we can obtain $M_t{=}M_{t-1}+T_t$. So the per capita transfer payment is $\theta_t M_{t-1}$. Since the model assumes that consumer goods are only cash goods, the cash reserve constraint (CIA constraint) of the model is:

$$P_t c_t \leq M_{t-1} + T_t$$

Where P_t represents the price level in the period t. Two sides of the equation are divided by the price, and the CIA constraint is:

$$c_t \leq \frac{m_{t-1}}{\Pi_t} + \tau_t \tag{7.2}$$

where $\Pi_t = \frac{P_t}{P_{t-1}} = 1 + \pi_t$, Π_t is equal to 1 plus the inflation rate. It indicates that the cash held by the representative agent at the beginning of each period must at least meet the needs of purchasing consumer goods in the current period. When the economy enters an equilibrium state, the equation form of equation 7.2 holds.

Additionally, the representative agent is subject to budget constraint:

$$P_t \upsilon_t = P_t f(k_{t-1}) + (1-\delta)P_t k_{t-1} + I_{t-1}B_{t-1} + M_{t-1} + T_t \geq P_t c_t + P_t k_t + B_t + M_t$$

where υ_t represents the real resources owned by the representative agent in period t. It consists of the nominal income $P_t f(k_{t-1})$ formed by the production in period t, the nominal capital stock $(1-\delta)P_t k_{t-1}$ that has not yet been depreciated ($0 \leq \delta \leq 1$ is the depreciation rate), the principal and interest income $I_{t-1}B_{t-1}$ ($I_{t-1} = 1 + i_{t-1}$; i_{t-1} represents the nominal rate of margin period $t-1$ to period t) of the representative agent's nominal bond B_{t-1} in period $t-1$, holding money M_{t-1} and government transfer payments T_t. The representative agent uses these resources to purchase consumption and capital, bonds and nominal money holdings reserved for the $t+1$ period. Dividing both sides of equation 7.2 by the price P_t in period t, the budget constraint is:

$$y_t + (1-\delta)k_{t-1} + \left(\frac{1+i_{t-1}}{1+\pi_t}\right)b_{t-1} + \frac{m_{t-1}}{\Pi_t} + \tau_t \geq c_t + k_t + b_t + m_t \tag{7.3}$$

Chow and Li (2002) used Chinese macroeconomic data from 1952 to 2008 to estimate the aggregate production function and found that the Cobb–Douglas production function with constant returns to scale is in line with the reality. Therefore, this chapter considers a Cobb–Douglas production function. The per capita production function is:

$$y_t = e^{z_t} k_{t-1}^{\alpha} n_t^{1-\alpha} \tag{7.4}$$

Where α represents the output elasticity of capital, $0 \le \alpha \le 1$. The exogenous productivity shock z_t follows:

$$z_t = \rho z_{t-1} + e_t, e_t \sim i.i.d.N\left(0, \sigma_e^2\right) \tag{7.5}$$

where $0 \le \rho \le 1$. The mean of random variable e_t is zero, and its variance is σ_e^2.

When $u_t = \theta_t - \theta^{ss}$, u_t represents the difference between the nominal money supply growth rate and the steady-state growth rate in period t. According to the McCallum rule, there is a close connection between money supply and output. Liu (2003) and Xu and Ye (2009) proved that the monetary policy in China often aimed at stabilizing economic growth and focused on stimulating output. Therefore, this chapter will adapt the assumptions of Cooley and Hansen (1989) and add output factors to the shock equation in order to better simulate the Chinese economy. The modified money supply shock equation has the following form:

$$u_t = \sum_{\tau=1}^{k} \gamma_\tau u_{t-\tau} + \sum_{\tau=1}^{k} \xi_\tau \hat{y}_{t-\tau} + \omega_t, \quad \omega_t \sim i.i.d.N\left(0, \sigma_\omega^2\right)$$

Where k represents the number of possible lag periods. $\hat{y}_{t-\tau}$ represents the deviation of the output growth rate from the steady-state growth rate in each lag period. ω_t represents a white noise correction term, the mean value is 0, and the variance is σ_ω^2.

Through the analysis of the time difference between money and output, it is found that output and money have the strongest correlation within two periods, so u_t follows the random process:

$$u_t = \sum_{\tau=1}^{2} \gamma_\tau u_{t-\tau} + \sum_{\tau=1}^{2} \xi_\tau \hat{y}_{t-\tau} + \omega_t, \omega_t \sim i.i.d.N\left(0, \sigma_\omega^2\right) \tag{7.6}$$

According to $M_t = (1+\theta_t)M_{t-1}$, the equation of the real money balance is:

$$m_t = \frac{1+\theta_t}{1+\pi_t} m_{t-1} \tag{7.7}$$

Therefore, the programming problem faced by the representative agent is under the constraint, shown in equations 7.2 and 7.3, to choose the trajectory of c_t, k_t, b_t, m_t, n_t to achieve the maximization of equation 7.1.

This chapter uses the Lagrange multiplier method to solve the corresponding first-order condition and transversality condition of the model and then establishes a stochastic linear equation. In this programming problem, the parameters of the two shocks can be obtained through calibration. When λ_t represents the Lagrangian multiplier with regard to budget constraint, its economic meaning is the marginal utility of wealth; when μ_t represents the Lagrangian multiplier with regard to CIA constraint, its economic meaning is the marginal utility of real holding money. By maximizing the utility of the representative agent through the Lagrangian function, the first-order conditions about c_t, k_t, b_t, m_t, n_t can be obtained:

$$c_t^{-\Phi} - \lambda_t - \mu_t = 0 \tag{7.8}$$

$$-\lambda_t +_t \beta E_t \lambda_{t+1}(\frac{\partial y_{t+1}}{\partial k_t} + (1-\delta)) = 0 \tag{7.9}$$

$$-\lambda_t + \beta E_t(\frac{1+i_t}{1+\pi_{t+1}})\lambda_{t+1} = 0 \tag{7.10}$$

$$-\lambda_t + \beta E_t(\frac{\lambda_{t+1} + \mu_{t+1}}{\Pi_{t+1}}) = 0 \tag{7.11}$$

$$-\psi(1-n_t)^{-1} + \lambda_t \frac{\partial y_t}{\partial n_t} = 0 \tag{7.12}$$

If the real return on capital in period t is set as R_t, and$y_t = e^{z_t} k_{t-1}^{\alpha} n_t^{1-\alpha}$, the following can be obtained:

$$R_t = E_t \frac{\partial y_{t+1}}{\partial k_t} + 1 - \delta = \alpha \frac{E_t y_{t+1}}{k_t} + 1 - \delta \tag{7.13}$$

It can be seen from equation 7.13 that the real return on capital R_t in period t is composed of the current capital output rate and capital depreciation surplus.

In this way, the linear programming problem's constraint conditions shown by equations 7.2–7.7 and first-order conditions shown by equations 7.8–7.13 together constitute a nonlinear differential equation set.

The existence of the solutions to the equation set requires the following boundary conditions: First, the initial capital investment k_0 is given. Second, the transversality conditions of the economy $\lim_{i\to\infty} \beta^i E_t c_{t+i}^{-\Phi} k_{t+i+1} = 0$, $\lim_{i\to\infty} \beta^i E_t c_{t+i}^{-\Phi} m_{t+i} = 0$, and $\lim_{i\to\infty} \beta^i E_t c_{t+i}^{-\Phi} b_{t+i} = 0$ indicate that the representative agent's infinite utility level cannot be further improved and that at the same time it has a certain amount of capital accumulation (either money or bonds). Third, the representative agent's amount of labor supply in the steady state remains a constant.

The economic system equilibrium defines the following: Given the preferences, technology and resource constraints in the economy, under the given state variables and exogenous shock variables, the representative agent maximizes the expected utility, and the manufacturer maximizes the expected profit and market clearing. This is a dynamic stochastic programming problem, and its equilibrium solution can be expressed as a strategy set of k_t, c_t, m_t, y_t, n_t, r_t, π_t and i_t.

Satisfying the first-order conditions and boundary conditions at the same time is a sufficient and necessary condition for the optimal solution of the programming problem. However, in general, there are no analytical solutions to nonlinear differential equations, so numerical solutions are often used as reasonable alternatives. In solving the numerical solutions, the first-order Taylor formula expansion method and the numerical equivalent substitution are adopted, and the constraint conditions and the first-order conditions are processed logarithmically in the vicinity of the steady state. After logarithmic linearization, the economic system described by the economic programming problem can be approximated represented by the ten stochastic linear equations shown in equation 7.14. These ten equations have ten variables, among which the endogenous state variables are k_t and m_t, the exogenous state variables are z_t and u_t, and the endogenous jump variables are y_t, r_t, π_t, i_t, c_t and n_t.

$$\begin{cases} \bar{y}\cdot\hat{y}_t = \bar{c}\cdot\hat{m}_t + \bar{k}\cdot\hat{k}_t - (1-\delta)\bar{k}\cdot\hat{k}_{t-1} \\ \hat{y}_t = z_t + \alpha\hat{k}_{t-1} + (1-\alpha)\hat{n}_t \\ \hat{r}_t = \alpha\frac{\bar{y}}{\bar{k}}\left(\dfrac{\rho z_t + (1-\alpha)(1-\bar{n})\hat{\lambda}_t + \bar{n}(\alpha-1)\hat{k}_t}{\alpha + (1-\alpha)\bar{n} + (1-\alpha)(1-\bar{n})\alpha\frac{\bar{y}}{\bar{k}}}\right) \\ \hat{i}_t = \hat{r}_t + E_t\hat{\pi}_{t+1} \\ \hat{\lambda}_t = \hat{r}_t + E_t\hat{\lambda}_{t+1} \\ \left(\dfrac{1}{1-\bar{n}}\right)\hat{n}_t = \hat{\lambda}_t + \hat{y}_t \\ \hat{\lambda}_t = (\Phi-1)E_t\hat{\pi}_{t+1} - \Phi\hat{m}_t - \Phi\left(\sum_{\tau=0}^{1}\gamma_{1+\tau}u_{t-\tau} + \sum_{\tau=0}^{1}\xi_{1+\tau}\hat{y}_{t-\tau}\right) \\ \hat{m}_t = u_t + \hat{m}_{t-1} - \hat{\pi}_t \\ z_t = \rho z_{t-1} + e_t, e_t \sim i.i.d.N\left(0,\sigma_e^2\right) \\ u_t = \sum_{\tau=1}^{2}\gamma_\tau u_{t-\tau} + \sum_{\tau=1}^{2}\xi_\tau\hat{y}_{t-\tau} + \omega_t, \omega_t \sim i.i.d.N\left(0,\sigma_\omega^2\right) \end{cases} \tag{7.14}$$

7.4 Parameter calibration

7.4.1 First, output elasticity and technology shocks

Suppose the production function is a Cobb–Douglas type with constant returns to scale:

$$Y_t = A_t K_t^\alpha L_t^{1-\alpha} = e^{z_t + \mu\cdot T} K_t^\alpha L_t^{1-\alpha}$$

Where T represents the time trend variable, $T = 1,2,....$ μ is the parameter value of the variable T. To eliminate the linear correlation between the regression variables, the production function is transformed by the intensive form of output and capital and log-linearization. The output and capital stock data use the real output and capital stock calculated at constant prices in 1978; labor time in the existing research is replaced by employed population. The data on the employed population comes from National Bureau of Statistics (2011).[5] The production function estimated in this chapter is:

$$\ln\frac{Y}{L} = 3.566 + 0.422\ln\frac{K}{L} + 0.044T$$
$$(9.062) \quad (7.376) \quad (9.194)$$
$$R^2 = 0.9978,\ S.E. = 0.036,\ F = 7061.01$$

The value in parentheses below the estimated value of these measurement model parameters is the t-test value; the goodness of fit reaches 99.78%, and both the parameters and the model pass the test. The measurement results show that the output elasticity of capital α is 0.422, so the output elasticity of labor is $1 - 0.422 = 0.578$.

According to the preceding equation, the time series of the Solow residual A_t can be further obtained:

$$\ln A_t = \ln\frac{Y}{L} - 0.422 * \ln\frac{K}{L} - 0.044 * T \quad .$$

In this way, a time series data on technology shocks A_t is obtained. Since it was assumed that technology shocks followed the first-order autoregressive progress, the first order autoregressive progress of technology shocks can be obtained by regression analysis of this time series. The first-order autoregressive coefficient of technology shocks ρ is 0.735, the correction term e_t approximately conforms to normal distribution, and the standard deviation σ_e is 2.26%.

7.4.2 *Second, money supply shocks*

Using the VAR model to solve equation 7.6, the final equation is as follows:

$$u_t = 0.91u_{t-1} - 0.195583u_{t-2} + 0.121629\hat{y}_{t-1} - 0.176083\hat{y}_{t-2} + \omega_t$$

After estimating the equation, the residual sequence can be obtained. Since the model setting requires the residual sequence ω_t to follow a normal distribution, this chapter does a Jarque–Beta (JB) test on the residual sequence. The JB statistics show that the residual sequence conforms to the normal distribution with a probability of 82.05%. The standard deviation σ_ω obtained by the residual sequence ω_t is estimated as 0.041039. The estimated value of the correlation coefficient is $\gamma_1 = 0.91$, $\gamma_2 = -0.195583$, $\xi_1 = 0.121629$, $\xi_2 = -0.176083$, and the standard deviation of the correction term is estimated as $\sigma_\omega = 4.1039\%$.

7.4.3 Third, the depreciation rate (δ)

Internationally, it is believed that the quarterly depreciation rate is generally 0.025 and that the annual depreciation rate is 0.1. This chapter assumes that the average useful life of the fixed assets in China is ten years and the depreciation rate is 0.1.

7.4.4 Fourth, the rate of return on capital ($\bar{R}$)

According to the calculation equation of the rate of return on capital $R = \left(\sum_{t=1978}^{2010} \frac{\alpha Y_t}{K_t} \right) /33 + 1 - \delta$, the estimated value of $\bar{R}$ is about 1.1658.

7.4.5 Fifth, the subjective discount rate (β)

According to the equilibrium condition, $\bar{R} = \frac{1}{\beta}$ of the first-order condition shown in equation 7.12, $\beta = 0.8578$.

7.4.6 Sixth, labor supply ($\bar{n}$)

According to the research by Huang (2005) on the equilibrium labor supply, the proportion of the employment population is relatively stable, and the fluctuation of this value is small. The average value of the proportion of the employment population in China from 1978 to 2010 is 0.553. Since the model analyzes the problem of the representative agent, suppose that the total time resources the representative agent has is 1, part of which is used for leisure consumption, and part is used for labor. Therefore, the value of the equilibrium labor supply $\bar{n}$ is 0.553.

7.4.7 Seventh, the steady-state inflation rate ($\bar{\pi}$)

This chapter agrees with the research results of Cooley and Hansen (1995) and uses the geometric average annual growth rate of the nominal capital stock M2 to estimate $\bar{\pi}$. The annual value of the steady-state inflation rate $\bar{\pi}$ is 21.55%.

7.4.8 Eighth, the relative risk aversion coefficient (Φ)

Regarding the relative risk aversion coefficient of consumption, this chapter will set Φ as 1.2875 based on the research on the relative risk aversion coefficient from 1978 to 2002 in China by Chen, Yang and Fang (2005).

Table 7.4 Parameter Values in the CIA Model

β	α	δ	Φ	ρ	σ_e
0.8578	0.422	0.1	1.2875	0.735	0.0226
γ_1	γ_2	ξ_1	ξ_2	σ_ω	
0.91	−0.195583	0.121629	−0.176083	0.041039	

Table 7.5 Steady-State Parameter Values Based on the Parameter Values in the Model

$\overline{R}$	$\overline{y}$	$\overline{c}$	$\overline{k}$	$\overline{m}$	$\overline{i}$	$\overline{n}$	$\overline{\pi}$
1.166	0.7746	0.6517	1.2288	0.6517	0.4173	0.553	0.2155

In summary, the model parameter values are shown in Table 7.4. According to the parameter values in the table, the value of the equilibrium labor supply $\overline{n}$ and the equilibrium equations, the equilibrium value of each variable can be obtained as shown in Table 7.5.

Substituting these parameters and steady-state values into the equation set shown in 7.14, the equation set in the numerical form can be obtained.[6]

7.5 Empirical results analysis

DYNARE 4.2.1 and MATLAB 7.5 are used to program the preceding economic system to obtain the following results: the standard deviation of each economic variable, the corresponding correlation coefficient of each economic variable with output, the impulse response of each economic variable to monetary shocks and technology shocks, and the variance decomposition of each economic variable with monetary and technology shocks.

7.5.1 Periodic characteristics of the simulated economy

This chapter compares the standard deviation of the economic variables of the simulated economy and the corresponding correlation coefficient with output with real economic results, as shown in Table 7.6.

From the perspective of output, the Kydland–Prescott ratio of output reaches 80.5%. It indicates that the output of the simulated economy can explain 80.5% of the fluctuations of the real economy, which explains well compared with other existing studies by Chinese scholars. It is clear that introducing monetary shocks into the model helps explain output volatility.

From the perspective of consumption, the standard deviation of consumption in the simulated economy is only 2.18%, smaller than that of the real economy, which is 3.54%. The main reason is that to use the transaction

Table 7.6 Cyclical Characteristics of Simulated Economy

Parameters	*Real Economy*		*Simulated Economy*		*Kydland–Prescott Ratio*
	Standard Deviation (%)	*Corresponding Correlation Coefficient with Output*	*Standard Deviation (%)*	*Corresponding Correlation Coefficient with Output*	
Output	3.1429	1.000	2.53	1.000	80.5
Consumption	3.5405	0.66	2.18	0.6487	61.6
Capital	2.4725	0.428	1.95	0.6777	78.9
Labor	0.5935	−0.1194	1.09	0.5107	183.7
Real Money	5.6314	0.076	2.18	0.6487	38.7
Inflation Rate	6.3613	0.4253	5.24	−0.3322	82.4
Nominal Interest Rate	2.9912	0.1719	2.68	−0.2094	89.6

function of money to introduce monetary shocks into the model, the model assumes that all consumer goods need to be transacted through cash and that the volatility of consumption in the simulated economy is restricted by the fluctuations of cash. But in reality, with the increase in e-commerce and credit card consumption, consumption fluctuations are less restricted by cash.

From the perspective of capital, its Kydland–Prescott ratio is 78.9%, indicating that the model can better explain the fluctuations of the capital stock of the real economy.

In terms of labor, the fluctuations of labor in the simulated economy are much greater than that in the real economy, and the standard deviation of labor in the simulated economy is 1.837 times that of the real economy. In addition, the correlation coefficient of labor with output in the simulated economy is 0.5107, significantly different from −0.1194 in the real economy. The fundamental reason is that, under the RBC framework, it is assumed that labor time can be flexibly adjusted to perform the intertemporal substitution of labor, so that the fluctuations of labor under shocks is highly correlated with that of output. In the real economy, due to the reform and opening-up policy institutionalized in 1978, there is high unemployment in the rural areas of China, which can be mobilized to meet production needs in time. In addition, the defects of the employment statistics method make the volatility of labor and the correlation with the volatility of output both low.

In terms of real money, the simulated economy does not well explain this variable in the real economy. First, the volatility of real money in the simulated economy is small, and the Kydland–Prescott ratio is only 38.7%. Second, there is also a large gap between the correlation coefficient of real money with output in the simulated economy with that in the real economy. And in the real economy, the current real money has almost nothing to do with output. In response to these problems, this chapter makes the following analysis: First, in terms of the small Kydland–Prescott ratio, since 1978, monetary policy in China has been in the process of continuous development and improvement. Real money fluctuates very sharply at this stage, and it is difficult to simulate its fluctuations with a smooth model estimation. In order to test this judgment, the standard deviation of real money after the initial maturity of the monetary policy is calculated, and it is obtained that the Kydland–Prescott ratio increases significantly to 74%. This shows that our judgment is correct and that the model can better explain the real economy at the initially mature period of monetary policy. Second, in terms of the large difference in the correlation coefficient of real money with output, it is assumed that the time lag of monetary policy was not taken into account in the process of model building. To test this assumption, the time difference between the volatility of real money and output volatility is analyzed. It is found that the correlation coefficients of the time difference lagging two periods and one period between them are 0.654 and 0.617, which is close to that of the simulated economy, 0.6487. This probably is in line with the assumption.

In terms of the two nominal variables—the inflation rate and the nominal interest rate—their Kydland–Prescott ratios reaches 82.4% and 89.6%, respectively. This shows that the model with the money supply shocks can better explain the volatility of the nominal variables. However, the correlation coefficients of them with output are all negative, which is exactly the opposite of the real economy. This formation mechanism is as follows: Under the framework of the RBC model, the representative agent can well anticipate the impact of money supply shocks on the inflation rate. When encountering a positive money supply shock, the inflation rate in the simulated economy has risen rapidly and household wealth has shrunk, so that people will reduce consumption and increase savings. Also, because money is used to trade consumer goods in the model, the reduction in consumption on the one hand reduces output; on the other hand, it increases the relative money supply in reality, and the inflation rate exceeds the level caused by a positive monetary shock. Therefore, the money supply shocks will initially lead to a positive inflation rate, a positive nominal interest rate, and negative output changes. Then, as time goes by, the monetary shocks will gradually weaken, and the inflation rate, output and other variables will gradually return to state values. In this dynamic path, the inflation rate and nominal interest rate show a negative correlation with output. In the real economy, people's ability to predict monetary policy is poor, and at the same time they have poor expectations of the impact of monetary policy on macroeconomic variables such as the inflation rate. In the case of confronting a positive monetary shock, an increase in holding money increases consumption and investment, which in turn increases output and interest rates. Therefore, in reality, inflation and interest rates are positively correlated with output. In short, this problem is rooted in the fact that the representative agent in the model is assigned to have rational expectations.

Through the analysis of the standard deviation of these variables and their corresponding correlation coefficients with output, the model cannot well simulate the standard deviation of labor and that of the real money and the correlation coefficients of inflation and nominal interest rates with output. Nevertheless, the model simulates well, and the lowest Kydland–Prescott ratio can reach 61.6%.

7.5.2 ***Impulse response analysis***

To more intuitively illustrate the impact of money supply shocks and technology shocks, the impulse responses of variables to two types of shocks are shown in Figures 7.2 and 7.3.

It can be seen from Figure 7.2 that when the economy is accidentally hit by a positive money supply growth rate of about 4%, the inflation rate is very sensitive, with an increase of more than 5%. Along with it, the nominal interest rate increases by close to 3%; for the sake of resistance to inflation, the representative agent increases the holding of physical capital, and the capital shows a positive growth. Under high inflation expectations, the representative agent reduces the current labor input and consumption (that is, the amount of real money), and thus the current output also shows a negative growth. As the money supply shocks continue to slow down, the role of rational expectations is obvious. The inflation rate and nominal interest rate continue to decline. The increase in capital holdings in the early stage of the shocks leads to an increase in early output and consumption; when the positive money supply shocks cannot meet the emerging demand for money transaction, the real capital, output, consumption etc. approach the steady state, along with the shocks until the steady state. The whole process lasts about 25 periods, which is 25 years in reality.

The impulse response under the technology shocks is shown in Figure 7.3. When the economy is accidentally hit by a positive technology shock of more than 2%, the real output, labor, capital, consumption etc. all increase positively; due to the increase in real money demand at this time, in the case that there is no positive money supply, the inflation rate is negative. During the entire shock process, output will gradually stabilize as the technology shocks weaken. The continuous increase in output in the previous periods (about five periods) brings about an increase in capital and consumption (real money), and then as output cannot satisfy them, they will continue to increase and tend to stabilize with output. In the process of increasing capital and consumption, the representative agent reduces the labor input and increases labor when the capital input declines faster than the output. When capital increases, the real rate of return decreases, and because the increase in output exceeds the increase in the amount of real money, the nominal interest rate shows a downward trend. As capital gradually approaches a steady state, the real rate of return increases; thus the nominal interest rate has also gradually moved from a negative value to a steady state. The inflation rate is gradually

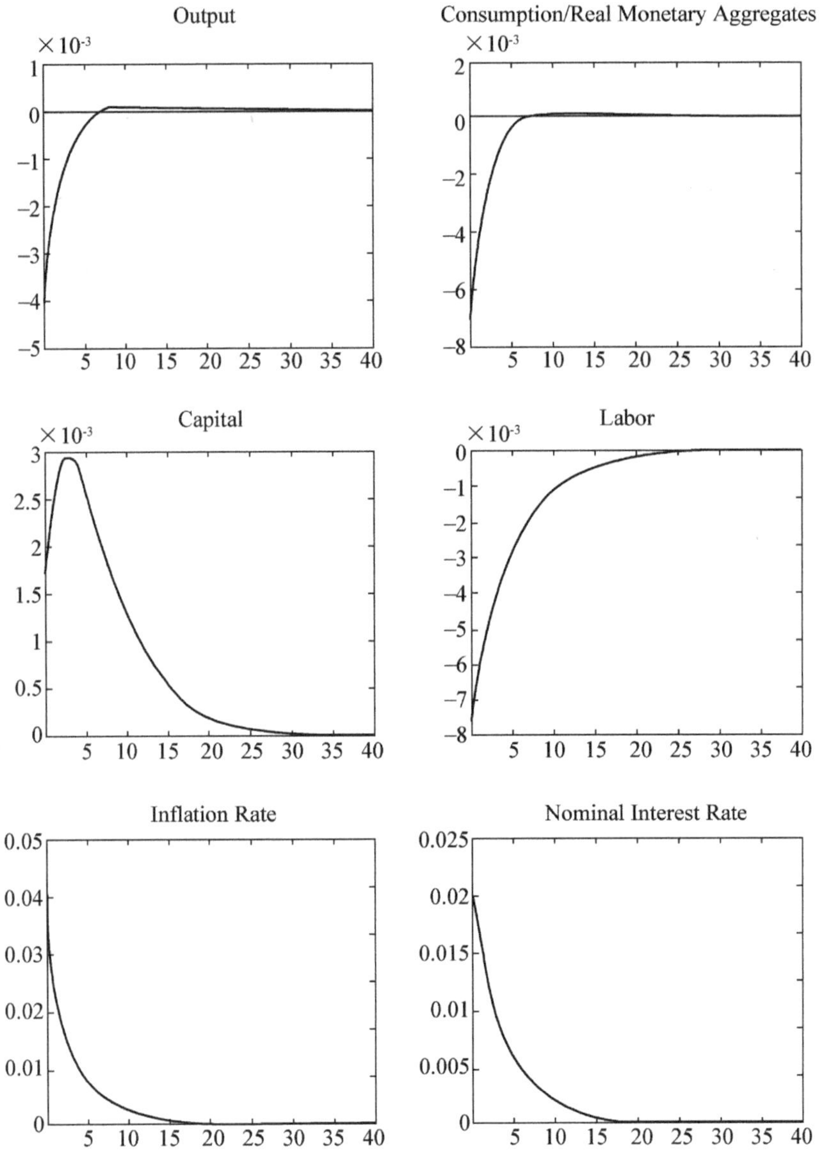

Figure 7.2 Impulse Responses of Variables to Money Supply Shocks.

approaching a steady state after the increase in the amount of real money exceeds the increase in output. The entire economy regains its steady state in about 30 periods.

Through the comparative analysis of Figures 7.2 and 7.3, it can be found that the impact of technology shocks on output and capital is greater than

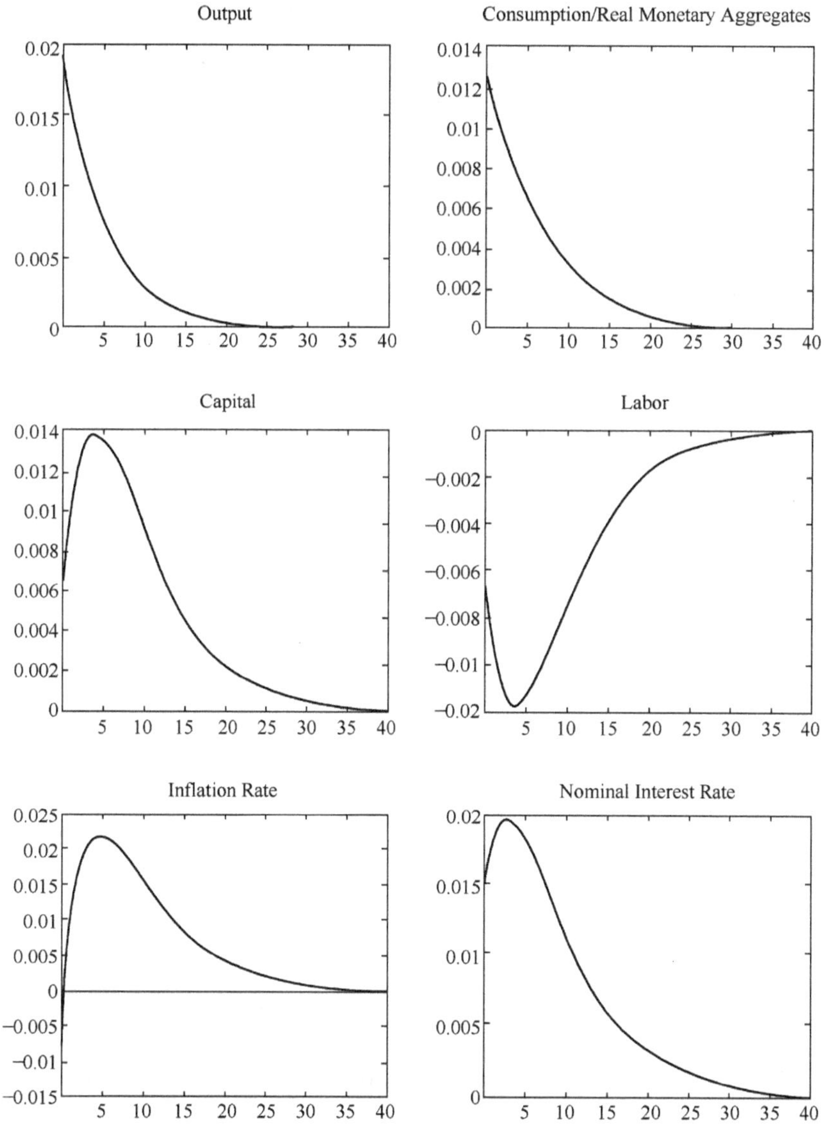

Figure 7.3 Impulse Responses of Variables to Technology Shocks.

that of money supply and that money supply shocks have a greater impact on the real money, labor, nominal interest rate and inflation. It can be accurately seen from Table 7.7 that monetary policy in China is still focused on affecting nominal variables and that its influence on real variables is relatively weak. The technology shocks can last longer, and the dynamic changes of various variables it causes are more complicated.

Table 7.7 Variance Decomposition of Variables

Variables / *Shocks*	*Output*	*Real Aggregate Money*	*Capital*	*Labor*	*Inflation Rate*	*Nominal Interest Rate*
Technology Shock	93.05	37.22	82.11	16.87	1.91	2.64
Monetary Shock	6.95	62.78	17.89	83.13	98.09	97.36

7.6 Policy recommendations and research prospects

In the comparative analysis with the real economy, it is found that the model economy can reasonably explain the real economy. After introducing money supply shocks, the model can explain 80.5% of fluctuations in output. This demonstrates that there is indeed a correlation between money and output in China. This also verifies that monetary policy in China indeed considers achieving economic growth goals. But in the long term, the non-neutrality of money means that when policymakers pay attention to the stimulus effect of monetary policy, they should pay more attention to its impact on inflation and use monetary policy cautiously. Meanwhile, monetary policy reform should be thoroughly explored, clarify the objectives and reduce inconsistencies. It is necessary to enhance people's policy predictions so as to shorten the time lag of monetary policy and eliminate harmful fluctuations caused by monetary policy as much as possible.

This chapter attempts to use the CIA model to incorporate monetary factors into the analysis of Chinese economic fluctuations. It imposes some strict assumptions: The representative agent is rational, the simulated economy is a closed economy with two sectors, and consumer goods can only be bought by cash. Nevertheless, this chapter posits that the representative agent bases decisions on rational expectations, causing simulations to conflict with the real economy. Along with policy recommendations and wishes to improve the real situation, a more direct method is to find ways to reduce the constraints of the assumptions in the model. For instance, one can consider using the VAR model to construct an inflation rate prediction equation to eliminate expectations rather than through the assumption of rational expectations.

In addition, the money supply shock equation can also be improved. Its construction is mainly based on the reaction function of the central bank. In this chapter, we focus on promoting output growth according to the current monetary policy and only use output as the independent variable of the money supply shock equation. But, in fact, many factors impact the monetary policy reaction function. It is possible to rebuild the money supply shock equation and continue to explore the RBC model that introduces monetary factors, to be able to achieve more satisfactory results.

Notes

1 Xu Gao, "Quantitative Analysis on China's Business Fluctuations Based on the DSGE Model," PhD Dissertation, Beijing: Peking University, 2008, p. 38.

2 Xia and Liao (2001) believed that due to the existence of a distorted monetary transmission mechanism, the expected policy effects cannot be achieved through the adjustment of the money supply, and therefore it is not appropriate to use the money supply as an intermediate target. However, some scholars, such as Liu (2006), believed that adopting the interest rate as an intermediary target of monetary policy has its merits. However, given the fact that the current interest rate formation mechanism is imperfect and the interaction between interest rate and output is not strong, the money supply should still be used as an intermediary target. Taking into account that in recent years, China's central bank has used monetary policy to carry out macroregulations mainly through affecting the money supply, so this chapter still analyzes the impact of monetary policy on economic fluctuations by analyzing the money supply.

3 This chapter selects these three indexes from a total of 33 samples from 1978 to 2010. The data of M_2 from 1978 to 1998 are extracted from the thesis of Zuo (1999), and the data of M_0 and M_1 from 1978 to 1989 are extracted from the doctoral dissertation of Hu (2011). All other data are obtained from the statistical database of China Economic Information Network.

4 Here the Granger test table is absent due to limited space.

5 It is important to note that, due to the changes in the statistical method in 1990, two sets of data resulted on the employed population in the whole society that year, which was 567.4 million according to the old statistical method and 647.4 million according to the new statistical method. In order to make the data consistent, the employment data of the whole society before 1990 are adjusted by using an adjustment coefficient (= 64 749/56 740) to multiply the old number of employed population in each year before 1990.

6 To eliminate the remaining expected factors in the linear equation set and to use the software DYNARE 4.2.1 to solve, this model assumes that the representative agent is assigned to have rational expectations.

Bibliography

Chen, Kunting, and Gong Liutang 陈昆亭, 龚六堂. "Numerical Simulation for the Chinese Economy in a Sticky-Price Model" 粘滞价格模型以及对中国经济的数值模拟—对基本RBC模型的改进. *The Journal of Quantitative & Technical Economics* no. 8 (2006): 106–117.

Chen, Xuebin, Yang Ling, and Fang Song 陈学彬, 杨凌, 方松. "The Micro-Foundation Studies of Monetary Policy Effect: An Empirical Analysis of the Chinese Residents' Consumption-Savings Behavior" 货币政策效应的微观基础研究—我国居民消费储蓄行为的实证分析. *Fudan Journal* (Social Sciences Edition) no. 1 (2005): 42–54.

Chow, Gregory C., and Kui-Wai Li. "China's Economic Growth: 1952–2010." *Economic Development and Cultural Change* no. 1 (2002): 247–256.

Clower, Robert W. "A Reconsideration of the Microfoundations of Monetary Theory." *Western Economic Journal* no. 1 (1967): 1–9.

Cooley, Thomas F., and Gary D. Hansen. "The Inflation Tax in a Real Business Cycle Model." *The American Economic Review* no. 4 (1989): 733–748.

Cooley, Thomas F., and Gary D. Hansen. "Equilibrium Business Cycles with Idle Resources and Variable Capacity Utilization. *Economic Theory* no. 1 (1995): 35–49.

Cooley, Thomas F., and Gary D. Hansen. "Money and Business Cycle." In *Frontiers of Business Cycle Research*, edited by T. F. Cooley. Princeton: Princeton University Press (1995): 175–216.

Huang, Zelin 黄赜琳. "A Study on Business Cycle and the Effects of Fiscal Policy in China: An Empirical Study on a RBC Model with Three Sections" 中国经济周期特征与财政政策效应——一个基于三部门RBC模型的实证分析. *Economic Research Journal* no. 6 (2005): 27–39.

Kiyotaki, Nobuhiro, and Randall Wright. "On Money as a Medium of Exchange." *Journal of Political Economy* no. 4 (1989): 927–954.

Kydland, Finn E., and Edward F. Prescott. "Time to Build and Aggregate Fluctuations." *Econometrica* no. 6 (1982): 1345–1370.

Liu, Bin 刘斌. "Empirical Research on the Relationship Among Output, Price and Monetary Aggregates" 我国货币供应量与产出、物价间相互关系的实证研究. *Journal of Financial Research* no. 7 (2002): 10–17.

Liu, Bin 刘斌. "Choice and Implementation of the Optimal Monetary Policy Rules in China" 最优货币政策规则的选择及在我国的应用. *Journal of Financial Research* no. 9 (2003): 3–13+92.

Liu, Jinquan, and Zhang Ailian 刘金全, 张艾莲. "The Effectiveness of Monetary Policy in Different Periods of Business Cycle and Testing of the Money–Output Relationships" 我国货币政策作用机制的阶段性与货币—产出之间影响关系检验. *Statistical Research* no. 8 (2003): 60–63.

Liu, Mingzhi 刘明志. 2006. "Monetary Aggregate or Interest Rate Taken as an Intermediate Target" 货币供应量和利率作为货币政策中介目标的实用性. *Journal of Financial Research* no. 1 (2006): 51–63.

Long, John B., and Charles I. Plosser. "Real Business Cycles." *Journal of Political Economy* no. 1 (1983): 39–69.

Lu, Jun, and Shu Yuan 陆军, 舒元. "Long-Run Monetary Neutrality in China: Theories and Evidence" 长期货币中性: 理论及其中国的实证. *Journal of Financial Research* no. 6 (2002): 32–40.

Lucas, Robert E., Jr., and Nancy L. Stokey. "Money and Interest in a Cash-in-Advance Economy." *Econometrica* no. 3 (1987): 491–513.

National Bureau of Statistics 国家统计局. *China Statistical Yearbook 2011*中国统计年鉴2011. Beijing: China Statistics Press, 2011.

Samuelson, Paul A. "An Exact Consumption–Loan Model of Interest with the Social Contrivance of Money." *Journal of Political Economy* no. 6 (1958): 467–482.

Sidrauski, Miguel. "Rational Choice and Patterns of Growth in a Monetary Economy." *American Economic Review* no. 2 (1967): 534–544.

Svensson, Lars E. O. "Money and Asset Prices in a Cash-in Advance Economy." *Journal of Political Economy* no. 5 (1985): 919–944.

Xia, Bin, and Liao Qiang 夏斌, 廖强. "Money supply Is No Longer Suitable as the Intermediary Target of the Monetary Policy in China" 货币供应量已不宜作为当前我国货币政策的中介目标. *Economic Research Journal* no. 8 (2001): 33–43.

Xu, Bing, and Ye Yafen 许冰，叶娅芬. "Implementation of Optimal Monetary Policy in Rational Expectations Models in China" 基于理性预期模型的最优货币政策的选择及应用. *Statistical Research* no. 5 (2009): 25–32.

Xu, Gao 徐高. "Quantitative Analysis on Chinese Business Fluctuations Based on the DSGE Model" 基于动态随机一般均衡模型的中国经济波动数量分析. PhD Dissertation, Beijing: Peking University, 2008.

Zuo, Xiaoshun 左孝顺. "The Changes in the Velocity of Money: An Example from China" 货币流通速度的变化:中国的例证, 1978–1997. *Journal of Financial Research* no. 6 (1999): 39–45.

8 Energy prices and the Chinese macroeconomy

The effects of rising energy prices and large fluctuations on Chinese macroeconomy has become increasingly prominent. It is of great significance to explore the transmission mechanism of energy price fluctuations and their impact on Chinese macroeconomy. This chapter first analyzes some stylized facts of Chinese macroeconomy. It then builds a DSGE model of energy price changes influencing macroeconomy by introducing energy price shocks into the RBC model. The model parameters will be calibrated to be consistent with the typical facts of Chinese economic development in order to address the degree of resemblance of the model economy to the real economy. As a result, the findings indicate that after introducing energy price shocks, the RBC model can ideally simulate the real economy. The initial impact of energy price shocks is greater than that of technology shocks, though the latter lasts longer.

8.1 The relationship between energy prices and macroeconomy

The global oil crisis in the 1970s and the stagflation of developed countries that stemmed from this crisis caused the issue of energy prices to become an important subject in the field of macroeconomics. For its scarcity and non-renewability, energy becomes an important resource and a basic guarantee for the economic development of all countries in the world. The issue of energy security has become the primary factor affecting the world's political and economic order and the focus of governmental diplomacy. The Chinese economy has maintained its rapid growth for decades. Whether this will continue in the future depends whether energy can support the growth rate of the macroeconomy.

The energy consumption of China is in the top rank worldwide. The total energy consumption of China in 2020 was 4.98 billion tons of standard coal, accounting for 26.1% of the world's total energy consumption. However, compared with the global average per capita energy possession, the per capita energy possession of China reached about 45%. According to statistics from British Petroleum in 2021, as of the end of 2020, the remaining recoverable coal reserves of China were 143.197 billion tons, accounting for 13.3% of

DOI: 10.4324/9781003305651-8

the world's remaining recoverable reserves, with a reserve/production ratio[1] of 37 years; crude oil recoverable reserves were 26 billion barrels, accounting for 1.5% of the world's remaining recoverable reserves, with a reserve/production ratio of 18.2 years; the remaining recoverable reserves of natural gas were 8.4 trillion cubic meters, accounting for 4.5% of the world's remaining recoverable reserves, with a reserve/production ratio of 43.4 years; and the world's average reserve/production ratios of coal, natural gas and oil were 139 years, 48.8 years and 53.5 years, respectively. The coal, natural gas and oil reserve/production ratios in China were 26.6%, 88.7% and 34.0% of the world average, respectively.[2]

The substantial increase in the energy demand of China since 2002 has led to a substantial increase in energy prices. For instance, the price of oil has risen to US$61.92 per barrel on December 31, 2009, from the close of US$19.48 per barrel in January 2002. As of January 22, 2021, the price of oil has risen to US$84.9 per barrel. Since China became a net oil importer in 1993, the oil dependence of China on foreign sources has continued to increase. In addition, due to the strengthening of expectations of the arrival of the peak of world oil production, the sharp increase in oil demand for economic development and the difficulty of replacing conventional energy with new energy sources in the short term, the pressure on oil prices has intensified.

In the 1970s, scholars in the developed countries started to explore the relationship between energy prices and economic fluctuations. Fried and Schultze (1975) and Dohner (1981) proposed that rising oil prices will cause net oil exporters to increase their own consumption demand and reduce the aggregate consumption demand of net importers. The increase in demand will be lower than the decrease in the latter's demand, so the total global consumer demand will fall, which in turn will reduce the rate of economic growth and trigger economic recessions. Hamilton (1983) found that, since World War II, with the exception of economic recessions in 1960, oil prices had almost been related to every economic recession, which also made the research on the effects of oil price shocks on macroeconomy shift from the demand side to the supply side.

Balke, Brown and Yucel (2002) used the vector auto-regression (VAR) model to introduce the US federal funds rate, short-term and long-term interest rates, GDP deflator index, etc. Assuming that the federal funds rate remains unchanged, the response of short-term interest rates and GDP to oil price shocks is asymmetrical. They concluded that the following was the mechanism by which oil price affects output: The impact of oil price on interest rates is asymmetrical, and the impact of interest rates on output is significant, so the impact of changes in oil prices on output is also asymmetrical. Hooker (2002) focused on the relationship between oil prices and inflation and found that there was a significant relationship between oil price fluctuations and inflation during the period 1962–1980, which was no longer significant in the following period.

Chinese scholars' research on the impact of energy prices on the economy started relatively late. Wei (2002) used a calculable general equilibrium model to quantitatively study the impact of rising international oil prices on the Chinese economy and found that for every 10% increase in world oil prices, the GDP of China will drop by approximately 0.1%, while prices will increase by 0.1%. Xu et al. (2005) used the method adopted by Hamilton (1983) to analyze Chinese economic data and found that rising oil prices would indeed lead to a decline in GDP, and the output elasticity of oil price was between −0.07 and −0.14. Sun (2007) analyzed the impact of energy price shocks on the Phillips curve of China by using the C-D production function combined with the operating mode of monetary policy; he found that a 10% increase in energy price would push the inflation rate up by 0.35% and that the output gap also rose by 0.05%. Lin and Mou (2008) found that the negative impact of rising oil prices on the economy is less than the negative impact of rising coal prices on the economy, and the two will also have an impact on the adjustment of industrial structure, though the degree of impact is different.

This chapter attempts to examine the mechanism and effects of energy prices on the Chinese macroeconomy by building a DSGE model. The model parameters were calibrated to be consistent with the stylized facts of Chinese economic development, and the values of each economic variable were calculated when the simulated economy reached a stable state through the calibrated model economy. Kydland and Prescott (1982) were the first to use the calibration method in macroeconomic research and thus won the Nobel Prize in Economics in 2004. Canova (1994) believed that the calibration method started with the definition of the problem, including model selection, parameter assignment, data sequence generation, characterization, comparison with the same characteristics of the real economy and even economic policy analysis. Adopting the DSGE model is to make the built macroeconomic model have microfoundations and an intertemporal dynamic vision and to overcome the so-called Lucas critique. The DSGE model and calibration method have not been adopted in the previous literature analyzing energy prices and the Chinese economy. Therefore, this chapter presents a new approach.

8.2 Data sources and stylized facts

Generally, adopting the DSGE model and calibration method to analyze the problem follows several steps: First, determine the stylized facts of economic growth and fluctuations. Secondly, build a general equilibrium model that can present these facts, solve the equilibrium solution of the model and calibrate the parameters, and then compare the model simulation results and the real economy to draw conclusions and policy recommendations.

Before processing the variables, first introduce the data sources:

First, output: Based on the gross domestic product (GDP) data of *China Statistical Yearbook 2009*, the consumer price index (CPI) is used to calculate the output to the real value of the base year 1978.

Second, consumption: Consumption includes government consumption and household consumption. The data come from *China Statistical Yearbook 2009*. The CPI is used to convert the government and household consumptions to the actual value of the base year 1978.

Third, employment: The original data comes from *China Statistical Yearbook 2009*. Since China has no specific statistics on working hours, previous studies have used the number of employees instead. In addition, the method of statistics has changed since 1990, so employment has undergone major changes around 1990. In order to make the data comparable and continuous, the employment data from 1978 to 1989 was revised according to the average growth rate from 1990 to 1994.

Fourth, investment: The original data come from *China Statistical Yearbook 2009*, and the fixed asset price index is used to adjust the original data to the actual value of the base year 1978.

Five, capital stock: Referring to the estimation of Zhang (2002), the capital stock of the fixed assets in China from 1978 to 2001 is obtained, and the data from 2002 to 2008 are also obtained according to Zhang's method of estimating the capital stock.

Six, energy consumed: According to *China Statistical Yearbook 2009*, the energy consumed in China was obtained and adjusted by using the fuel and power price index from 1989 to 2008. As the *China Statistical Yearbook* did not provide the fuel and power price index from 1978 to 1988, providing only the price index of oil, coal and electricity, the price index from 1978 to 1988 is calculated by using the proportion of these three kinds of energy consumed to the total energy consumed as the weight.

After using the H-P filter to process the main variables of Chinese economic fluctuations from 1978 to 2005 and detrending, the fluctuation data of the variables can be obtained as discussed next.

According to the results shown in Figures 8.1–8.6, the following stylized facts are made clear: Since 1978, output, investment, consumption and employment population have experienced several large fluctuations. The fluctuations of these variables show greater consistency; each component of total demand and output shows pro-cyclicality, especially the fluctuations in fixed asset investment, in household consumption and in output, while energy price fluctuation and output fluctuation show weak pro-cyclicality. The correlation between labor input fluctuation and output fluctuation represented by working population is not high, and it shows non-cyclicality.

8.3 Model building and parameter calibration

To examine the mechanism of energy prices and the sources of economic fluctuations involved in the stylized facts of the Chinese economy, energy price

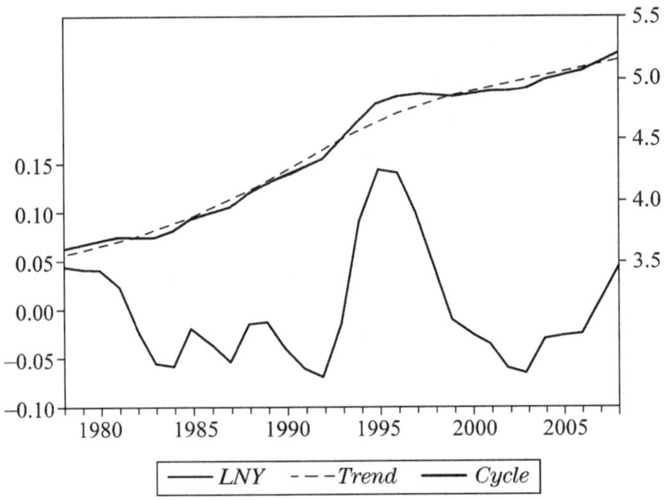

Figure 8.1 Output Fluctuations from 1978 to 2008.[a]

[a] From Figures 8.1–8.6, the horizontal axis is time (year), and the vertical axis is percentage (%).

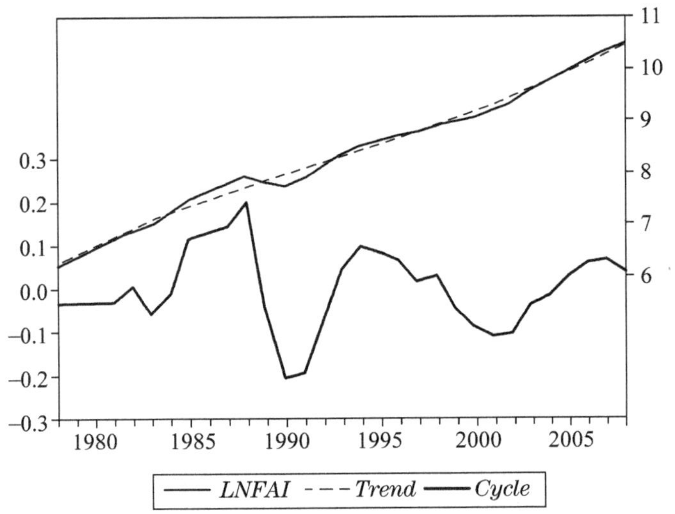

Figure 8.2 Fixed Asset Investment Fluctuations from 1978 to 2008.

shocks are introduced into the DSGE model with classical assumptions and the assumptions of constant returns to scale. It is assumed that the representative household has an infinite life span, and its utility comes from consumption and leisure. The utility function adopts the form of relative risk aversion; the production function considers constant returns to scale; energy prices

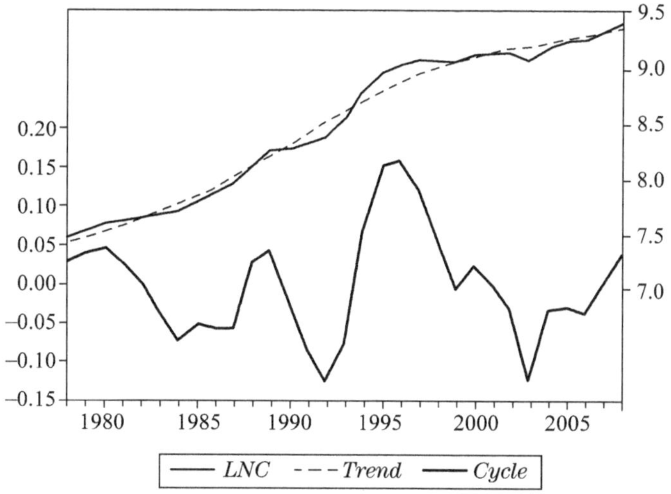

Figure 8.3 Household Consumption Fluctuations from 1978 to 2008.

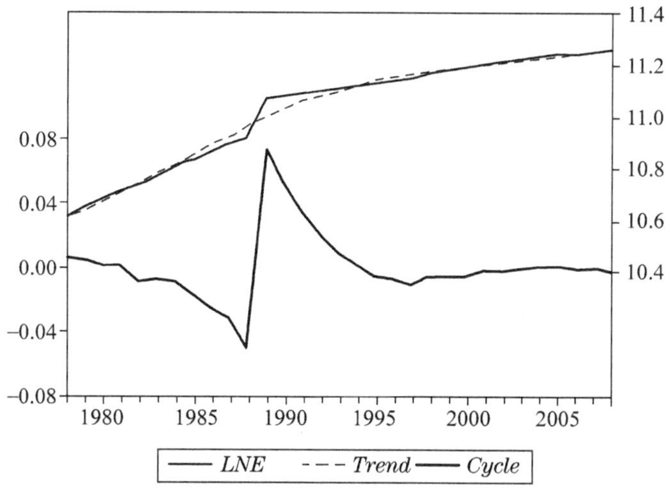

Figure 8.4 Employment Fluctuations from 1978 to 2008.

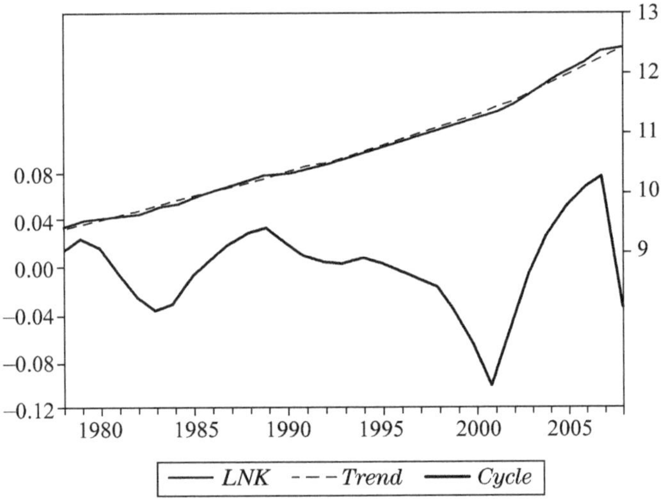

Figure 8.5 Capital Stock Fluctuations from 1978 to 2008.

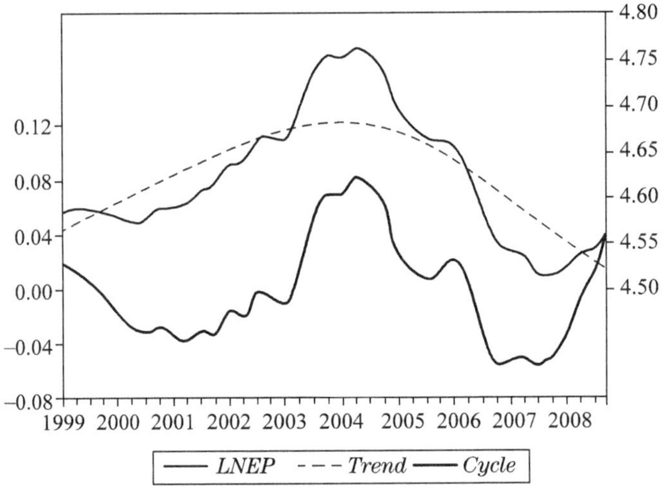

Figure 8.6 Energy Price Fluctuations from 1998 to 2009.

and technology are regarded as exogenous random shock variables and are assumed to be subject to the law of the logarithmic first-order autoregression process. The specific form of the utility function is:

$$U(C_t, P_t, N_t) = \frac{C_t^{1-\xi} - 1}{1-\xi} + \eta \ln(1 - N_t) \tag{8.1}$$

where C_t and N_t, respectively, represent the consumption and labor of the representative household in period t. If the available labor supply is normalized as 1, $1 - N_t$ represents leisure in the period t. ξ represents the coefficient of relative risk aversion for consumption, and η reflects the degree of preference for labor in the utility function, $\eta \in (0,1)$.

The objective function of intertemporal utility is:

$$\max E \sum_{t=0}^{\infty} \omega^t [\frac{C_t^{1-\xi} - 1}{1-\xi} + \eta \ln(1 - N_t)] \tag{8.2}$$

$$\text{s.t. } Y_t^d = C_t + K_{t+1} - (1-\delta)K_t + P_t Q_t \tag{8.3}$$

where E represents the expectation operator; ω represents the subjective discount rate, $\omega \in (0, 1)$; Y_t^d represents the household disposable income; K_t and K_{t+1} represent the capital stock in periods t and $t+1$, respectively; δ represents the rate of depreciation, $\delta \in [0, 1]$; P_t and Q_t represent the price and amount of energy consumed in period t, respectively.

The investment equation is:

$$K_{t+1} = I_t + (1-\delta) K_t \tag{8.4}$$

Chow and Li (2002) estimated the production function based on the data from 1952 to 1998 and found that the Cobb–Douglas production function with constant returns to scale was applicable to the situation of China. So they based the estimate on the Cobb–Douglas production function, and the production function in this chapter is improved:

$$Y_t = A_t K_t^{\alpha} N_t^{\beta} (P_t Q_t)^{\gamma} \tag{8.5}$$

Y_t represents output; α, β and γ, respectively, represent the share of capital, labor and energy input, and $\alpha + \beta + \gamma = 1$; A_t represents an exogenous random technology shock, which is subject to the law of logarithmic first-order autoregressive process:

$$\ln A_t = (1-\rho_A)\ln \bar{A} + \rho_A \ln A_{t-1} + e_t^A, \quad e_t^A \sim i.i.d.N(0,\sigma_A^2) \tag{8.6}$$

$\bar{A}$ represents the steady-state value of the technology shock variable, e_t^A represents the stochastic disturbance of technology shocks, and the mean is zero and serially uncorrelated. ρ represents the correlation coefficient of two adjacent periods, $|\rho| < 1$.

Energy price shocks also are subject to the law of logarithmic first-order autoregressive process:

$$\ln P_t = (1-\rho_P)\ln \bar{P} + \rho_P \ln P_{t-1} + e_t^P, \quad e_t^P \sim i.i.d.N(0,\sigma_P^2)\,, \tag{8.7}$$

$\bar{P}$ represents the steady-state value of the energy price shock variable, P_t. e_t^P represents the stochastic disturbance of price shocks, and the mean is zero and serially uncorrelated.

In a perfect competitive market, if corporate profits are to be maximized, the income of production factors equals the marginal productivity of production factors. The representative household is homogeneous, so when the utility of the representative household is maximized, the overall welfare of the society is maximized. The Lagrange function of the representative household's utility maximization is:

$$L = E\left\{\sum_{t=0}^{\infty} \omega^t \left[\frac{C_t^{1-\xi}-1}{1-\xi} + \eta \ln(1-N_t) - \lambda_t (C_t + K_{t+1} - (1-\delta) K_t \right.\right.$$
$$\left.\left. + P_t Q_t - A_t K_t^{\alpha} N_t^{\beta} P_t^{\gamma} Q_t^{\gamma})\right]\right\} \tag{8.8}$$

To solve the first-order conditions of the state variable in the preceding equation, the following equations can be obtained:

$$C_t^{-\xi} - \lambda_t = 0 \tag{8.9}$$

$$-\frac{\eta}{1-N_t} + \lambda_t \beta A_t K_t^{\alpha} N_t^{\beta-1} (P_t Q_t)^{\gamma} = 0 \tag{8.10}$$

$$-\lambda_t + \lambda_{t-1}\omega[1-\xi + A_{t+1}\alpha K_{t+1}^{\alpha-1} N_{t+1}^{\beta} (P_{t+1}Q_{t+1})^{\gamma}] = 0 \tag{8.11}$$

$$P_t - A_t \gamma K_t^{\alpha} N_t^{\beta} P_t^{\gamma} Q_t^{\gamma-1} = 0 \tag{8.12}$$

$$R_t = \alpha \frac{Y_t}{K_t} + 1 - \delta \tag{8.13}$$

where R_t represents the rate of capital return, which can be seen from equation 8.13. R_t includes the capital output rate and the residual capital after capital depreciation. In addition, the equation is subject to the following three boundary conditions: First, the initial capital stock is given; second, $\lim_{i\to\infty} E_t \omega^i C_{t+i}^{-\eta} K_{t+i+1} = 0$ means that, in an infinite period, the discounted marginal utility of the rational economic man is equal to zero; third, the supply of labor at a steady state is a constant.

The definition of the equilibrium of this economic system is as follows: Given the preferences and technology and resource constraints in the economy, under the established state variables and exogenous shock variables, the household maximizes the expected utility, and the manufacturer maximizes the expected profit, ensuring the market clearing. This is a stochastic dynamic programming problem, and its equilibrium solution is $\{Y_t, C_t, I_t, K_t, N_t, Q_t, P_t, R_t, A_t\}_{t=0}^{\infty}$.

Since there are no analytical solutions for nonlinear differential equations, this chapter uses the numerical solution as an alternative, through log-linearization, and numerical equivalent substitutions should be performed. After log-linearization, the following equations are shown:[3]

$$
\begin{aligned}
&\bar{Y} y_t = \bar{C} c_t + \bar{I} i_t + \bar{P}\bar{Q}(p_t + q_t + p_t q_t) \\
&\bar{K} k_{t+1} = \bar{I} i_t + (1-\delta)\bar{K} k_t \\
&y_t \approx a_t + \beta n_t + \alpha k_t + \gamma p_t + \gamma q_t \\
&a_t = \rho_A a_{t-1} + e_t^A \\
&p_t = \rho_P p_{t-1} + e_t^P \\
&n_t \approx (1-\bar{N})(y_t - \xi c_t) \\
&E[\xi(c_t - c_{t+1}) + r_{t+1}] = 0 \\
&\bar{R} r_t \approx \alpha \frac{\bar{Y}}{\bar{K}}(y_t - k_t) \\
&q_t = \gamma y_t - p_t
\end{aligned}
\tag{8.14}
$$

There are nine equations and nine variables: Among them, a_t and p_t are exogenous state variables, y_t, r_t, l_t, i_t and q_t are systematic state variables, and k_t and c_t are endogenous control variables. The parameters in the model are calibrated next.

Generally, there are two ways to calibrate parameters: Either determine the relevant parameters based on the previous research results, or use measurement tools, such as regression methods, to estimate the parameters. This chapter involves these two methods to assign parameters based on historical data in China.

First, the coefficient of relative risk aversion for consumption (ξ)

When Chen (2005) conducted an empirical analysis on the consumption and saving behaviors of Chinese residents, the relative risk aversion coefficient of consumption was estimated to be about 0.77. However, when studying credit constraint, Chen et al. (2010) pointed out that, under the form of the utility function used by Chen et al. (2005), the coefficient of relative risk aversion is no longer the reciprocal of the intertemporal substitution elasticity of consumption. Here the estimation of Chen et al. (2010) is adopted, and ξ is set as 3.5.

Second, the relative price of consumption and labor (η)

When Li and Zax (2003) estimated the 1995 survey data of Chinese residents' income, it was found that the labor supply elasticity of the urban population relative to wage changes was 0.054, so in this chapter η is set as 20.

Third, the depreciation rate (δ)

Internationally, it is believed that the depreciation rate is 0.025 and the annual depreciation rate is 0.1. Here it is assumed that the average service life span of the fixed assets in China is ten years, and the rate of depreciation δ is 0.1.

Fourth, the capital share (α), labor share (β) and energy share (Υ)

Like many models that study the Chinese real business cycle, this chapter also assumes that the production function follows the Cobb–Douglas form with constant returns to scale. The capital data are based on the estimation method of Zhang (2003), using *Y*, *K* and *E*, respectively, to represent the actual output, capital stock and energy consumption value calculated at constant prices in 1978. The energy consumption value is calculated based on total energy consumption and the fuel and power price index. Since the energy consumption value accounts for a low proportion of the actual output, this chapter does not exclude the energy consumption value from the capital stock value. The result of this estimation does not have much of an effect on the result of the equation estimation. Employment (*N*) refers to the data from *China Statistical Yearbook 2008*. Since the employment data provided by the statistical yearbook changed in 1990, to make the data comparable and continuous throughout the whole period, the original employment data were revised, and the method of revision was to move the 1978–1989 employment data upward based on the average growth rate of employment from 1990 to 1993.

The regression equation obtained by the estimation method of Zhang (2003) is:

$$\log(Y/N) = -2.048 + 0.158 * \log(E/N) + 0.493 * \log(K/N) + 0.105 * T$$

$$(-12.903) \qquad (3.429) \qquad (-2.929) \qquad (13.012)$$

$R^2 = 0.997$ S.E. = 0.029 F = 1610.207(1978–2008)

The test values are shown in parentheses. The goodness of fit of the model reaches 99.7%. The equation and the variables have passed the t-test. It can be seen from the model that output is positively correlated with energy consumption, capital stock and labor. The output elasticity of energy (γ) is 15.8%, the output elasticity of capital (α) is 49.3%, and the output elasticity of labor (β) is 34.9%.

Five, other parameters

N represents the equilibrium value of labor supply. Zeng and Yu (2006) found that the natural rate of unemployment in China fluctuates between 0.048 and 0.052. According to the record of China's urban registered unemployment rate, the unemployment rate of China is about 4.2%, so the value of N in this chapter is set as 0.95, that is, the equilibrium value of labor supply ($\bar{N}$) is 0.95. According to the research of Chen et al. (2010), calculated from the Solow residual, the value of ρ_A is 0.718, and the value of σ_A is 0.019. $\bar{A}$ represents a balanced technical level, with only level effect and without volatility effect, so it is taken as 1. According to the calculation equation $R=(\sum_{t=1978}^{2008}\frac{(1-\alpha)Y_t}{K_t})/31+1-\delta$ of the rate of capital return, the value of R can be estimated to be about 1.081. From the equilibrium state $\beta=\frac{1}{\bar{R}}$ and $\bar{R}$ = 1.081, it can be seen that the subjective discount rate ω is 0.925. Based on the energy price data from 1978 to 2008, the first-order autoregressive coefficients and standard deviations of energy price shocks and energy consumption shocks can be calculated: the first-order autoregressive coefficient of energy price shock $\rho_P = 0.957$, its standard deviation $\sigma_P = 0.01562$, and the equilibrium value of energy price $\bar{P} = 1$.

From the above analysis, the calibration results of the model parameters are shown in Table 8.1.

8.4 Empirical results

According to the equation set of 8.14, the standard deviation of each macroeconomic variable in the equilibrium state and the correlation coefficient

Table 8.1 Calibrated Values of Variable Parameters

ξ	η	δ	α	β	γ	$\bar{N}$	ρ_A	$\bar{A}$
3.5	20	0.1	0.493	0.349	0.158	0.95	0.718	1
ω		ρ_P		σ_P		$\bar{P}$	σ_A	$\bar{R}$
0.925		0.957		0.01562		1	0.019	1.081

Table 8.2 Periodic Characteristics of Simulated Economy

Variables	*Real Economy*		*Simulated Economy*		*Kydland–Prescott Ratio*
	Standard Deviation (%)	*Corresponding Correlation Coefficient with Output*	*Standard Deviation (%)*	*Corresponding Correlation Coefficient with Output*	
Output	3.1	1	2.9	1	93.55%
Capital	3.8	0.650	1.1	0.524	28.94%
Consumption	3.8	0.819	3.0	0.631	78.95%
Labor	0.7	−0.694	0.6	0.312	85.71%
Investment	11.6	0.871	9.2	0.624	79.31%

between these variables are obtained by using MATLAB, as shown in Table 8.2.[4] Through comparing the results obtained by the model with the data of actual macroeconomic variables, it can be judged whether the RBC model that introduces energy price shocks can reflect the real economic fluctuations.

The data in Table 8.2 are all obtained using the H-P filter to detrend the variables. The Kydland–Prescott ratio is the standard deviation obtained by the model simulation divided by the standard deviation of the real economic data, which reflects the explanatory effect of the model. The larger the ratio, the better the fitting effect of the model.

In terms of output fluctuations, the standard deviation of real economic output is 0.031, and the standard deviation of simulated economic output is 0.029. It can be seen that the fluctuations of the two are approximately the same.

In terms of capital fluctuations, the standard deviation of real economic capital is 0.038, while the standard deviation of simulated economic capital is 0.011, which can only explain approximately 28.94% of real fluctuations. The corresponding correlation coefficients with output are relatively similar.

In terms of consumption fluctuations, the standard deviation of real economic consumption is 0.038, and the standard deviation of simulated economic consumption is 0.030. The model can explain approximately 78.95% of real fluctuations. The corresponding correlation coefficient with output of the simulated economy is 0.631, and that of the real economy is 0.819, both of which are procyclical.

In terms of labor fluctuations, the standard deviation of real economic consumption is 0.007, and the standard deviation of simulated economic labor is 0.006. The model can explain approximately 85.71% of the real fluctuations. The corresponding correlation coefficient with output of the simulated labor is 0.312, showing weak procyclicality, while the corresponding correlation coefficient with output of the real labor is −0.694, showing countercyclicality, which can possibly be associated with the changes of the statistical method

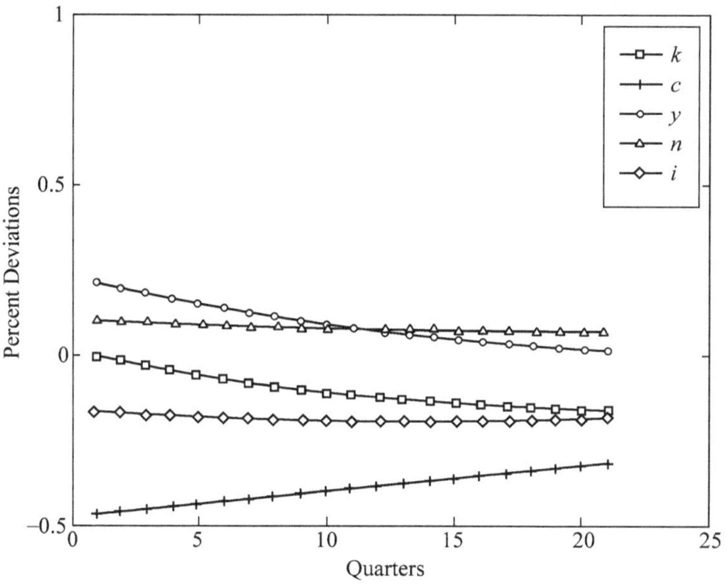

Figure 8.7 Impulse Responses to Energy Price Shocks.[a]

[a] The horizontal axis of Figures 8.7–8.9 is the quarter, and the vertical axis is percentage (%).

of the employed population after 1990. This has little to do with the pros and cons of the model.

In terms of investment fluctuations, the standard deviation of the real economic investment is 0.116, and the standard deviation of the simulated economic investment is 0.092. The results can explain about 79.31% of the real fluctuations. The corresponding correlation coefficient with output of the simulated investment is 0.624, and that of the real investment is 0.871, both showing strong procyclicality.

The preceding analysis shows that the RBC model involving energy price shocks can better explain Chinese economic fluctuations. According to the simulated data obtained after parameter calibration, the impulse response of different variables to shocks can be established, as shown in Figures 8.7 and 8.8.

It can be seen from Figure 8.7 that when the economic system is impacted by a unit of energy price (price reduction), output and capital stock decrease significantly and recover to the equilibrium level after about 19 quarters; labor and investment in the economic system are almost unchanged; consumption has significantly increased, and it will take more than five years to return to the balanced growth path. It can be seen from Figure 8.8 that when the economic system is hit by a unit of technology, investment immediately drops sharply, and the effect of output reduction is also obvious. After about four years, investment and output can return to a balanced growth path; energy

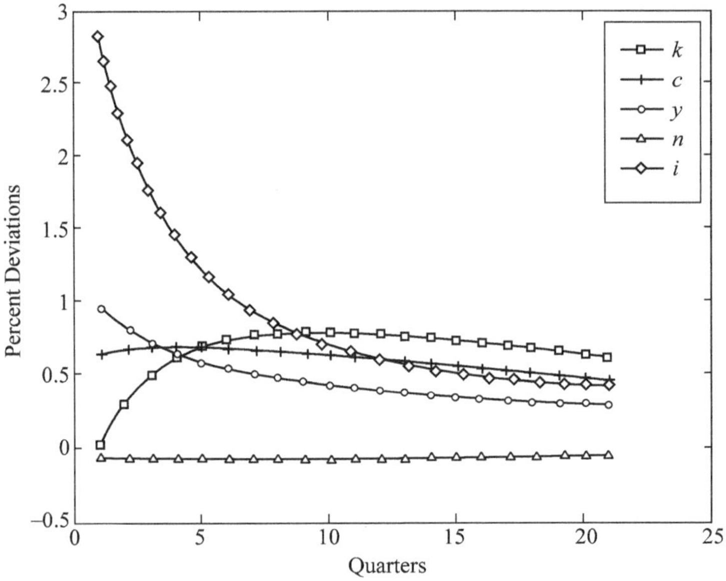

Figure 8.8 Impulse Responses to Technology Shocks.

prices and consumption are not significantly affected by technology shocks, while the capital stock appears to increase sharply at first, then slowly decline after two years, and return to equilibrium after five years.

Although both energy prices and technology are exogenous shocks, the responses they cause are quite different:

First of all, on the whole, the initial impact of energy price shocks is greater than that of technology shocks, which is easier to understand. Changes in energy prices will quickly affect the production costs of enterprises, consumer expenditures and the overall price level of the economy. It has a relatively significant impact on the economy, while the transmission process of technology shocks is relatively slow, and the initial impact on the entire economy is not obvious.

Second, from the perspective of duration, the impact of technology shocks lasts longer. At the end of the 20th quarter, technology shocks still have a certain influence. The influence of energy prices at this time is already very weak, however, considering that in the same period of time, the magnitude and frequency of energy price fluctuations are much higher than that of technological fluctuations. Therefore, the impact of energy price fluctuations cannot be ignored in the study of Chinese economic growth and economic fluctuations.

Figure 8.9 is a variable fluctuation figure derived from model simulation (after the H-P filter). It can be seen that output fluctuates the most, followed

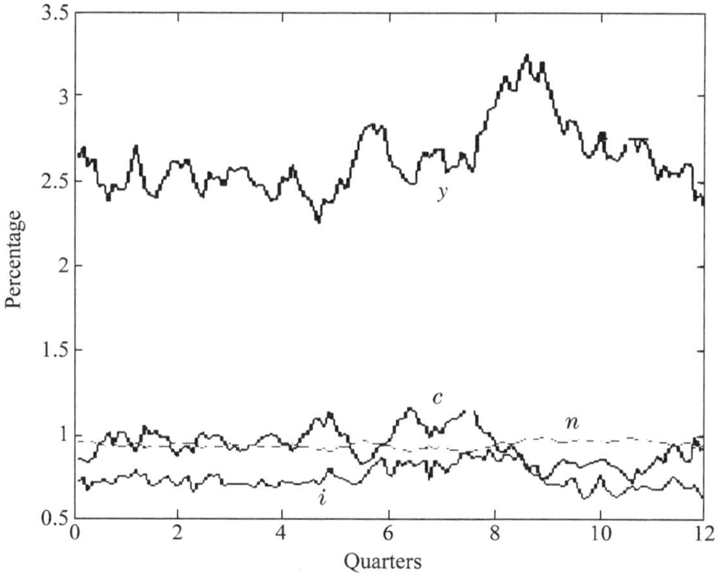

Figure 8.9 Variable Fluctuations Derived from Simulation.

successively by consumption, investment and labor; output, consumption and investment are all procyclical, while labor does not fluctuate too much. According to Figures 8.7–8.9, it can be seen that output, investment and consumption are more consistent with real fluctuations. Only labor is quite different from the actual fluctuations, which can possibly be associated with the changes of the statistical scale of the employed population in China after 1990, so that the actual fluctuation changes drastically, and the model built in this chapter does not consider this factor. The results thus obtained are different from the real ones but do not affect the applicability of the model.

8.5 Conclusion and policy recommendations

Energy is an important resource for the development of the national economy, and it is also a driving force for economic growth. Accompanying the rapid economic development of China is the rapid growth of energy demand. China has become a net importer of oil since 1993. As of 2006, China was still a net exporter of coal but became a net importer of coal in 2007. Due to the extensive pattern of economic growth in China, high input, high consumption, low output and low energy utilization efficiency have caused excessive consumption of energy, especially the coal-based energy structure, which has a great impact on the environment. Sulfur dioxide and carbon dioxide emissions rank first and second in the world, respectively. The per capita energy resources in

China are relatively insufficient, and energy consumption per unit of output value is high. A large amount of coal burning has caused serious air pollution. China is facing huge resource and environmental pressures, and the issue of energy security is severe.

This chapter introduces the energy price shocks into the RBC model, calibrates the model parameters, compares the model economy with the real economy and evaluates the effectiveness of the model. It is found that after the introduction of energy price shocks, the model can perform well in simulating the real economy. Except for the capital stock, the model economy can explain more than 79% of real economic fluctuations, which is higher than the Kydland–Prescott ratio in the existing domestic literature; for example, the Kydland–Prescott ratio calculated by Huang (2005) is 70%. It is also found that the impact of energy price shocks on the macroeconomy is greater than that of technology shocks, but the duration of the impact is shorter than that of technology shocks.

The energy import sources of China are scarce. Take, as an example, oil, which is mainly imported from countries and regions like the Middle East, Africa and Southeast Asia. The political situations in these countries and regions are turbulent, and the quantities and prices of oil supply are extremely uncertain. Although China has become a major energy consumer, it does not have the discursive privilege in international energy pricing. Developed countries, large multinational corporations and international hot money all attempt to raise the energy import prices of China, lower the export energy prices of China in the international markets and use price scissors to benefit from Chinese economic development. What can be expected is that the international and domestic energy prices faced by Chinese companies will be volatile in the future. The impact of energy prices on the macroeconomy cannot be ignored.

This DSGE model, by introducing energy price shocks, can well explain Chinese economic fluctuations. In the future, the model can be further improved by considering government purchases, import and export and other factors or by introducing shocks such as market imperfections and consumer preferences in the model to make it more consistent with the facts of the Chinese economy.

Notes

1 The remaining reserves at the end of the year are divided by the output of the year to get the number of years that the remaining reserves can be exploited at the current production level, that is, the reserves-to-production ratio.

2 Data refers to bp's Statistical Review of World Energy 2020. For more information, please visit the following website: //www.bp.com/en/global/corporate/energy-economics/statistical-review-of-world-energy.html

3 The specific derivation of log-linearization is omitted; whoever may be of interest can contact the author for it.

4 The MATLAB program is rewritten on the basis of the program provided by Uhlig (1997).

Bibliography

Adland, David A. "High Frequency Real Business Cycles." *Journal of Monetary Economics* no. 2 (2001): 271–292.

Balke, Nathan S., Stephen P. A. Brown, and Mine K. Yucel. "Oil Price Shocks and the US Economy: Where Does the Asymmetry Originate?" *The Energy Journal* no. 3 (2002): 27–52.

Bernanke, Ben S., Mark Gertler, and Mark Watson. "Systematic Monetary Policy and the Effects of Oil Price Shocks." *Brookings Papers on Economy Activity* no. 1 (1997): 91–157.

Brown, Stephen P. A., and Mine K. Yucel. "Energy Prices and Aggregate Economic Activity: An Interpretative Survey." *The Quarterly Review of Economics and Finance* no. 2 (2002): 193–208.

Canova, Fabio. "Statistical Inference in Calibrated Models." *Journal of Applied Econometrics* no. 9 (1994): S123–S144.

Chen, Kunting, and Gong Liutang 陈昆亭, 龚六堂. "Growth and Fluctuations in China Economy" 中国经济增长的周期与波动的研究——引入人力资本后的RBC模型. *China Economic Quarterly* no. 4 (2004): 803–803.

Chow, Gregory C., and Kui-Wai Li. "China Economic Growth: 1952–1998." *Economic Development and Culture Change* no. 1 (2002): 247–256.

Dohner, Robert S. "Energy Prices, Economic Activity and Inflation: A Survey of Issues and Results." In *Energy Prices, Inflation and Economic Activity*, edited by Knut Anton Mork. Cambridge: Ballinger, 1981.

Ferderer, J. Peter. "Oil Price Volatility and the Macroeconomy: A Solution to the Asymmetry Puzzle." *Journal of Macroeconomics* no. 1 (1996): 1–16.

Finn, Mary G. "Perfect Competition and the Effects of Energy Price Increases on Economy Activity." *Journal of Money Credit and Banking* no. 3 (2000): 400–416.

Fried, Edward R., and Charles L. Schultz. *Higher Oil Prices and the World Economy: The Adjustment Problem*. The Brookings Institution Press, 1975, p.105.

Gong, Gang 龚刚. "Real Business Cycle: Theory, Empirics and Disputes" 实际商业周期: 理论、检验与争议. *China Economic Quarterly* no. 4 (2004): 785–802.

Greenwood, Jeremy Z., and Gregory W. Hoffman. "Tax Analysis in a Real-Business-Cycle Model." *Journal of Monetary Economics* no. 2 (1991): 167–190.

Hall, Robert E. "The Relation Between Price and Marginal Cost in U.S Industry." *Journal of Political Economics* no. 96 (1988): 309–327.

Hamilton, James D. "Oil and the Macroeconomy Since World War Ⅱ." *Journal of Political Economy* no. 2 (1983): 228–248.

Hansen, Gary D. "Indivisible Labor and the Business Cycle." *Journal of Monetary Economics* no. 3 (1985): 309–327.

He, Xiaoqun, and Wei Taoyuan 何晓群, 魏涛远. "The Impact of the World Oil Price Rise on the Chinese Economy" 世界石油价格上涨对我国经济的影响. *Economic Theory and Business Management* no. 4 (2002): 11–15.

Hooker, Mark A. "Are Oil Shocks Inflationary? Asymmetric and Nonlinear Speciation Versus Changes in Regime." *Journal of Money, Credit and Banking* no. 2 (2002): 540–561.

Huang, Zelin 黄赜林. "A Study on Business Cycle and the Effects of Fiscal Policy in China: An Empirical Study on a RBC Model with Three Sections" 中国经济周期特征与财政政策效应. *Economic Research Journal* no. 6 (2005): 27–39.

Khan, Aubhik, and Julia K. Tomas. "Inventories and the Business Cycle: An Equilibrium Analysis of (S, s) Policies." *The American Economic Review* no. 4 (2007): 1165–1188.

Kydland, Finn E., and Edward F. Prescott. "Time to Build and Aggregate Fluctuations." *Econometrica* no. 6 (1982): 1345–1370.

Li, Haizheng, and Jeffrey S. Zax. "Labor Supply in Urban China." *Journal of Comparative Economics* no. 4 (2003): 795–817.

Lin, Boqiang, and Mou Dunguo 林伯强, 牟敦国. "The Impact of Energy Price Rise on Macroeconomy: An Analyses Based on CGE Method" 能源价格对宏观经济的影响——基于可计算一般均衡的分析. *Economic Research Journal* no. 8 (2008): 88–101.

Long, John B., and Charles I. Plosser. "Real Business Cycles." *Journal of Political Economy*, no. 1 (1983): 39–69.

Pan, Huifeng, and Zhang Jinshui 潘慧峰, 张金水. "The Analysis of Domestic Oil Price Fluctuation Based on ARCH Models" 基于ARCH类模型的国内油价波动分析. *Statistical Research* no. 4 (2005): 16–20.

Sun, Wencun 孙稳存. "Effects of Energy Price Shocks on Chinese Macroeconomy" 能源价格冲击对中国宏观经济的影响. *Economic Theory and Business Management* no. 2 (2007): 31–36.

Xu, Jiangang, Song Peng, and Li Zhiguo 徐剑刚, 宋鹏, 李治国. "Oil Price Shocks and Macroeconomy" 石油价格冲击与宏观经济. *Shanghai Management Science* no. 11 (2006): 6–9.

Zhang, Jun 张军. "Growth, Capital Formation and Technological Choice" 增长、资本形成与技术选择. *China Economic Quarterly* no. 1 (2002): 301–338.

Zhang, Jun, and Zhang Yuan 张军, 章元. "Recalculating the Capital Stock of China" 对中国资本存量K的再估. *Economic Research Journal* no. 7 (2003): 35–90.

9 DSGE analysis with the CNY real exchange rate

Determining the equilibrium real exchange rate of CNY accurately is of great theoretical and policy significance. The factors affecting the CNY exchange rate are numerous and complex, but previous studies capture mainly major variables. Under the framework of new open economy macroeconomics, this chapter builds a dynamic general equilibrium model involving the equilibrium real exchange rate of CNY. It improves the theoretical modeling based on microfoundations and covers as many variables or parameters as possible to examine the formation mechanism of the CNY exchange rate. The results indicate that the improvement or increase of sectoral technological progress, foreign consumption, total volume of export commodities, government nontradable expenditure, foreign real money balance and trade conditions will make the equilibrium real exchange rate of CNY appreciate and that the increase or acceleration of domestic consumption, domestic real currency holding balance and current account balance will make the equilibrium real exchange rate of CNY depreciate. It is found that the model with the CNY exchange rate is in line with economic intuition.

9.1 The CNY real exchange rate

Since 1997, the issue of the CNY exchange rate has become the focus of attention at home and abroad. From 1997 to 2000, people argued about whether CNY was devalued and about its impact on the export trade of China. Since 2002, developed countries, represented by Japan, the United States, and the European Union countries, have insisted that the CNY was seriously undervalued in consideration of China's own interests and that China has dumped Giffen goods into the international market. These countries intended to demand that the CNY be appreciated. There have been many disputes in the theoretical and real worlds both at home and abroad, and it is difficult to reach a quick conclusion.

The nominal exchange rate is affected by many factors and fluctuates frequently. Therefore, it is of little academic value and practical significance to simply argue about the appreciation or stability of the nominal exchange rate of CNY, while it is not the case with the real exchange rate. The real effective

DOI: 10.4324/9781003305651-9

exchange rate (multilateral real exchange rate) is the weighted value of the bilateral real exchange rate of one country and all its important trading partners and competitors, and it measures the average changes of one country's currency relative to the exchange rate of multiple countries. Obstfeld (2002) argued that the most important asset value in an economy is the real exchange rate and that changes in the real exchange rate would adjust the prices of factors of production in the tradable and nontradable sectors of a country and promote the transfer of these factors from sectors with low efficiency to sectors with high efficiency, thus affecting the economic growth of a country.

The equilibrium real exchange rate works as a frame of reference to judge whether the real exchange rate is reasonable. Williamson (1985) explained equilibrium real exchange rate as the real exchange rate that achieves internal equilibrium and external equilibrium simultaneously. An internal equilibrium means the supply and demand of the market for nontradables can be balanced at present and in the future, and the unemployment rate is in a "natural" state. An external equilibrium is the budget constraint in which the discounted sum of a country's current account is equal to zero and is bound to match the current account balance with long-term sustainable capital flows. With the rise of the Chinese economy in the world, CNY should also become an international currency. Determining the equilibrium real value of CNY accurately is conducive not only to international trade balance, the optimal allocation of resources in the global world, but also to mutual understanding between China and the world economy.

The international literature reviewing equilibrium real exchange rate mainly includes four aspects.

First, purchasing power parity theory (PPP) and its extension: Kassel, a Swedish economist, proposed the PPP theory, which claims that a basket of goods is priced in the same currency in different countries and that the final price is the same; that is, the real exchange rate is equal to constant 1, or it will quickly return to 1 under the condition of external shocks. Nevertheless, this is based on the international trade theory and only considers the mutual pricing of currencies in the process of the exchange of goods and services between two countries, without considering the influence of other factors on exchange rate pricing. In response to the limits of the PPP theory, Balassa–Samuelson (1964) proposed the role of productivity in determining the long-term exchange rate. When the productivity of a country's tradable sector grows faster than that of its nontradable sector, the price level of its nontradable goods will rise faster than that of the other country, leading to an appreciation trend of its currency relative to the other country's currency. Sector productivity difference, instead of purchasing power parity, determines the real exchange rate. According to this hypothesis, the countries with rapid economic growth are accompanied by real appreciation of their currencies, known as the Balassa–Samuelson effect.

Second, an empirical model of equilibrium exchange rate under the partial equilibrium framework: Williamson (1985) proposed the theory of fundamental equilibrium exchange rate (FEER), which refers to a standardized equilibrium exchange rate that is expected on the basis of macroeconomic equilibrium. Zhang (1999) contended that FEER theory gave up short-term cyclical conditions and temporary factors, focused on fundamental economic factors and measured the standardized exchange. While adopting the FEER method, many macroeconomic equilibrium models need to be built, and a large number of parameters need to be estimated. For developed countries and regions with complete and detailed economic data, it is a feasible method to estimate equilibrium exchange rate. However, it does not work in the case of developing countries.

Third, a single-equation model under the framework of reduced general equilibrium: Instead of calculating the real exchange rate when both an internal equilibrium and an external equilibrium are realized, the behavioral equilibrium exchange rate (BEER) uses the determinants of the real exchange rate to estimate FEER. Clark and MacDonald (1998) argued that, in the behavioral sense, the real exchange rate is in equilibrium, which means that, in the statistical sense, the change of realistic real exchange rate reflects the change of related economic factors. Due to BEER's strong applicability, some Chinese scholars have studied the real exchange rate of CNY based on this method.

Fourth, an empirical model of equilibrium exchange rate under the general equilibrium framework: The main steps of this method are as follows: Build a general equilibrium analytical framework, define the determinants and determine the mechanisms of the equilibrium exchange rate level, and then calculate the corresponding equilibrium exchange rate under the general equilibrium framework. The popular empirical model of the exchange rate under the general equilibrium framework is the Devarajan–Lewis–Robinson (DLR) model. It consists of eight equations. The key is to calculate two kinds of elasticity: demand substitution elasticity and supply transfer elasticity.

Chinese scholars' research on the CNY exchange rate can be summarized in terms of the following three aspects:

First, system and institutional analysis: In light of the system and institutional limits and obstacles in China, such as the partly opened capital account, the incomplete foreign exchange market (including forward transactions), the rigid exchange rate adjustment mechanism, and ineffective exchange rate policies, Li and Yu (2005), Zhang (2005), Xia and Chen (2006), Chen and Wang (2002), Yang (2003), Zhang (2000) and Zhang (2004) pointed out that the currency mismatch posed a major risk in the course of the exchange rate reform in China and proposed to reform the foreign exchange management system, return to the managed floating exchange rate regime, expand the floating range of the CNY exchange rate at the right time and strengthen the prudential supervision for currency mismatches.

Second, mathematical model research: Few Chinese scholars have adopted this method. Pu and Tyers (2001) estimated the equilibrium real effective exchange rate of CNY by building the extended DLR three-commodity general equilibrium model. They were the first to adopt the general equilibrium analysis method, which incorporated the microbehaviors of enterprises into the analysis of the equilibrium CNY exchange rate by introducing a production function. Their analysis, however, is static or comparative static. Yao (2007) built the structural model of the CNY exchange rate system selection, which took into consideration the influence of the microbehavior of consumers and manufacturers on the equilibrium CNY exchange rate. The macromodel thus had microfoundations. Unfortunately, the final equation of exchange rate was not obtained, and the paper only carried out the simulation analysis of the CNY exchange rate.

Third, econometric empirical research: Jin (1995), Zhang (1999), Lin (2002), Shi and Yu (2005) and others established the cointegration function of the equilibrium CNY exchange rate by means of cointegration analysis, the BEER method and the Hsiao program, figured out the medium- and long-term factors affecting the equilibrium CNY exchange rate, and estimated the equilibrium CNY real exchange rate and the degree of exchange rate mismatch.

The previous literature has done a lot of research in relation to the overvaluation or undervaluation of the CNY real exchange rate, but there are also several limits: First, the foundation of the existing mathematical model for the measurement of the CNY exchange rate is not solid enough, reducing the effectiveness of the model and even resulting in "the lack of theories" in the quantitative analysis.[1] Second, the mathematical model is based on the Keynesian economic framework, lacks microfoundations, and only carries out static or comparative static analysis; concerning dynamic analysis, it often does not distinguish between long- and short-term factors that affect the real exchange rate. Third, in reality, the factors that affect the real exchange rate level include external factors, such as trade terms, sustainable current account balance, foreign interest rate etc., and also domestic policy factors, such as money supply, government expenditure structure, tax rate, domestic supply side factors, such as labor productivity and the speed of technological progress. In the process of building the model with the CNY exchange rate, some factors are always captured through the hypotheses of researchers, while some quite important factors are ignored, thus making the variable selection and parameter determination of the model more subjective and arbitrary.

This chapter uses the method of intertemporal dynamic general equilibrium analysis under the new open-economy macroeconomics framework to build the model with the CNY real exchange rate. It aims to involve as many variables and parameters as possible in order to present the microfoundations. It is more general than previous models and can capture the ways that various variables and parameters affect exchange rate—the exchange rate formation mechanism. In the analysis of external equilibrium, this method does not require the absolute equilibrium of the balance of payments; that is, the current account is zero in each period, but only the intertemporal net present value of the current account is zero. In this aspect, this method is in agreement with the stylized facts of the Chinese economy.

9.2 Model building

The model in this chapter is built under the framework of the new open-economy macroeconomics (Obstfeld and Rogoff, 1995, 1999), combined with the equilibrium real exchange rate theory of developing countries proposed by Elbadawi and Soto (2005). For the convenience of description and calculation, the real exchange rate in the model is defined as the relative price of nontradables versus tradables. Thus an increase in the value of the real exchange rate indicates an appreciation of the real exchange rate; otherwise, a depreciation. The equilibrium exchange rate is defined as the real exchange rate at which the domestic market of nontradables reaches equilibrium and the current account balance reaches sustainable balance. There are some similarities and differences between the internal and external equilibria of this model and the previous exchange rate equilibrium theories. Similarly, the realization of the equilibrium exchange rate must be based on the realization of internal and external equilibria. This equilibrium differs from the previous exchange rate equilibrium in that the external equilibrium of this model is not the absolute equilibrium of the balance of payments but the sustainable balance of the current account. The absolute equilibrium of the balance of payments means that the current account balance has to be zero in each period and that the sustainable balance of the current account only requires that the intertemporal net present value of the current account is zero.

9.2.1 Fundamental assumptions

The main assumptions of this model are as follows. First, there are only two categories of countries in the world—the country and its foreign counterparts. The country is the receiver of the international market price relative to its foreign counterparts. The model assumes that China is the receiver of world commodity prices for the following reasons: the insufficient negotiation ability of China in the world commodity market and financial market, the unaccomplished integration of the financial market and the closed capital account. Second, there are three categories of goods in the market: exports (X), imports (M) and nontradables (N). The country produces exports and nontradables. The representative household consumes these three kinds of goods at the same time, but the government consumes only imports and nontradables; the government levies residents on three categories of goods at the tax rates τ^X, τ^M, τ^N (the first two mainly refer to tariff tax, and the latter mainly refers to consumption tax). The government's tax revenue is still returned to the public in order to maintain a balanced government budget. Third, the property held by households consists of two parts: bond (b) and money (m). Bond can be freely transferred internationally, but there is a certain transfer cost (μ). The size of (μ) reflects the degree of capital control, and the larger μ is, the more severe capital control is. Fourth, households everywhere are risk averse, seeking to maximize expected utility; enterprises are of a risk-neutral type, pursuing the maximization of current profits; households' expectation of tariff rate is assumed to be static, or constant. This model determines the consumption behaviors of households and labor demand behaviors of enterprises through the intertemporal optimization of households and the periodic optimization of enterprises and then obtains the equilibrium value of the internal real exchange rate under the conditions of specific government policies and external constraints.

9.2.2 Household optimization behavior

The utility function of the representative household is:

$$u(C_t, m_t, n_t) = \frac{c_t^{1-\sigma} - 1}{1-\sigma} + \kappa \frac{m_t^{1-\chi} - 1}{1-\chi} + \eta \frac{(1-n_t)^{1-\gamma} - 1}{1-\gamma} \tag{9.1}$$

where c_t represents consumption set, and m_t represents real money holding. The representative household provides the nontradable goods sector and the export sector, respectively, with labor n_t^N and n_t^X, and $n_t = n_t^N + n_t^X$. In view of the stylized facts of the Chinese economy, it is assumed total labor supply is not fixed.

The total consumption of households consists of nontradables c_t^N and international tradables c_t^T, while $c_t^T = (c_t^X)^{1-\omega}(c_t^M)^{\omega}$. The total household consumption is:

$$c_t = (c_t^N)^{1-\alpha}(c_t^T)^{\alpha} = (c_t^N)^{1-\alpha}[(c_t^X)^{1-\omega}(c_t^M)^{\omega}]^{\alpha} \tag{9.2}$$

where α and ω, respectively, represent the interperiod elasticity of substitution between tradable and nontradable sectors and within tradable sectors, and $0 < \alpha,\ \omega < 1$.

Households hold negotiable bonds b_t and domestic money m_t in the international market in order to proceed with intertemporal wealth distribution. The household budget constraint is:

$$\begin{aligned}&(1 + i_t - \mu_t)b_{t-1} + m_{t-1} + w_t(n_t^N + n_t^X)\\ &= b_t + m_t + (1 + \tau_t^N)p_t^N c_t^N + (1 + \tau_t^M)p_t^M c_t^M + (1 + \tau_t^X)p_t^X c_t^X\end{aligned} \tag{9.3}$$

The left side of the budget constraint equation represents the sources of household wealth: the bond principal of the previous period and its return part (the interest rate i_t is the rate of return, and μ_t is the transaction cost), the currency holding balance of the previous period, and the current labor income (w_t is the real wage level, which is the same in all sectors).[2] The right side of the equation represents the use of household wealth, which consists of bond purchases and consumption (tax included). $1 + r_t - \mu_t$ represents the cost of raising funds.

Under the constraints of equations 9.2 and 9.3, the household maximizes equation 9.1, and the arbitrage conditions of relative prices within the period can be represented as:

$$\frac{p_t^M}{p_t^N} = \frac{(1+\tau_t^N)}{(1+\tau_t^M)} \frac{\alpha\omega}{1-\alpha} \frac{c_t^N}{c_t^M} \tag{9.4a}$$

$$\frac{p_t^M}{p_t^X} = \frac{(1+\tau_t^X)}{(1+\tau_t^M)} \frac{\omega}{1-\omega} \frac{c_t^X}{c_t^M} \tag{9.4b}$$

These arbitrage conditions indicate how consumption of different goods should be redistributed when relative prices or taxes change.

The domestic general price index P_t can be obtained by minimizing the unit cost of household consumption:

$$P_t = \frac{\left[(1+\tau_t^N)P_t^N\right]^{1-\alpha}\left[(1+\tau_t^M)P_t^M\right]^{\alpha\omega}\left[(1+\tau_t^X)P_t^X\right]^{\alpha(1-\omega)}}{(1-\alpha)^{1-\alpha}(\alpha\omega)^{\alpha\omega}\left(\alpha(1-\omega)\right)^{\alpha(1-\omega)}} \tag{9.5}$$

where P_t^N, P_t^M and P_t^X (represented by capital letters) represent the nominal price levels of the corresponding goods:

$$p_t^N = \frac{P_t^N}{P_t} = \frac{\alpha^\alpha(1-\alpha)^\alpha}{(1+\tau_t^N)^{1-\alpha}} RER_t^\alpha \tag{9.6a}$$

$$p_t^X = \frac{P_t^X}{P_t} = \frac{(1-\alpha)^{1-\alpha}\alpha^\alpha\omega^\omega(1-\omega)^{1-\omega}}{(1+\tau_t^M)^\omega(1+\tau_t^X)^{1-\omega}(1+\tau_t^N)^{1-\alpha}} \frac{TOT_t^\omega}{RER_t^{1-\alpha}} \tag{9.6b}$$

where $TOT_t = P_t^X / P_t^M$ represents the trade terms, and $RER_t = P_t^N / P_t^T$ represents the internal real exchange rate. A rise in this value means appreciation, while a decline means depreciation.

9.2.3 Enterprise production behaviors

It is assumed that the production function of domestic nontradable goods and export tradable goods follow the following equations:

$$y_t^N = A_t^N(n_t^N)^\gamma \tag{9.7a}$$

$$y_t^X = A_t^X(n_t^X)^\vartheta \tag{9.7b}$$

A_t represents the total factor productivity (TEP) of each sector; γ and ϑ represent the labor intensity of nontradable and export tradable sectors, respectively; and $0 < \vartheta < \gamma < 1$. Given the production function, the relative output of domestic sectors can be obtained by maximizing the profits of enterprises:

$$\frac{y_t^X}{y_t^N} = \frac{A_t^{X\frac{1}{1-\vartheta}}}{A_t^{N\frac{1}{1-\gamma}}} \frac{\vartheta^{\frac{\vartheta}{1-\vartheta}}}{\gamma^{\frac{\gamma}{1-\gamma}}} \frac{\left(p_t^X\right)^{\frac{\vartheta}{1-\vartheta}}}{\left(p_t^N\right)^{\frac{\gamma}{1-\gamma}}} w_t^{\left(\frac{\gamma}{1-\gamma}-\frac{\vartheta}{1-\vartheta}\right)} \tag{9.8}$$

It shows that, relative to the nontradable goods sector, the output of the export goods sector depends on relative technological progress, the relative price and real wages. If $\gamma = \vartheta$, that is, when the labor intensity of the nontradable and tradable sectors is equal, real wages have no effect on relative output.

9.2.4 Government behavior

The government receives revenue from the consumption tax on tradables and nontradables and spends the income on nontradables N and imports M, represented by g_t^N, g_t^M respectively (it is assumed that the government does not consume exports X). The government is subject to the budget constraint:

$$m_t - m_{t-1} + \tau_t^N p_t^N c_t^N + \tau_t^X p_t^X c_t^X + \tau_t^M p_t^M c_t^M - p_t^N g_t^N - p_t^M g_t^M = 0 \tag{9.9}$$

9.2.5 Current account balance

Combining the household budget constraint and government budget constraint, the following can be obtained:

$$b_t - (1 + r_t - \mu_t) b_{t-1} = p_t^N (y_t^N - c_t^N - g_t^N) + p_t^X (y_t^X - c_t^X) - p_t^M (c_t^M + g_t^M) \tag{9.10}$$

In equilibrium, the supply of domestic nontradable goods should equal the demand. Therefore, the first term on the right side of the equation is zero, and the last two terms reflect the balance of the trade balance. Using the interperiod arbitrage condition (referred as equation 9.4b), the consumption demand of nontradable goods is used to represent the consumption demand of domestic exported tradable goods, and it is assumed that the government's consumption of imported goods is θ_M times that of household's consumption of imported goods, i.e., $g_t^M = \theta_M c_t^M$, so the following can be obtained:

$$b_t - (1 + r_t - \mu_t) b_{t-1} = p_t^X y_t^X - p_t^M c_t^M \phi_t \tag{9.11}$$

of which

$$\phi_t = \left[\frac{(1+\tau_t^M)}{(1+\tau_t^X)} \frac{(1-\omega)}{\omega} + (1+\theta_M) \right].$$

Based on the definition of current account balance and the preceding equation, the following can be obtained:

$$ca_t = b_t - b_{t-1} = p_t^X y_t^X + (r_t - \mu_t) b_{t-1} - p_t^M c_t^M \phi_t \tag{9.12}$$

9.2.6 Equilibrium price and equilibrium exchange rate

Based on the arbitrage conditions of imports and exports of tradables and nontradables, referred to as equations 9.4a and 9.4b, and the budget constraint of households and governments, referred to as equations 9.3 and 9.9, the equilibrium price of nontradables can be:

$$(p_t^N)^{\frac{1}{1-\gamma}} = \frac{k_1}{y_t^X} (p_t^X)^{\frac{\vartheta}{1-\vartheta}} \left(\frac{(1-n_t)^{-\xi}}{c_t^{1-\sigma}} \right)^{\left(\frac{\gamma}{1-\gamma} - \frac{\vartheta}{1-\vartheta}\right)} (k_2)^{\left(\frac{1}{1-\gamma} - \frac{\vartheta}{1-\vartheta}\right)} \tag{9.13}$$

of which

$$k_1 = \frac{A_t^{X\frac{1}{1-\vartheta}} \vartheta^{\frac{\vartheta}{1-\vartheta}}}{A_t^{N\frac{1}{1-\gamma}} \gamma^{\frac{\gamma}{1-\gamma}}} \left(\frac{\eta(1+\tau_t^N)}{(1-\alpha)(1+\theta_N)} \right)^{\left(\frac{\gamma}{1-\gamma} - \frac{\vartheta}{1-\vartheta}\right)}, \theta_N = \frac{g_t^N}{c_t^N}$$

$$k_2 = \frac{(1-\alpha)(1+\tau_t^M)(1+\theta_N)[p_t^X y_t^X + (r_t - \mu_t) b_{t-1} - ca_t]}{\alpha\omega(1+\tau_t^N)\phi_t}$$

where y_t^X is composed of domestic consumption c_t^X and the final exports of one country; that is, $y_t^X = c_t^X + c_t^{M*}$. c_t^{M*} represents the final exports of one country or imports of the rest of the world.

The foreign representative household is faced with the optimization problem similar to the domestic representative household.

According to the first-order conditions of household optimization, the following can be obtained:

$$\kappa m_t^{-\gamma} = \lambda_t - \beta\lambda_{t+1}, \lambda_t - \beta\lambda_{t+1} = \beta\lambda_{t+1}(i_{t+1} - \mu_{t+1}), \lambda_t = \frac{\alpha\omega c_t^{1-\sigma}}{(1+\tau_t^M) p_t^M c_t^M}$$

Thus

$$c_t^M = \frac{\alpha\beta\omega c_t^{1-\sigma}}{(1+\tau_t^M)p_t^M \kappa m_{t-1}^{-\gamma}}(i_t - \mu_t)$$

Similarly,

$$c_t^{M*} = \frac{\alpha\beta\omega(c_t^*)^{1-\sigma}}{(1+\tau_t^{M*})p_t^{M*}\kappa(m_{t-1}^*)^{-\gamma}}(i_t - \mu_t)$$

when

$$k_3 = \left(\frac{(1-\omega)c_t^{1-\sigma}}{m_{t-1}^{-\gamma}} + \frac{\omega(c_t^*)^{1-\sigma}}{(m_{t-1}^*)^{-\gamma}}\right)(i_t - \mu_t)$$

the following equation is obtained:

$$y_t^X = \frac{\alpha\beta k_3}{\kappa(1+\tau_t^X)p_t^X}$$

Thus the equilibrium real price of nontradables can be:

$$(p_t^N)^{\frac{1}{1-\gamma}} = \frac{k_1}{\dfrac{\alpha\beta k_3}{\kappa(1+\tau_t^X)p_t^X}}(p_t^X)^{\frac{\vartheta}{1-\vartheta}}\left(\frac{(1-n_t)^{-\xi}}{c_t^{1-\sigma}}\right)^{\left(\frac{\gamma}{1-\gamma}-\frac{\vartheta}{1-\vartheta}\right)}(k_2)^{\left(\frac{1}{1-\gamma}-\frac{\vartheta}{1-\vartheta}\right)} \quad (9.14)$$

Substituting the preceding equation into the equations for p_t^N (9.6a) and for p_t^X (9.6b), the real exchange rate can be:

$$[RER_t]^{\frac{1-\alpha}{1-\theta}+\frac{\alpha}{1-\gamma}} = \frac{k_1\kappa}{\alpha\beta k_3}\left(\frac{(1-n_t)^{-\xi}}{c_t^{1-\sigma}}\right)^{\left(\frac{\gamma}{1-\gamma}-\frac{\vartheta}{1-\vartheta}\right)} TOT_t^{\frac{\omega}{1-\vartheta}}(k_2)^{\left(\frac{1}{1-\gamma}-\frac{\vartheta}{1-\vartheta}\right)}\cdot \frac{\alpha^{\frac{\alpha}{1-\vartheta}-\frac{\alpha}{1-\gamma}}(1-\alpha)^{\frac{1-\alpha}{1-\vartheta}-\frac{\alpha}{1-\gamma}}\omega^{\frac{\omega}{1-\vartheta}}(1-\omega)^{\frac{1-\omega}{1-\vartheta}}(1+\tau_t^N)^{\frac{1-\alpha}{1-\gamma}-\frac{1-\alpha}{1-\vartheta}}}{(1+\tau_t^M)^{\frac{\omega}{1-\vartheta}}(1+\tau_t^X)^{\frac{1-\omega}{1-\vartheta}-1}} \quad (9.15)$$

Equation 9.15 is exactly the equilibrium real exchange rate of CNY. This equation generally presents the relationship between the numerous variables and parameters affecting the exchange rate and the equilibrium real exchange rate.

9.3 Factors affecting the equilibrium real exchange rate

According to equation 9.15, the factors affecting the equilibrium real exchange rate can be summarized into four kinds.

First, the factors of supply:

$$\frac{\partial \log RER_t}{\partial \log A_t^N} = -\frac{\dfrac{1}{1-\gamma}}{\dfrac{1-\alpha}{1-\theta}+\dfrac{\alpha}{1-\gamma}} < 0 \tag{9.16}$$

Equation 9.16 shows the effect of a country's overall technological progress on the equilibrium exchange rate when the sectoral relative technological progress remains unchanged. Overall, technological progress usually affects the equilibrium real exchange rate in two ways: On the one hand, it increases the international competitiveness of the country's tradable goods sector and improves trade balances; achieving the sustainable current account balance as the external equilibrium constraint requires the real exchange rate's appreciation; on the other hand, it will lead to an increase in the supply of nontradable goods. In order to achieve internal equilibrium, the real exchange rate is required to depreciate. The results of this model show that overall technological progress has a smaller effect on the equilibrium real exchange rate's appreciation than on its depreciation. It means overall technological progress will lead to the equilibrium exchange rate's depreciation.

Second, the factors of demand: The domestic and foreign consumption's effects on the equilibrium real exchange rate can be represented as:

$$\frac{\partial \log RER_t}{\partial c_t} = \frac{(1-\sigma)c_t^{-1}}{\dfrac{1-\alpha}{1-\theta}+\dfrac{\alpha}{1-\gamma}}\left[-\left(\frac{\gamma}{1-\gamma}-\frac{\vartheta}{1-\vartheta}\right)-1\right] < 0 \tag{9.17}$$

$$\frac{\partial \log RER_t}{\partial c_t^*} = \omega(1-\sigma)(c_t^*)^{-\sigma}(m_{t-1}^*)^{\gamma}\frac{1}{k_3} > 0 \tag{9.18}$$

As can be seen, an increase in domestic consumption leads to the equilibrium real exchange rate's depreciation; an increase in foreign consumption leads to the equilibrium real exchange rate's appreciation.

In terms of the effect of the change in the total amount of exports ($p_t^X y_t^X$) on the real exchange rate, when $p_t^X y_t^X = X_t$, the following equation is obtained:

$$\frac{\partial \log RER_t}{\partial X_t} = \frac{\dfrac{1}{1-\gamma}-\dfrac{\theta}{1-\theta}}{\dfrac{1-\alpha}{1-\theta}+\dfrac{\alpha}{1-\gamma}}\cdot\frac{1}{p_t^X y_t^X+(r_t-\mu_t)b_{t-1}-ca_t} > 0 \tag{9.19}$$

It can be seen that an increase in the total amount of exports causes the equilibrium real exchange rate's appreciation.

Third, the factors of policy needs: The effect of structural changes of government consumption expenditure on the equilibrium real exchange rate can be represented as:

$$\frac{\partial \log RER_t}{\partial \theta_{Nt}} = \frac{1}{\dfrac{1-\alpha}{1-\theta} + \dfrac{\alpha}{1-\gamma}} \cdot \frac{1}{1+\theta_N} > 0 \tag{9.20}$$

Equation 9.20 reflects the effect of government consumption expenditure of nontradables, that is, the effect of changes in the ratio of government consumption expenditure of nontradables on the equilibrium real exchange rate. The increase in the ratio of government consumption expenditure on nontradables causes the equilibrium exchange rate's appreciation: The increase in the ratio of government consumption expenditure on nontradables will reinforce the demand for nontradables, reduce the demand for imports, and cause the price of nontradables to rise and the price of imports to fall, eventually leading to the appreciation of the equilibrium real exchange rate. The impact of changes in the ratio of government spending of imports (θ_{Mt}) on the real exchange rate cannot be determined as positive or negative.

The effect of the changes of real money supply on equilibrium real exchange rate can be represented as:

$$\frac{\partial \log RER_t}{\partial m_{t-1}} = \frac{1}{\dfrac{1-\alpha}{1-\theta} + \dfrac{\alpha}{1-\gamma}} \cdot \frac{1}{k_3} (\omega - 1) c_t^{1-\sigma} \gamma m_{t-1}^{\gamma-1} < 0 \tag{9.21}$$

$$\frac{\partial \log RER_t}{\partial m^*_{t-1}} = \frac{1}{\dfrac{1-\alpha}{1-\theta} + \dfrac{\alpha}{1-\gamma}} \cdot \frac{1}{k_3} \omega\gamma (c_t^*)^{1-\sigma} (m^*_{t-1})^{\gamma-1} > 0 \tag{9.22}$$

Equations 9.21 and 9.22 represent domestic real money balance effect and foreign real money balance effect. The former refers to the effect of the changes of domestic real money holding balance on the equilibrium real exchange rate, while the latter refers to the effect of the change of the foreign real money holding balance on the equilibrium real exchange rate. According to equations 9.21 and 9.22, the rise of the domestic real money holding balance will lead to the depreciation of the equilibrium real exchange rate, while the rise of the foreign real money holding balance will lead to the appreciation of the equilibrium real exchange rate.

Fourth, the factors of external environment: The effect of changes of trade terms on the equilibrium real exchange rate can be represented as:

$$\frac{\partial \log RER_t}{\partial TOT_t} = \frac{\frac{\omega}{1-\theta}}{\frac{1-\alpha}{1-\theta}+\frac{\alpha}{1-\gamma}} \cdot \frac{1}{TOT_t} > 0 \tag{9.23}$$

An improvement in the trade terms will lead to an appreciation of the equilibrium real exchange rate. Generally speaking, the effect of the improvement in the trade terms on the real exchange rate is uncertain. On the one hand, if imports and exports are inelastic, the improvement in trade terms will increase export income relative to import expenditure, thereby improving the current account balance. Achieving the sustainable current account balance as the external equilibrium constraint requires the real exchange rate's appreciation. On the other hand, if the imports and exports are of the elastic type, the improvement in trade terms will be offset by the income effect and the substitution effect, and the final effect on the current account balance will be uncertain. Thus the effect on the equilibrium real exchange rate becomes uncertain. However, in this model, the improvement of the trade terms will lead to the appreciation of the equilibrium real exchange rate.

The effect of the changes in the current account balance on the equilibrium real exchange rate can be represented as:

$$\frac{\partial \log RER_t}{\partial ca_t} = \frac{\frac{1}{1-\gamma}-\frac{\theta}{1-\theta}}{\frac{1-\alpha}{1-\theta}+\frac{\alpha}{1-\gamma}} \cdot \frac{-1}{p_t^X y_t^X + (r_t - \mu_t) b_{t-1} - ca_t} < 0 \tag{9.24}$$

According to equation 9.24, an increase in the current account balance will lead to the depreciation of the equilibrium real exchange rate.

9.4 Conclusion

Through the modeling research on the CNY equilibrium real exchange rate, it is found that foreign consumption, government expenditure on nontradables, the total volume of exports, foreign real money balance, the improvement of the terms of trade terms will make the CNY equilibrium real exchange rate appreciate. The overall technological progress, domestic consumption, domestic real money balance and the rise of the current account balance will make the CNY equilibrium real exchange rate depreciate. The research results of the model involving the exchange rate matches with economic intuition.

The policy implication is that the CNY equilibrium real exchange rate is a dynamic concept. The central bank should establish a dynamic monitoring system for the CNY equilibrium real exchange rate, have a sense of the effect of exchange rate levels in a period on macroeconomic indexes and use various macroeconomic indexes to calculate the real equilibrium of the period to predict trends of the market-oriented exchange rate in the next period. This will work as a reference for adjusting the exchange rate policy. The mathematical model in this chapter works as a significant reference for understanding the formation mechanism of the CNY exchange rate and constructing the exchange rate monitoring system.

Future research of the CNY equilibrium real exchange rate can introduce economic structural factors, for the industrial structure, the labor market structure and the urban–rural dual structure all largely affect the real exchange rate. The interactive mechanism between the CNY real exchange rate and these structural factors is worth further exploring.

Notes

1 For instance, Lin (2002), Shi and Yu (2005) and others had no theoretical models in the selection of explanatory variables of the quantitative model.

2 In this model, except the nominal interest rate, the capital letters represent the nominal variables, and the lowercase letters represent the real variables corresponding to the nominal variables after adjusting the total price level.

Bibliography

Balassa, Bela. "The Purchasing Power Parity Doctrine: A Reappraisal." *Journal of Political Economy* no. 6 (1964): 584–596.

Bu, Yongxiang, and Rod Tyers 卜永祥,. "The Equilibrium Real Exchange Rate: An Aggregated General Equilibrium Analysis" 中国均衡实际有效汇率: 一个总量一般均衡分析. *Economic Research Journal* no. 6 (2001): 21–32+96.

Chen, Ping, and Wang Xi 陈平, 王曦. "A Non-Equilibrium Analysis of CNY Exchange Rate and the Macro-Efficiency of Exchange Rate System" 人民币汇率的非均衡分析与汇率制度的宏观效率. *Economic Research Journal* no. 6 (2002): 23–31+94.

Clark, Peter B., and Ronald MacDonald. "Exchange Rates and Economic Fundamentals: A Methodological Comparison of BEERs and FEERs." IMF Working Paper 9867, 1998.

Edwards, Sebastian. "Real Exchange Rate in the Developing Countries: Concept and Measurement." NBER Working Paper 2950, 1989.

Elbadawi, Ibrahim, and Raimundo Soto. "Theory and Empirics of Real Exchange Rates in Sub-Saharan Africa and Other Developing Countries" (unpublished mimeo). Development Economic Research Group, World Bank, November 2005.

Jin, Zhongxia 金中夏. "The Reform of Real Exchange Rate Management in China" 论中国实际汇率管理改革. *Economic Research Journal* no. 3 (1995): 63–71.

Li, Yang, and Yu Weibin 李扬, 余维彬. "The Reform of CNY Exchange Rate System: Return to Managed Floating" 人民币汇率制度改革：回归有管理的浮动. *Economic Research Journal* no. 4 (2005): 24–31+53.

Lin, Boqiang 林伯强. "Estimating the CNY Equilibrium Real Exchange Rate and Measuring Real Exchange Rate Misalignment" 人民币均衡实际汇率的估计与实际汇率错位的测算. *Economic Research Journal* no. 12 (2002): 60–69+92.

Lu, Feng, and Han Xiaoya 卢锋, 韩晓亚. "Economic Growth and Real Exchange Rate Changes: Balassa-Samuelson Effect Hypothesis and Empirical Evidence" 长期经济成长与实际汇率演变—巴拉萨-萨缪尔森效应假说及其经验证据. *Economic Research Journal* no. 7 (2006): 4–14.

Obstfeld, Maurice. "Inflation-Targeting, Exchange-Rate Pass-Through, and Volatility." *The American Economic Review* no. 2 (2002): 102–107.

Obstfeld, Maurice, and Kenneth Rogoff. "Exchange Rate Dynamics Redux." *Journal of Political Economy* no. 3 (1995): 624–660.

———. "New Direction for Stochastic Open Economy Models." NBER Working Paper 7313, 1999.

Samuelson, Paul A. "Theoretical Notes on Trade Problem." *Review of Economics and Statistics* no. 2 (1964): 145–154.

Shi, Jianhuai, and Yu Haifeng 施建淮, 余海丰. "Equilibrium CNY Exchange Rate and Exchange Rate Misalignment: 1991–2004" 人民币均衡汇率与汇率失调：1991-2004. *Economic Research Journal* no. 4 (2005): 34–45.

Williamson, John. *The Exchange Rate System.* Cambridge and London: MIT Press for the Institute of International Economics, 1985.

Williamson, John, and Molly Mahar. *A Survey of Financial Liberalization.* Princeton: Princeton Essays in International Finance, no. 211, 1998.

Xia, Bin, and Chen Daofu 夏斌，陈道富. "The Exchange Reform of China Under the Unbalance of International Monetary System" 国际货币体系失衡下的中国汇率政策. *Economic Research Journal* no. 2 (2006): 4–15.

Yang, Fan 杨帆. "Theory and Policy: Discussing the Trend of CNY Exchange Rate" 理论与政策：关于人民币汇率走势的讨论. *Management World* no. 6 (2006): 33–42.

Yao, Bin 姚斌. "Research on the Choice of CNY Exchange Rate Regime: A Quantitative Analysis Based on the Welfare" 人民币汇率制度选择的研究——基于福利的数量分析. *Economic Research Journal* no. 11 (2007): 45–57.

Zhang, Bin 张斌. "CNY Exchange Rate Revaluation and Exchange Rate Regime Reform from the Perspective of Equilibrium Exchange Rate Theory" 人民币汇率重估与汇率制度改革——基于均衡汇率理论的视角. *Management World* no. 3 (2004): 58–66.

Zhang, Shuguang 张曙光. "CNY Exchange Rate: Appreciation and Cost-Benefit Analysis" 人民币汇率问题: 升值及其成本—收益分析. *Economic Research Journal* no. 5 (2005): 17–30.

Zhang, Xiaopu 张晓朴. "Theory and Model of the CNY Equilibrium Exchange Rate" 人民币均衡汇率的理论与模型. *Economic Research Journal* no. 12 (1999): 70–77.

———. "Thoughts on the Mid- and Long-term Reform of CNY Exchange Rate Mechanism" 关于人民币汇率机制中长期改革的几点思考. *Management World* no. 1 (2000): 136–139.

Appendix

In terms of household maximization, under the budget constraint shown as equation 9.3, the maximization is represented by equation 9.1. According to the first-order condition, the following equations can be obtained:

$$\lambda_t(1+\tau_t^N)p_t^N c_t^N = (1-\alpha)c_t^{1-\sigma},\quad \lambda_t(1+\tau_t^X)p_t^X c_t^X = \alpha(1-\omega)c_t^{1-\sigma},$$
$$\lambda_t(1+\tau_t^M)p_t^M c_t^M = \alpha\omega c_t^{1-\sigma}$$
$$\lambda_t w_t = \eta(1-n_t)^{-\xi},\quad \lambda_t = \beta\lambda_{t+1}(1+i_{t+1}-\mu_{t+1}),\quad \lambda_t = \beta\lambda_{t+1} + \kappa m_t^{-\gamma},$$

Of which λ_t represents the Lagrange multiplier. Equations 9.4a and 9.4b in the text can be obtained based on the preceding equations. According to the first-order conditions of consumers' cost minimization, the following equation can be obtained:

$$P_t^N = \lambda P_t \frac{c_t}{c_t^N}\frac{1-\alpha}{1+\tau_t^N},\quad P_t^M = \lambda P_t \frac{c_t}{c_t^M}\frac{\alpha\omega}{1+\tau_t^M},\quad P_t^X = \lambda P_t \frac{c_t}{c_t^X}\frac{\alpha(1-\omega)}{1+\tau_t^X}, \tag{A1}$$

Substituting equation A1 into $P_t\left(c_t^N\right)^{1-\alpha}\left[\left(c_t^M\right)^{\omega}\left(c_t^X\right)^{1-\omega}\right]^{\alpha} = 1$, the domestic price index is:

$$P_t = \frac{\lambda\left[(1+\tau_t^N)P_t^N\right]^{1-\alpha}\left[(1+\tau_t^M)P_t^M\right]^{\alpha\omega}\left[(1+\tau_t^X)P_t^X\right]^{\alpha(1-\omega)}}{(1-\alpha)^{1-\alpha}(\alpha\omega)^{\alpha\omega}\left(\alpha(1-\omega)\right)^{\alpha(1-\omega)}} \tag{A2}$$

Similarly, the price index of tradables is:

$$P_t^T = \frac{\lambda\left[(1+\tau_t^M)P_t^M\right]^{\omega}\left[(1+\tau_t^X)P_t^X\right]^{1-\omega}}{\omega^{\omega}(1-\omega)^{(1-\omega)}} \tag{A3}$$

$$\text{Then } p_t^N = \frac{P_t^N}{P_t} = \frac{P_t^N}{\dfrac{\left[(1+\tau_t^N)P_t^N\right]^{1-\alpha}(P_t^T)^{\alpha}}{(1-\alpha)^{1-\alpha}\alpha^{\alpha}}} = \frac{\alpha^{\alpha}(1-\alpha)^{\alpha}}{(1+\tau_t^N)^{1-\alpha}}\left(\frac{P_t^N}{P_t^T}\right)^{\alpha}$$
$$= \frac{\alpha^{\alpha}(1-\alpha)^{\alpha}}{(1+\tau_t^N)^{1-\alpha}}RER_t^{\alpha} \tag{A4}$$

$$p_t^X = \frac{P_t^X}{P_t} = \frac{P_t^X / P_t^T}{P_t / P_t^T} = \frac{(1-\alpha)^{1-\alpha}\alpha^{\alpha}\omega^{\omega}(1-\omega)^{1-\omega}}{(1+\tau_t^M)^{\omega}(1+\tau_t^X)^{1-\omega}(1+\tau_t^N)^{1-\alpha}}\frac{TOT_t^{\omega}}{RER_t^{1-\alpha}} \tag{A5}$$

where $TOT_t = P_t^X / P_t^M$ represents the trade terms, and $RER_t = P_t^N / P_t^T$ represents the internal real exchange rate. The rise of this value means appreciation, while decline means depreciation.

Through the maximization conditions of the maximization of profits of nontradable enterprises and export tradable enterprises, the labor needed by the two types of enterprises can be represented as:

$$n_t^N = \frac{\gamma p_t^N y_t^N}{w_t}, \quad n_t^X = \frac{\vartheta p_t^X y_t^X}{w_t} \tag{A6}$$

The supply price of the goods can be represented as:

$$p_t^N = \frac{w_t}{\gamma}\left[\frac{(y_t^N)^{1-\gamma}}{A_t^N}\right]^{1/\gamma}, \quad p_t^X = \frac{w_t}{\vartheta}\left[\frac{(y_t^X)^{1-\vartheta}}{A_t^X}\right]^{1/\vartheta} \tag{A7}$$

The real wage level is:

$$w_t = \eta(1-n_t)^{-\xi}\frac{(1+\tau_t^N)}{(1-\alpha)}\frac{p_t^N c_t^N}{c_t^{1-\sigma}} \tag{A8}$$

Then equation 9.8 in the text can be obtained. Based on equation 9.8 and the constraint condition $g_t^N = \theta_N c_t^N$, the following equation is obtained:

$$\frac{y_t^X}{y_t^N} = \frac{A_t^{X\frac{1}{1-\vartheta}}}{A_t^{N\frac{1}{1-\gamma}}}\frac{\vartheta^{\frac{\vartheta}{1-\vartheta}}}{\gamma^{\frac{\gamma}{1-\gamma}}}\frac{(p_t^X)^{\frac{\vartheta}{1-\vartheta}}}{(p_t^N)^{\frac{\gamma}{1-\gamma}}}\left(\eta(1-n_t)^{-\xi}\frac{(1+\tau_t^N)p_t^N c_t^N}{(1-\alpha)c_t^{1-\sigma}}\right)^{\left(\frac{\gamma}{1-\gamma}-\frac{\vartheta}{1-\vartheta}\right)} \tag{A9}$$

Substituting $g_t^N = \theta_N c_t^N$ and $y_t^N = c_t^N + g_t^N = (1+\theta_N)c_t^N$ into equation A9, the following equation is obtained:

$$\frac{y_t^X}{y_t^N} = k_1 (p_t^X)^{\frac{\vartheta}{1-\vartheta}}(p_t^N)^{\frac{-\vartheta}{1-\vartheta}}\left(\frac{(1-n_t)^{-\xi}y_t^N}{c_t^{1-\sigma}}\right)^{\left(\frac{\gamma}{1-\gamma}-\frac{\vartheta}{1-\vartheta}\right)} \tag{A10}$$

10 Foreign direct investment and business cycles in China

For developing countries, foreign direct investment (FDI) can not only cover the funding gaps but also provide a demonstrator model involving technology and institutions through spillover effects. However, it inevitably brings about consequences, including environmental pollution, crowding-out effect, profit outflow and even financial risk. This chapter first analyzes some stylized facts of the Chinese macroeconomy and then adopts the DSGE approach to build the RBC model with FDI shocks. It aims to study the ways and extent to which FDI impacts Chinese economic growth and fluctuations. The model parameters are calibrated to be consistent with the stylized facts of Chinese economic development. The similarity between the model economy and the real economy is then examined. The research findings indicate that the RBC model with FDI shocks well simulates the characteristics of Chinese real economic fluctuations. The impulse response function of FDI shocks shows that FDI has a negative effect on output, domestic investment, labor, etc., though it has a positive effect on consumption.

10.1 Reasons for building the RBC model with FDI shocks

Since the reform and opening up in 1978, the average GDP growth rate of China has reached more than 9.2%, making it one of the fastest growing countries in the world. Accompanying the rapid economic growth of China comes the stylized fact that the economy fluctuates sharply. In 1984, the GDP growth rate of China was as high as 15.18%, while in 1990, it was only 3.84%. The range and standard deviation of GDP growth rate was 11.34% and 2.74% respectively. During this period, Chinese macroeconomic variables, such as investment, consumption and export, all experienced growth and fluctuations respectively. The average annual growth rate of Chinese final consumption was 8.96%, with the final consumption growth rate as 8.96% in 1979 and -3.85% in 1989, and the range and standard deviation of the final consumption growth rate was 19.28% and 3.47% respectively. The average annual growth rate of investment (real gross fixed capital formation) was 11.87%, with the growth rate of investment as 27.43 % in 1992 and -16.4% in 1989, and the range and standard deviation of the growth rate of investment was 43.83%

DOI: 10.4324/9781003305651-10

and 8.04% respectively. According to the above data, China is confronted with a fast growth rate as well a large range of economic fluctuations.

It has been observed that since the 1980s, China's FDI inflows increased from US $30 million in 1978 to US $144.3693 billion in 2020. From 1978 to 2010, foreign direct investment inflows stood at US $2314.029 billion. The FDI inflows increases with the growth of the Chinese economy. Economic intuitions illustrate that in the process of the economic transition of China, FDI not only covers the funding gaps in the early stage of the economic take-off in China, but also provides technology demonstrations, institution samples and market space. Inevitably, it also brings about many negative effects, such as environmental pollution, crowing-out effect, profit outflow, regional development imbalance, and even financial risk. Therefore, it is of great significance to discuss FDI's impact on Chinese economic growth and fluctuations.

Economists and scholars have long been concerned about the effects of FDI on the economy of host countries. Hirschman (1958) first proposed the correlation effects and analyzed the impact of the FDI's correlation effects on economic growth. When flowing into a certain industrial sector in the host country, foreign capital leads to the expansion of this sector, which will drive the development of other industrial sectors and which remains the forward and backward linkage with the specific industrial sector, in turn stimulating domestic investment. Therefore, the inflow of foreign capital has a crowd-in effect on the domestic capital of the host country. Barro and Sala (1995) introduced FDI into long-term growth on the basis of Solow's model. They argued that the promotion effect of FDI on economic growth depends on technology spillover, and the spillover effect promotes the technological progress of the host country and drives the increase of domestic capital of the host country. Borensztein et al. (1998) built the endogenous growth model involving technology spillover into FDI; it was proved that FDI worked as the main channel of technology transfer and could promote the long-term growth of developing countries under the condition that the human capital of the host country must reach a certain level. Rama (2001) believed that, in developing countries, the inflow of FDI will increase the dispersion level of wage income and increase the inequality of income distribution. McDonald et al. (2002) believed that FDI had long- and short-term effects on employment among European Union members. FDI plays a minor role in promoting employment in the short term but provides a large number of jobs in the long term. Zhang (2006) carried out the empirical research based on the interprovincial panel data of China from 1992 to 2004 and demonstrated that the regional inequality of FDI inflows could cause the regional income gap to widen.

Chinese scholars also have done a lot of research on FDI. Cai and Wang (2004) believed that, although the employment share of FDI is relatively small, the rapid growth of FDI makes FDI a high contributor to the overall employment growth in China. With abundant labor, China can turn to FDI to absorb employment. They also contended that the development level of the labor market could explain the fact that FDI is mainly concentrated in the eastern part of China. Based on the regression model built by Agosin and Mayer (2000), Yang and Shen (2002) analyzed the crowd-in (crowd-out) effect of FDI by referring to the total investment of China, based on GDP and FDI data from 1985 to 1999. They figured out that FDI had already had the crowding-out effect on domestic investment in the long run. Zhong (2010) built a spatial dynamic econometric model to empirically analyze the regional effect of investment by multinational companies. It was found that foreign capital produced not only intraregional spillovers but also interregional spillovers, indicating that foreign capital in a certain regional investment not only stimulated and improved the productivity performance of the region but also indirectly led to the improvement of productivity in other regions. Wan, Lu and Chen (2005) referred to a semilogarithm income determination function and found that FDI had a significant positive effect on the regional income gap, which was increasingly intensified. Wu (2002) adopted a multidimensional variance analysis model to analyze the key variables including the regional GDP gap of China, domestic aggregate investment gap, domestic investment efficiency difference, FDI quantity difference and FDI efficiency difference. Wu contended that FDI's regional distribution difference cannot effectively explain the economic imbalances of various regions. On the contrary, the regional distribution difference of domestic investment, especially the significant difference in investment efficiency, is the main factor causing the long-term regional economic gap.

By reviewing the literature in relation to FDI, it is clear that a lot of research has been conducted on the effect of FDI on economic growth, investment, and employment of the host country, as well as the regional distribution of FDI. However, research concerning the relationship between FDI and Chinese economic fluctuations is rarely to be found.

Kydland and Prescott (1982) and Long and Plosser (1983) are pioneers in working out the RBC theory. As the mainstream research method of macroeconomics, the RBC theory is associated with the microagent's spontaneous selection; builds the DSGE model, making it possible to take economic growth and economic fluctuation under a unified research framework; and overcomes the problem of Lucas critique. Hansen (1985) introduced the form of indivisible labor in the RBC model, which improved the model's interpretation of labor volatility. Christiano and Eichenbaum (1992) introduced government expenditure shocks into the simple RBC model, studied separately the cases of the divisibility and indivisibility of labor, and found that the explanation degree of real labor productivity has been greatly improved when the government shocks were added in the case of the indivisibility of labor. Khan and Thomas (2004) introduced inventory investment into the RBC model, and their research showed that inventory accumulation is procyclical and that inventory changes are consistent with final product changes.

The research and application of RBC theory in China is still in the initial stage, which can be roughly divided into two aspects: One is the theoretical research on the RBC model itself, which tends to emphasize the inherent consistency of the model; for instance, Gong and Semmler (2003) considered the RBC model under the disequilibrium labor market, thus breaking through the original equilibrium assumption of market clearing and extending the basic model. The other is to use the RBC theoretical model to study Chinese macroeconomic problems. Bu and Jin (2002) introduced monetary factors into the exogenous labor model to build the model of the money and economic cycle in China and analyzed the relationship between Chinese economic growth and monetary indicators during 1980–2001. Chen, Gong and Zou (2004) used the basic RBC model to explain the changes in the Chinese economy since the establishment of PRC and found that the RBC model well simulated the fluctuations of most macrovariables and could explain more than 80% of output fluctuations. Huang (2005) regarded government expenditure as an exogenous random shock variable and examined the effect of government expenditure shocks on the economic cycle in the model, thus providing a theoretical basis for the formulation and implementation of fiscal policy. Li and Zhong (2008) added trade surplus shocks into the RBC model to analyze the relationship between trade surplus and Chinese real economic cycle. Wu (2009) introduced energy consumption shocks into the RBC model, took energy price as the exogenous random shocks, built the model involving energy efficiency under the DSGE framework, and investigated the impact of technology shocks, government consumption shocks and energy price shocks on Chinese energy efficiency fluctuations.

This chapter builds a theoretical model of the RBC model involving FDI shocks, empirically analyzes the relationship between FDI and Chinese economic fluctuations and examines the dynamic impact of FDI on various macroeconomic variables through impulse response analysis.

10.2 Data sources and stylized facts

In his chapter, the author selects the real data of gross domestic product (GDP), household consumption, government consumption, total investment and annual data of labor employment from 1978 to 2010. In terms of the capital stock, this chapter adopts the perpetual inventory method using the equation $K_{t+1} = I_t + (1-\delta)K_t$. For the annual investment flows, this chapter agrees with Shan (2008) and Zhang, Wu and Zhang (2004), taking gross fixed capital formation as the annual investment flows that affect capital formation during the year. For the capital stock of 1978 as the base period, by referring to a large number of existing literature, this chapter adopts the research of Huang et al. (2002), who set the capital stock of the base year 1978 as CNY 582.166 billion. Sun and Ren (2005) also supported the research results of Huang et al. (2002). In terms of the depreciation rate, this chapter sets the depreciation rate of capital as 10% because typically the depreciated rate of

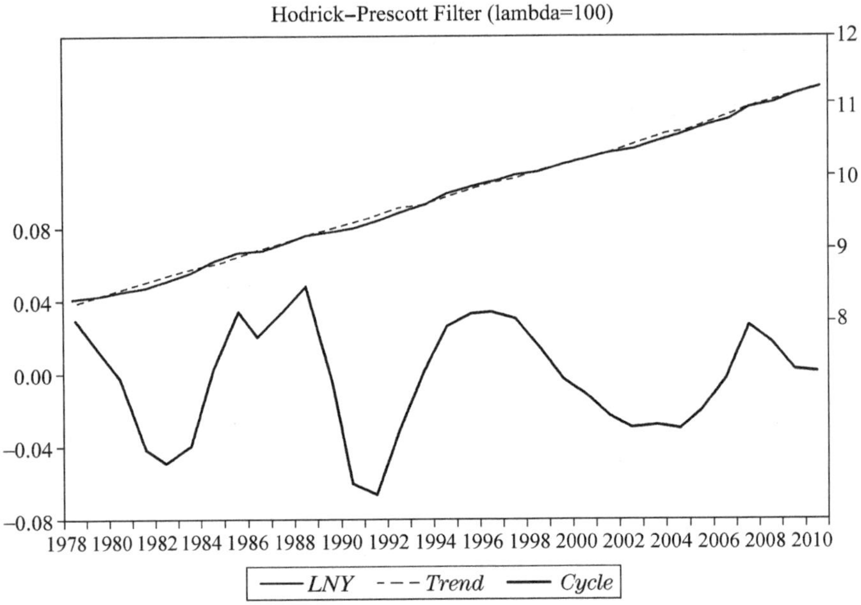

Figure 10.1 Output Fluctuations from 1978 to 2008.

capital is set around 10% by scholars both at home and abroad. Regarding FDI, to unify the units, this chapter converts it according to the average annual exchange rate of CNY against USD in the corresponding year. It uses the price index of the fixed asset investment to deflate and finally obtain the real FDI data of the base period 1978. For domestic investment data, this chapter uses the just mentioned total investment data minus FDI data.

In view of the data of Chinese economic variables from 1978 to 2010, the Chinese economy has shown significant fluctuations. After logarithmization, the data are then processed by the H-P filter using Eviews. Different macroeconomic variables' fluctuations are be shown in Figures 10.1 to 10.7.

As can been seen from the H-P filter fluctuation figures, since 1978, these macroeconomic variables have shown several cyclical fluctuations, and the fluctuations have also shown strong cooperation. The fluctuations of foreign direct investment and the fluctuations of output show obvious consistency. The fluctuations of other macrovariables and the fluctuations of output are procyclical: The fluctuations of household consumption and gross fixed assets investment are also remarkably consistent with the fluctuations of output; the correlation between the fluctuations of government consumption and the fluctuations of output is relatively weak; the waveform of capital stock is similar to that of output but lagging behind that of output. The fluctuations of labor represented by employment are less relevant than those of output.

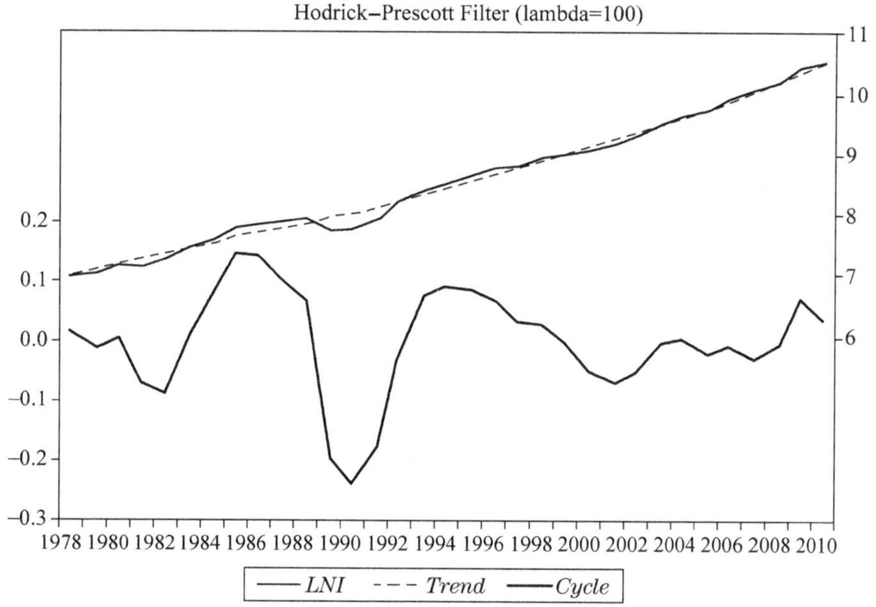

Figure 10.2 Gross Fixed Assets Investment Fluctuations from 1978 to 2008.

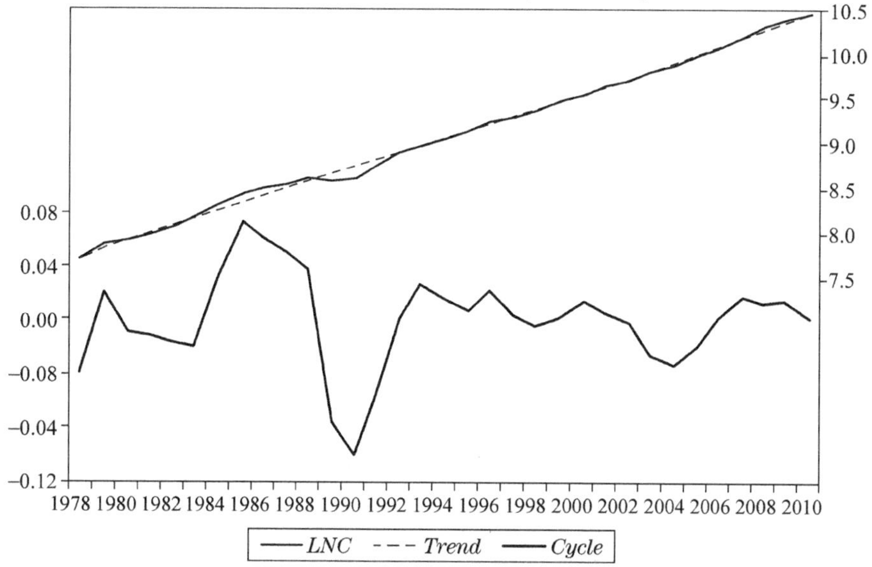

Figure 10.3 Household Consumption Fluctuations from 1978 to 2008.

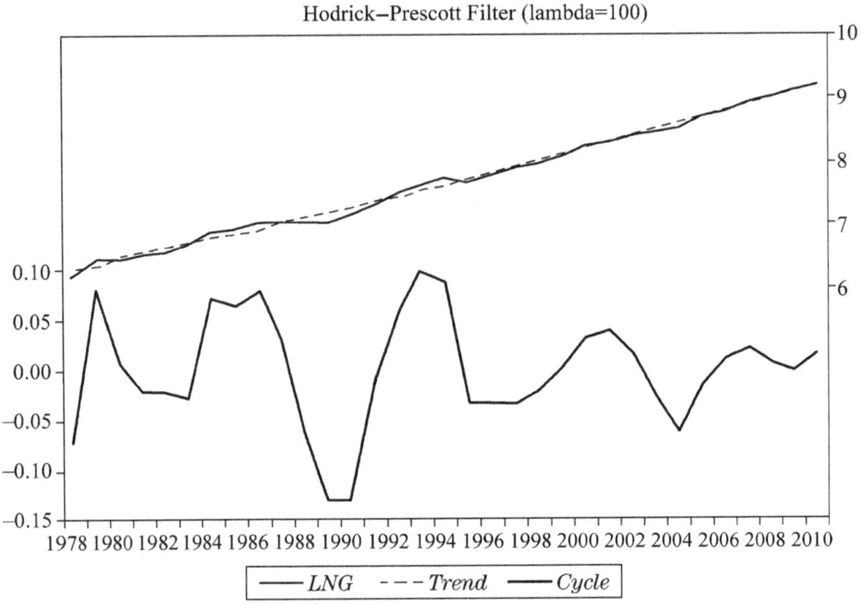

Figure 10.4 Government Consumption Fluctuations from 1978 to 2010.

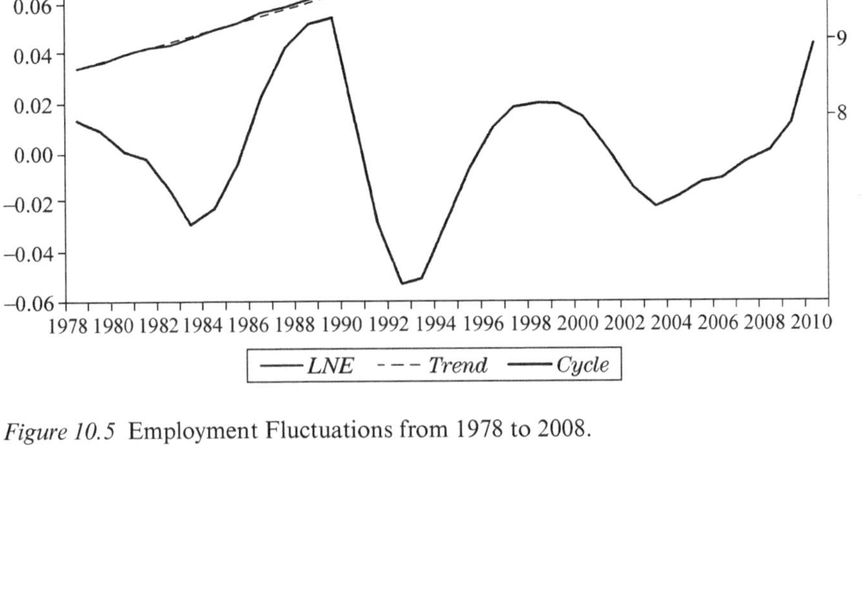

Figure 10.5 Employment Fluctuations from 1978 to 2008.

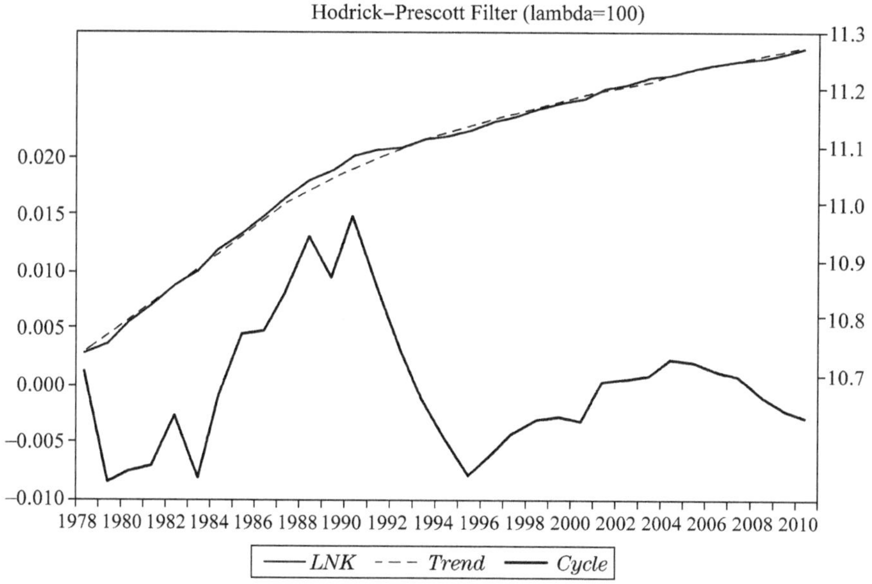

Figure 10.6 Capital Stock Fluctuations from 1978 to 2008.

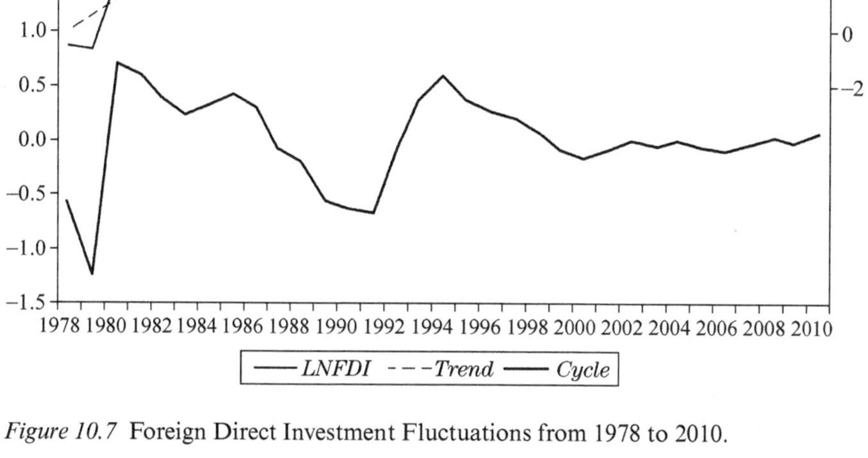

Figure 10.7 Foreign Direct Investment Fluctuations from 1978 to 2010.

10.3 Model building and parameter calibration

Before building the theoretical model, it is necessary to set up several assumptions contained in the model: First, the production function considers constant returns to scale; second, the utility function of the economic agent is the constant relative risk aversion (CRRA); third, technology, FDI and government consumption are all regarded as exogenous random shocks and subject to first-order autoregression AR(1).

Assume that the agents in the economy are homogeneous; that is, they are subject to the same consumption constraint and have the same utility function, so a single agent can represent the entire economy. Here, the typical agent is used to represent the overall economy, and its utility function can be expressed in the following ways:

$$E_0 \sum_{t=0}^{\infty} \beta^t U(C_t, L_t) \tag{10.1}$$

$$U(C_t, L_t) = \frac{C_t^{1-\eta} - 1}{1-\eta} + \theta \ln(1 - \mathrm{L}_t)$$

where β^t represents the subjective discount rate of period t, $\beta \in (0,1)$; C_t represents the consumption of the actor of period t; L_t represents the labor time of the agent of period t; and η represents the relative risk aversion coefficient, $\eta > 0$. In particular, when $\eta = 1$, the first term $\frac{C_t^{1-\eta} - 1}{1-\eta}$ of the CRRA utility function becomes logarithmic $\ln C_t$, which can be regarded as a special form; θ represents the relative value of consumption and leisure, and $\theta \in (0,1)$ reflects the agent's preference for consumption or leisure in the utility function.

The production function in this chapter adopts the Cobb–Douglas form, and the function form is as follows:

$$Y_t = A_t K_t^{\alpha} L_t^{1-\alpha} \tag{10.2}$$

where A_t represents the exogenous technical variable, K_t represents the real amount of capital input, and α represents the output elasticity of capital. Since the production function considers constant returns to scale, the output elasticity of labor is $1-\alpha$. A represents the traditional Solow residual.

The budget constraint faced by the actor in period t is:

$$Y_t = C_t^p + G_t + I_t^d \tag{10.3}$$

That is, the budget constraint faced by the actor in period t is expressed as the sum of household consumption C_t^p, government consumption G_t and investment I_t^d.

For consumption C_t in the utility function, this chapter draws on the settings of Christiano and Eichenbaum (1992) and Chen, Gong and Zou (2004), i.e.:

$$C_t = C_t^p + \varphi G_t \tag{10.4}$$

Consumption C_t in the utility function is composed of two parts, one is from the private consumption C_t^p selected by the representative agent, and the other is from the consumption G_t provided by the government. In the utility function of the representative agent, private consumption and government expenditure are inequivalent. According to classical economics, the agent's own choice obeys the principle of maximum utility, and the utility of the government to provide consumption will be lower than the individual's choice, so it is considered that $0 \le \varphi \le 1$. φ represents the ratio of one-unit government consumption utility to one unit private consumption utility.

The capital stock evolves according to:

$$\begin{aligned} K_{t+1} &= I_t + (1-\delta)K_t \\ I_t &= I_t^d + I_t^f \end{aligned} \tag{10.5}$$

where δ represents the capital depreciation rate $\delta \in (0,1]$, reflecting the depreciation of capital. I_t represents the investment of period t. I_t^d represents the domestic investment, and I_t^f represents the FDI.

This chapter focuses on the effect of I_t^f on the model and introduces I_t^f into the RBC model as exogenous shocks. I_t^f is set to evolve according to:

$$\begin{aligned} \ln I_t^f &= (1-\rho_f)\ln \bar{I}^f + \rho_f \ln I_{t-1}^f + \varepsilon_t^f \\ \varepsilon_t^f &\sim i.i.d.N(0, \sigma_f^2) \end{aligned} \tag{10.6}$$

where $\bar{I}^f$ represents the steady-state level of the FDI shock variable I_t^f; ρ_f represents the regression coefficient and indicates the relationship between the variable value of the current period and that of the previous period, $\rho_f \in (-1,1)$; ε_t^f represents the random disturbance, subject to white noise process, and reflects the impact of exogenous random shocks on FDI.

Technology evolves according to:

$$\begin{aligned} \ln A_t &= (1-\rho_A)\ln \bar{A} + \rho_A \ln A_{t-1} + \varepsilon_t^A \\ \varepsilon_t^A &\sim i.i.d.N(0, \sigma_A^2) \end{aligned} \tag{10.7}$$

where $\bar{A}$ represents the steady-state value of technology shocks A_t; ρ_A represents the regression coefficient and indicates the relationship between the variable value of the current period and that of the previous period, $\rho_A \in (-1,1)$; ε_t^A

represents the random disturbance, subject to the white noise process, and reflects the influence of exogenous random shocks on technology.

Government consumption is also a shock, and it evolves according to:

$$\begin{aligned} &\ln G_t = (1-\rho_g)\ln \bar{G} + \rho_A \ln G_{t-1} + \varepsilon_t^g \\ &\varepsilon_t^A \sim i.i.d.N(0,\sigma_g^2) \end{aligned} \tag{10.8}$$

Based on the assumptions of the preceding equations, the Lagrange function of the representative household's utility maximization is:

$$L = E\left\{\sum_{t=0}^{\infty}\beta^t \left[\begin{matrix} \dfrac{(C_t^p + \varphi G_t)^{1-\eta} - 1}{1-\eta} + \theta \ln(1-\mathrm{L}_t) - \lambda_t \\ \left(C_t^p + G_t + K_{t+1} - (1-\delta)K_t - I_t^f - A_t K_t^{\alpha} L_t^{1-\alpha}\right) \end{matrix}\right]\right\} \tag{10.9}$$

To solve the first-order conditions of the state variable in equation 10.9, the corresponding first-order conditions are:

$$\frac{\partial L}{\partial C_t^p} : (C_t^p + \varphi G_t)^{-\eta} - \lambda_t = 0 \tag{10.10}$$

$$\frac{\partial L}{\partial L_t} : \frac{-\theta}{1-L_t} + \lambda_t (1-\alpha) A_t K_t^{\alpha} L_t^{-\alpha} = 0 \tag{10.11}$$

$$\frac{\partial L}{\partial K_{t+1}} : -\lambda_t + \lambda_{t+1}\beta\left[\alpha \frac{Y_{t+1}}{K_{t+1}} + (1-\delta)\right] = 0 \text{ [1]} \tag{10.12}$$

$$\text{when } \alpha \frac{Y_t}{K_t} + (1-\delta) = R_t \tag{10.13}$$

of equation 10.12,

where R_t represents the yield of actual capital of period t. From the economic indications of the equation, R_t not only contains the capital output ratio corresponding to the current period but also includes the residual capital after capital depreciation in the previous period.

According to equations 10.10 and 10.11, the following can be obtained:

$$\theta L_t = (1-\alpha)(1-L_t) Y_t (C_t^p + \varphi G_t)^{-\eta} \tag{10.14}$$

According to equations 10.10 and 10.12, the following can be obtained:

$$(C_t^p + \varphi G_t)^{-\eta} = (C_{t+1}^p + \varphi G_{t+1})^{-\eta} \beta E_t(R_{t+1}) \tag{10.15}$$

According to equations 10.10 and 10.15, the following can be obtained:

$$\beta E_t\left(\left(\frac{C_t^p + \varphi G_t}{C_{t+1}^p + \varphi G_{t+1}}\right)^{\eta} R_{t+1}\right) = 1 \tag{10.16}$$

The constraint of the linear programming problem and equations 10.13–10.16 generated by the first-order condition of Lagrange function constitute a nonlinear differential equation set.

The existence of the equation set also requires the following boundary conditions: First is the initial capital investment K_0 and $K_t\,|_{t=0} = K_0$. Second is the transversality condition of an economy:

$$\lim_{i\to\infty} E_t \beta^i C_{t+i}^{-\eta} K_{t+i+1} = 0$$

In the numerical solution, using the first-order Taylor expansion and the numerical equivalent substitution, the constraint and first-order conditions are log-linearized near the steady state. Thus the following equations can be obtained:

$$\overline{Y} \cdot y_t = \overline{C}^p \cdot c_t^p + \overline{G} g_t + \overline{I}^d \cdot i_t^d \tag{10.17}$$

$$\overline{K} \cdot k_{t+1} = \overline{I}^d \cdot i_t^d + \overline{I}^f \cdot i_t^f + (1-\delta)\overline{K} \cdot k_t \tag{10.18}$$

$$y_t \approx a_t + \alpha k_t + (1-\alpha) l_t \tag{10.19}$$

$$a_t = \rho_A a_{t-1} + \varepsilon_t^A \tag{10.20}$$

$$i_t^f = \rho_f i_{t-1}^f + \varepsilon_t^f \tag{10.21}$$

$$g_t = \rho_g g_{t-1} + \varepsilon_t^g \tag{10.22}$$

$$l_t \approx \left(1-\overline{L}\right)\left(y_t - \eta \frac{\overline{C}^p c_t^p + \varphi \overline{G} g_t}{\overline{C}^p + \varphi \overline{G}}\right) \tag{10.23}$$

$$E_t\{r_{t+1} + \eta[\frac{\overline{C}^p}{\overline{C}}(c_t^p - c_{t+1}^p) + \frac{\varphi \overline{G}}{\overline{C}}(g_t - g_{t+1})]\} = 0 \tag{10.24}$$

$$\overline{R}\cdot r_t = R_t - \overline{R} = \alpha\frac{\overline{Y}}{\overline{K}}(y_t - k_t) \quad (10.25)$$

After log-linearization, there are nine equations and nine variables as shown by equations 10.17–10.25, in which k_t and c_t are endogenous control variables, a_t, i_t^f and g_t are exogenous state variables, and y_t, r_t, l_t and i_t^d are systematic state variables, So the economic system described by the economic programming problem can be approximately represented by these nine stochastic linear equations.

The parameters will be calibrated by referring to the data in China and the research findings in the existing literature.

10.3.1 Firstly, the coefficient of relative risk aversion for consumption (η)

This chapter sets the calibrated value of η as 0.77 based on previous research. When Chen Xuebin, Yang Ling and Fang Song (2005) made an empirical analysis of the consumption saving behavior of Chinese residents, the estimated coefficient of relative risk aversion for consumption was about 0.77. Huang Zelin (2005) and Li Hao and Zhong Changbiao (2008) also set $\eta = 0.77$ when they applied the RBC model in their studies.

10.3.2 Secondly, the depreciation rate (δ)

This chapter sets the value of the depreciation rate δ as 10%. In terms of the value of the depreciation rate, domestic scholars set different values in their studies. Zhang, Wu and Zhang (2004) learned that China's weighted depreciation rate from 1952 to 2000 was 9.6% by referring to the proportion of capital goods in China, and Shan (2008) estimated that the annual weighted depreciation rate was 10.96%.

10.3.3 Thirdly, the share of capital income (α)

In order to calculate the output elasticity of capital and labor and the regression coefficient of technology shocks, it is necessary to estimate the production function. Assuming that the production function obeys the Cobb–Douglas type with constant returns to scale, the following production function can be obtained:

$$Y_t = e^{a_t + \mu \cdot T} K_t^{\alpha} L_t^{1-\alpha} \quad (10.26)$$

where T represents the trend of time variable, $T = 1, 2, \ldots$, and μ is the parameter value of T. To exclude the linear correlation between regression variables, the production function is transformed by the intensive form of output and capital. After logarithmic linearization, substituting the data of real output, capital stock and labor calculated at constant prices in 1978 into equation 10.26, the estimated production function can be:

$$\begin{aligned} &\ln\frac{Y}{L} = -1.7534 + 0.4224\ln\frac{K}{L} + 0.044T \\ &\qquad(-13.01)\ (7.377) \qquad\quad (9.194) \\ &R^2 = 0.9978, \quad S.E. = 0.0364 \end{aligned} \tag{10.27}$$

The values in the brackets below the parameters of this quantitative model are t-test values, and the goodness of fit reaches 99.78%. The measurement results of both parameters and model have passed the test and show that the output elasticity of capital α is 0.4224, so the output elasticity of labor is $1 - 0.4224 = 0.5776$.

10.3.4 Fourth, the autocorrelation coefficient of technology shocks, government expenditure shocks, FDI shocks and the standard deviation of residual term

According to equation 10.27, the time series of Solow residual A_t can be further obtained.

$$\ln A = \ln\frac{Y}{L} - 0.4224 \cdot \ln\frac{K}{L} - 0.044 \cdot T \tag{10.28}$$

According to the series data of technology shocks from 1978 to 2010 and equation 10.7, the first-order autoregressive coefficient of technology shocks can be calculated as $\rho_A = 0.7356$. Its standard deviation $\sigma_A = 2.23\%$. $\overline{A}$ represents the balanced technology level and is set as 1.

According to series data of FDI shocks from 1978 to 2010, the FDI data are processed through log-linearization and H-P filter. Then the first-order autoregressive coefficient of FDI fluctuations can be calculated as $\rho_f = 0.7741$ and $\sigma_f = 18.56\%$ by using the equation $i_t^f = \rho_f i_{t-1}^f + \varepsilon_t^f$.

According to the serial data of government expenditure shocks from 1978 to 2010, government expenditure data are processed through the log-linearization and the H-P filter. Then the first-order autoregressive coefficient of government expenditure fluctuations can be calculated as $\rho_g = 0.476$ and $\sigma_g = 4.78\%$ by using the equation $i_t^f = \rho_f i_{t-1}^f + \varepsilon_t^f$.

10.3.5 Fifth, labor supply (N)

For the selection of labor supply index, different researchers have different choices. Because of the comprehensive data statistics, international scholars often choose the number of hours to calculate the labor supply situation. However, in the case of China, only employment is counted, but the labor hours are not counted. Therefore, domestic scholars either set the labor hours subjectively or use the data of employment. In this chapter, the employed population proportion in the whole society is used to reflect the changes of labor input. Based on the employed population proportion from 1978 to 2010, the time series of the employed population proportion is obtained. Since the labor supply is normalized as 1, the labor input at the equilibrium level $\overline{N} = 0.553$.

10.3.6 Six, the rate of capital return (R)

According to the calculation equation of the rate of capital return,

$$R = (\sum_{t=1978}^{2010} \frac{(1-\alpha)Y_t}{K_t}) / 33 + 1 - \delta$$

And the value of R can be estimated to be 1.166.

10.3.7 Seventh, the subjective discount rate (β)

According to the relationship between the subjective discount rate and the rate of capital return obtained by the preceding model in equilibrium, the value of β can be obtained as 0.86.

10.3.8 Eighth, the relative value of consumption and leisure (θ)

According to equation $\theta\overline{L} = (1-\alpha)(1-\overline{L})\overline{Y}(\overline{C}^{p} + \varphi\overline{G})^{-\eta}$, as well as the calibrated parameters and the obtained equilibrium value, $\theta = 0.4943$.

The calibrated values of all variables and parameters are shown in Table 10.1.

10.4 Empirical results

According to the equation set from equations 10.17–10.25, MATLAB is used to solve the equations, and the standard deviation of each macroeconomic

Table 10.1 Calibrated Values of Variable Parameters

η	θ	δ	α	β	$\overline{N}$	ρ_A	σ_A
0.77	0.4943	0.1	0.4224	0.86	0.553	0.7356	0.0223
$\overline{R}$	ρ_f	σ_f	ρ_g	σ_g	φ	$\overline{A}$	
1.166	0.8842	0.3958	0.476	0.0478	0.8	1	

Table 10.2 Real Economy and Fluctuation Characteristics of Macroeconomic Variables in Simulated Economy with FDI Shocks

	Real Economy		*Simulated Economy with FDI Shock*		
	Standard Deviation (%)	*Correlation Coefficient*	*Standard Deviation (%)*	*Correlation Coefficient*	*K-P Ratio*
Output	3.09	1.00	2.68	1.00	0.87
Capital	2.55	0.43	1.74	0.76	0.68
Household Consumption	3.47	0.75	2.45	0.72	0.71
Gross Investment	10.83	0.74	10.27	0.91	0.95
Domestic Investment	10.05	0.70	10.97	0.90	1.09
Labor	0.58	−0.12	0.75	0.92	1.29

Table 10.3 Fluctuation Characteristics of Macroeconomic Variables in Simulated Economy with FDI Shocks and Without FDI Shocks

	Real Economy		*Simulated Economy with FDI Shock*		
	Standard Deviation (%)	*Correlation Coefficient*	*Standard Deviation (%)*	*Correlation Coefficient*	*K-P Ratio*
Output	3.09	1.00	2.68	1.00	0.87
Capital	2.55	0.43	1.74	0.76	0.68
Household Consumption	3.47	0.75	2.45	0.72	0.71
Gross Investment	10.83	0.74	10.27	0.91	0.95
Domestic Investment	10.05	0.70	10.97	0.90	1.09
Labor	0.58	−0.12	0.75	0.92	1.29

Note: Simulated economy data are obtained using DYNARE in MATLAB2007.

variable and the correlation coefficient among the macroeconomic variables are obtained. The model findings are compared with the data of the real macroeconomic variables in order to test whether the RBC model introducing the FDI shocks can better simulate real economic fluctuations. The empirical results are shown in Tables 10.2 and 10.3.

The K-P ratio is obtained by dividing the standard deviation of the model's economic variables by that of the corresponding variables of the real economy. It indicates the effects of the models' interpretation of the real economy. The closer the ratio is to 1, the better the effects of simulating the real economy are.

In terms of output fluctuations, the standard deviation of real economic output is 3.09%, and the standard deviation of simulated economic output without FDI shock is 2.54%, and the K-P ratio reaches 82%, as shown in

Table 10.3. The simulation of the real economy is quite good. The standard deviation of the simulated economic output with FDI shocks is 2.68%, and the K-P ratio reaches 87%. The simulation of the real economy is better; that is, the simulated economy with FDI shocks is more fitting to interpret the real economy than the simulated economy without FDI shocks. Therefore, FDI shocks have a certain impact on the fluctuations of the GDP of China.

In terms of capital fluctuations, the standard deviation of real economic capital is 2.55%, while that of simulated economic capital without FDI shocks is 1.58%, and the K-P ratio reaches 62%. The standard deviation of simulated economic capital with FDI shocks is 1.74%, and the K-P ratio reaches 68%. Moreover, the correlation coefficient between capital and output in the model economy is consistent with that of the real economy, both of which were highly procyclical. Therefore, it is found that the model well explains the real economy's fluctuations.

In terms of household consumption fluctuations, the standard deviation of household consumption in the real economy is 3.47%. The standard deviation of household consumption in the simulated economy without FDI shocks is 2.34%, and the K-P ratio is 67%. The simulation of the real economy is also good. The standard deviation of household consumption in the simulated economy with FDI shocks is 2.45%, and the K-P ratio is 71%. The simulation of the real economy is improved compared with that of the simulated economy without FDI shocks. The reason why the interpretation degree of the model for household consumption is not as high as that of output is that the individual's choice of consumption is affected by many factors. For example, Chen and Zhang (2010) believed that credit constraint also resulted in the large fluctuations of the real household consumption of China. They introduced the factor of credit constraint into the RBC model, which greatly improved the model's interpretation for the fluctuations of household consumption.

In terms of labor fluctuations, the standard deviation of labor in the real economy is 0.58%, the standard deviation of labor in the simulated economy without FDI shocks is 0.73%, and the K-P ratio reaches 126%. The labor volatility in the simulated economy exceeds that in the real economy. The standard deviation of labor in the simulated economy with FDI shocks is 0.75%, and the K-P ratio reaches 129%, slightly higher than that in the simulated economy without FDI shocks. In the real economy, the correlation coefficient between labor and output is −0.12, showing a weak correlation, while the correlation coefficient between labor and output in the simulated economy with or without FDI shocks both shows strong pro-cyclicality. The reason why the model economy differs greatly from the real economy in interpreting labor fluctuations is mainly related to the setting of the model and the real labor statistics. In the simulated economy, this chapter considers divisibility of labor, but only the statistics of the number of employed population is available, not the data of working hours in labor statistics. Therefore, the fluctuations of employment in the real economy refer to the fluctuations of the number of employment. In terms of the employment statistics in China, the rural population is employed by default, and only the urban population statistics register the unemployment rate, which obviously ignores the hidden unemployment in the rural areas of China. These statistical characteristics reduce the degree of fluctuations of the employment in China because the degree of labor fluctuations in the model economy reflects the fluctuation characteristics of working hours, and most enterprises in China have overtime employment, which was illustrated by the higher labor fluctuations in the model economy compared with the real economy.

In terms of the fluctuations of gross investment, the standard deviation of gross investment in the real economy is 10.83%, the standard deviation of gross investment in the simulated economy without FDI shocks is 9.06%, and the K-P ratio is 84%, indicating a very high degree of simulation of the real economy. The standard deviation of gross investment in the simulated economy with FDI shocks is 10.27%, and the K-P ratio is 95%. Compared with the simulated economy without FDI shocks, its interpretation degree to the real economy is greatly improved. In addition, the corresponding correlation coefficient of gross investment and output in the model economy are 0.91 and 0.89, respectively, and the corresponding correlation coefficient of investment and output in the real economy are 0.74, indicating strong agreement.

From the above analysis, it can be seen that the RBC model with FDI shocks can better explain Chinese macroeconomic fluctuations and that, after comparison with the RBC model without FDI shocks, it is found that the model with FDI shocks can better explain Chinese macroeconomic fluctuations.

According to the simulated data obtained after parameter calibration, the impulse response of FDI shocks and technology shocks can be obtained, as shown in Figures 10.8 and 10.9.

In terms of gross investment, when the economy is in the steady state and FDI increases by 1% due to exogenous random shocks in the period t, the gross investment in the current period will immediately increase by about 0.002%. FDI is a part of the gross investment. The impact of FDI shocks on gross investment was examined, and the impact can last for about 30 periods, though the degree of impact is gradually weakened.

In terms of domestic investment, when the economy is in the steady state and FDI increases by 1% due to exogenous random shocks in the period t, domestic investment in the current period will decrease by about 0.025%, which reflects the crowding-out effect of FDI on domestic investment, and the impact can last for about 25 periods, though the degree of impact is gradually weakened. The model in this chapter does well in explaining investment and also proved the crowding-out effect of FDI on domestic capital in the light of scholars' discussions on crowding-in and crowding-out effect of FDI.

In terms of household consumption, when the economy is in the steady state and FDI increases by 1% due to exogenous random shocks in the period t, household consumption will increase by about 0.005% in the current period, and the impact can last for about 40 periods. As for the positive effect of FDI

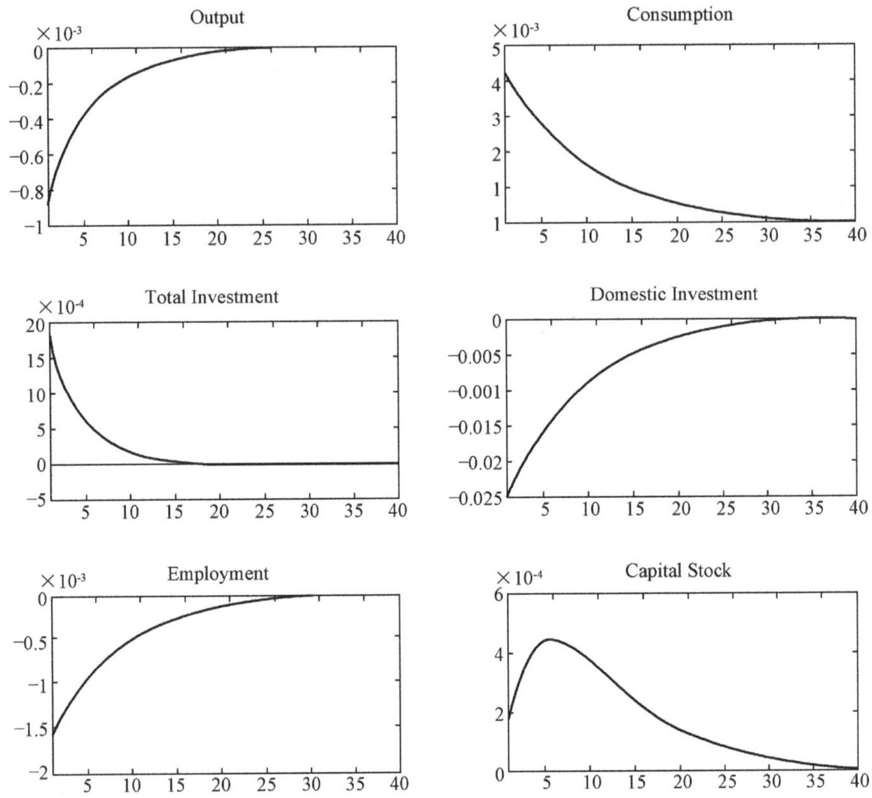

Figure 10.8 Impulse Responses of All Macroeconomic Variables to FDI Shocks.

on household consumption, the author believes that a large amount of foreign investment in China may play a certain role in narrowing the gap between the rich and the poor. Compared with some domestic enterprises, FDI enterprises have more advanced technology and equipment, but from the perspective of labor absorption, they are still labor-intensive enterprises. For example, electronic and textile enterprises have strong labor absorption capacity, which will help narrow the gap between the rich and the poor.

In terms of labor, when the economy is in the steady state and FDI increases by 1% due to exogenous random shocks in the period t, labor will decrease by about 0.0015% in the current period, and the impact can last for about 25 periods. Among the literature exploring the impact of FDI on the employment of the host country's labor, some hold that FDI reduces the employment level of the host country, while others hold that FDI improves the employment level of the host country. The research findings in this chapter show that FDI has a negative impact on the overall employment level of the host country.

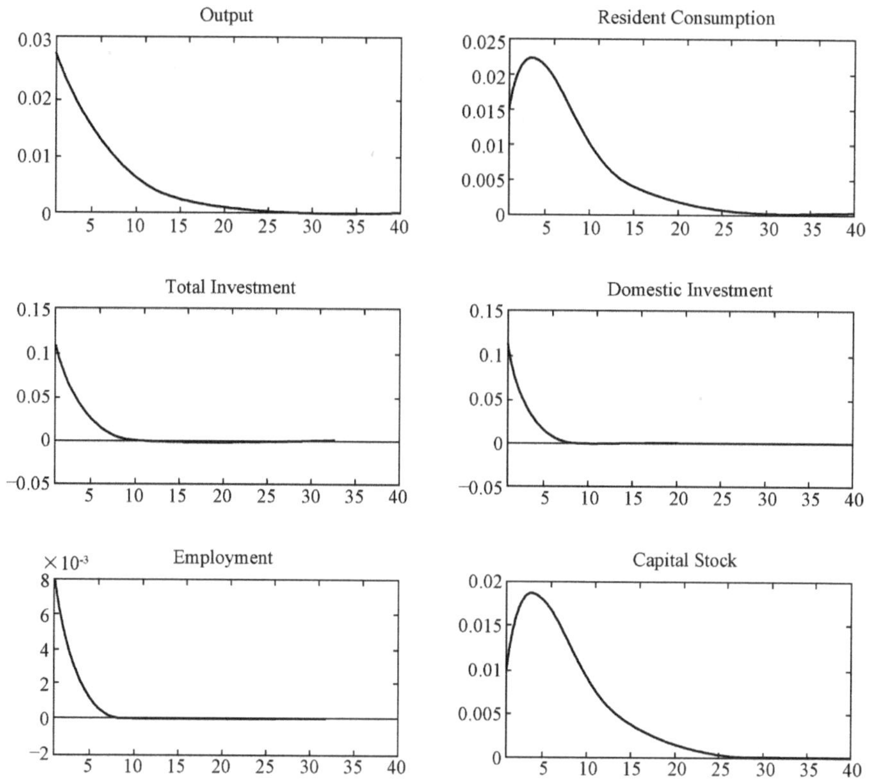

Figure 10.9 Impulse Responses of All Macroeconomic Variables to Technology Shocks.

In terms of capital stock, when the economy is in the steady state and FDI increases by 1% due to exogenous random shocks in the period *t*, the capital stock will increase by about 0.0003% in the current period, and the impact will reach the maximum around the fifth period, and then the impact will gradually weaken, lasting about 40 years. However, the impact of FDI is relatively small compared with the huge capital assets in China.

In terms of the total output, when the economy is in the steady state and FDI increases by 1% due to exogenous random shocks in the period *t*, the total output will decrease by about 0.001% in the current period, and the impact will last for about 20 periods. As can be seen from the results, FDI has a negative impact on the total output, though generally the impact is small, for FDI mainly affects the total output through affecting the labor level.

By comparing Figure 10.8 with Figure 10.9, it can be seen that, on the whole, the degree and duration of technology shocks on macroeconomic variables are less than those of FDI shocks on macroeconomic variables.

10.5 Conclusion

By introducing FDI shocks into the RBC model, it is found that the model economy with FDI shocks well explains the real economy, which is significantly better than the RBC model without FDI shocks. According to the impulse response effects of FDI shocks to various macroeconomic variables, FDI's influence on various macroeconomic variables provides a reference for formulating reasonable FDI absorption policies, including introducing FDI with technology spillover effect, guiding FDI to emerging industries, reasonably adjusting the regional distribution of FDI in China, improving financial services in China and reducing the dependence on low-efficient foreign capital.

The influence of FDI on macroeconomy has always been a concern of scholars at home and abroad, and a lot of theoretical and empirical studies have been done in this regard. In this chapter, FDI is included in the RBC model, and the DSGE method is used to solve the parameters of the model. The model in this chapter is mainly based on the RBC model, and some factors have not been considered in the model. In future research, the model needs to be further optimized to make it more consistent with Chinese real economic facts. For example, to further improve the rationality and forecasting ability of the model, the influence of FDI on technological progress should be separated, the capital utilization rate should be considered, the nonequilibrium of the market can be introduced, and the consumer utility function can be optimized. As an important part in world economic markets, China is bound to be affected by economic globalization. Although with the introduction of FDI, this chapter reflects part of the reality of economic globalization, the model does not, to some degree, consider the factors of import and export without considering the high and long-term dependence of China on foreign demand. Therefore, in the process of theoretical model research, it is necessary to incorporate the model into more open economic models to measure the impact of globalization on economic growth and fluctuations.

Note

1 The equation should be $\frac{\partial L}{\partial K_t}:(1-\delta)+\lambda_t \alpha A_t K_t^{\alpha} L_t^{1-\alpha}=0$, but for the sake of analysis, the Lagrange function is revised as the following form and then adopts the first-order condition:

$$L = E\left\{\sum_{t=0}^{\infty}\beta^t\left[\frac{C_t^{1-\eta}-1}{1-\eta}+\theta\ln(1-\mathrm{L}_t)-\lambda_t\left(C_t+K_{t+1}-I_t^f\right)+\right.\right.$$
$$\left.\left.\beta\lambda_{t+1}\left(A_{t+1}K_{t+1}^{\alpha}L_{t+1}^{1-\alpha}+(1-\delta)K_{t+1}\right)\right]\right\}$$

Bibliography

Agosin, Manuel R., and Ricardo Mayer. "Foreign Investment in Developing Countries: Does It Crowd in Domestic Investment?" UNCTAD Discussion Paper No. 146, 2000.

Barro, Robert J., and Xavier Sala-i-Martin. *Economic Growth*. New York: McGraw Hill, 1995: 312–320.

Borensztein, Eduardo, Jose De Gregorio, and Jong-Wha Lee. "How Does Foreign Direct Investment Affect Economic Growth." *Journal of International Economics* no. 1 (1998): 115–135.

Bu, Yongxiang, and Jin Yan 卜永祥, 靳炎. "Chinese Real Business Cycle (RBC): A Basic Explanation and Theoretical Expansion" 中国实际经济周期:一个基本解释和理论扩展. *World Economics* no. 7 (2002): 3–11.

Cai, Fang, and Wang Dewen 蔡昉, 王德文. "Foreign Direct Investment and Its Employment Effects in China: An Analysis of Human Capital" 外商直接投资与就业—个人力资本分析框架. *Collected Essays on Finance and Economics* no. 1 (2004): 1–14.

Chen, Kunting, and Gong Liutang 陈昆亭, 龚六堂. "Growth and Fluctuations in the Chinese Economy: Introducing Human Capital into RBC Model" 中国经济增长的周期与波动的研究---引入人力资本后的RBC模型. *China Economic Quarterly* no. 4 (2004): 803–818.

Chen Kunting, Gong Liutang, and Zou Hengfu 陈昆亭, 龚六堂, 邹恒甫. "Numerical Experiments of Basic RBC Method for Simulating the Chinese Economy" 基本RBC方法模拟中国经济的数值试验. *World Economic Papers* no. 2 (2004): 41–52.

Chen, Xiaoguang, and Zhang Yulin 陈晓光, 张宇麟. "Credit Constraint, Government Consumption and Real Business Cycle in China" 信贷约束、政府消费与中国实际经济周期. *Economic Research Journal* no. 12 (2010): 48–59.

Chen, Xuebin, Yang Ling, and Fang Song 陈学彬, 杨凌, 方松. "The Micro-Foundation Studies of Monetary Policy Effect: An Empirical Analysis of the Chinese Residents' Consumption-Savings Behavior" 货币政策效应的微观基础研究-我国居民消费储蓄行为的实证分析. *Fudan Journal* (Social Science Edition) no. 1 (2005): 42–54.

Cheng Peikun, Zhou Yingheng, and Yin Zhiyang 程培堃, 周应恒, 殷志扬. "Trade-off Between FDI and Domestic Investment: From the Industrial Organization Perspective FDI" 对国内投资的挤出(入)效应: 产业组织视角. *China Economic Quarterly* no. 4 (2009): 1527–1548.

Christiano, Lawrence J., and Martin Eichenbaum. "Current Real-Business-Cycle Theories and Aggregate Labor-Market Fluctuations." *American Economic Review* no. 3 (1992): 430–450.

Gong, Gang, and Willi Semmler 龚刚,. "Real Business Cycles with Labor Market Disequilibrium" 非均衡劳动力市场的真实经济周期模型. *China Economic Quarterly* no. 3 (2003): 591–604.

Hansen, Gary D. "Indivisible Labor and the Business Cycle." *Journal of Monetary Economics* no. 3 (1985): 309–327.

Hirschman, Albert O. *The Strategy of Economic Development*. New Haven: Yale University Press, 1958: 213–225.

Huang, Yongfeng, Ren Ruoen, and Liu Xiaosheng 黄勇峰, 任若恩, 刘晓生. "Capital Stock Estimations in Chinese Manufacturing by Perpetual Inventory Approach" 中国制造业资本存量永续盘存法估计. *China Economic Quarterly* no. 2 (2002): 377–396.

Huang, Zelin 黄赜琳. "A Study on Business Cycle and the Effects of Fiscal Policy in China: An Empirical Study on a RBC Model with Three Sections" 中国经济周期特征与财政政策效应: 一个基于三部门RBC模型的实证分析. *Economic Research Journal* no. 6 (2005): 27–39.

Khan, Aubhik, and Julia K. Thomas. "Modeling Inventories over the Business Cycle." Staff Report 343, Federal Reserve Bank of Minneapolis, 2004.

Kydland, Finn E., and Edward F. Prescott. "Time to Build and Aggregate Fluctuations." *Econometrica* no. 6 (1982): 1345–1370.

Li, Hao, and Zhong Changbiao 李浩, 钟昌标. "Trade Surplus and Chinese Real Business Cycle Analysis: A Study Based on the Open RBC Model" 贸易顺差与中国的实际经济周期分析: 基于开放的RBC模型的研究. *The Journal of World Economy* no. 9 (2008): 60–65.

Long, John B., Jr, and Charles I. Plosser "Real Business Cycles." *Journal of Political Economy* no. 1 (1983): 39–69.

McDonald, F., H. J. Tselman and A. Heise. "Foreign Direct Investment and Employment in Host Regions." *European Business Review* no. 1 (2002): 40–50.

Rama, Martin. "Globalization, Inequality and Labor Market Policies." Paper for Annual Bank Conference in Development Economics (ABCDE Europe), Washington, 2001.

Shan, Haojie 单豪杰. "Reestimating the Capital Deposit of China: 1952–2006" 中国资本存量K的再估算: 1952–2006. *The Journal of Quantitative and Technical Economics* no. 10 (2008): 17–31.

Sun, Linlin, and Ren Ruoen 孙琳琳, 任若恩. "China's Capital Investment and Total Factor Estimation" 中国资本投入和全要素生产率的估算. *The Journal of World Economy* no. 12 (2005): 3–13.

Wan, Guanghua, Lu Ming, and Chen Zhao 万广华, 陆铭, 陈钊. "Globalization and Regional Inequality: Chinese Evidence" 全球化与地区间收入差距:来自中国的证据. *Social Sciences in China* no. 3 (2005): 17–26.

Wu, Lixue 吴利学. "Fluctuations of China's Energy Efficiency: Theoretical Explains, Numerical Simulations and Policy Experiments" 中国能源效率波动:理论解释、数值模拟及政策含义. *Economic Research Journal* no. 5 (2009): 130–142.

Wu, Jian 武剑. "Regional Discrepancy of Foreign Direct Investment in China and Its Effect on Economic Growth" 外商直接投资的区域分布及其经济增长效应. *Economic Research Journal* no. 4 (2002): 27–35.

Yang, Liuyong, and Shen Guoliang 杨柳勇, 沈国良. "An Analysis of the Squeezing Out Effect of Foreign Direct Investment on Domestic Investment" 外商直接投资对国内投资的挤入挤出效应分析. *Statistical Research* no. 3 (2002): 6–8.

Zhang, Jun, Wu Guiying, and Zhang Jipeng 张军, 吴桂英, 张吉鹏. "Estimation of China's Provincial Capital Stock: 1952–2000" 中国省际物质资本存量估算: 1952–2000. Economic Research Journal no. 10 (2004): 35–44.

Zhang, Kevin H. "Foreign Direct Investment and Growth in China: A Panel Data Study for1992–2004." The Conference of "WTO, China and Asian Economies." Beijing, China, 2006, 24–25.

Zhong, Changbiao 钟昌标. "Empirical Evidence on the Regional Spillover Effects of FDI in China" 外商直接投资地区间溢出效应研究. *Economic Research Journal* no. 1 (2010): 80–89.

Afterword

My research on macroeconomics began in the summer of 2005 when I went to Tsinghua University to attend the Advanced Course in Modern Economics for Teachers. Hence, I learned from Prof. Xiaodong Zhu and Prof. Danyang Xie, who thoroughly reviewed the foundations and advanced developments in macroeconomics. I have been pretty fascinated by macroeconomic models since then. During my visit to the Department of Economics at Cornell University from January to June in 2009, I followed the ongoing conversations in the field of macroeconomics. Coauthored with Prof. Yi Du and Prof. Yongmiao Hong, the article titled "Labor Market Distortions, Efficiency Difference and the Urban–Rural Gap" (Chapter 3, this volume) was the first publication to apply what I had learned.

This well prepared me for the program titled Calibration of Chinese Macroeconomic Data and Its Improvement Methodology, sponsored by the National Social Science Fund of China in 2010, and further the course Cutting-Edge Literature Seminar on Macroeconomics for students of the School of Economics, Nanjing University, in 2012. I would also like to thank my grad students who have closely cooperated with me in extensive research on Chinese macroeconomic theories, problems and trends. For instance, in 2013, my graduate Lei Zeng and I published the article "Intermittent Institutional Changes and Chinese Economic Fluctuations: Calibrated Models and Dynamic Analysis" (Chapter 2, this volume) in the journal *Management World*; in 2015, another article "Informal Finance, A Duel Track Interest Rate and the Effects of Credit Policy: An Analysis Based on the New-Keynesian DSGE Model" (Chapter 5) was published again in *Management World*. In addition, a series of research results incorporated into this book were previously published in journals, including *Nankai Economic Research*, *International Trade Issues*, *Financial Issues Research*, *Contemporary Economic Research* and so forth.

I would like to express my gratitude to anyone who provided help for the publication of this book, including Mr. Jianping Fu and Ms. Tiantian Tang from Nanjing University Press, who already spared enormous efforts in terms of their excellent editing work on the publication of the Chinese version six years ago. This book would never have been completed without decades of discussions with my students, colleagues and other scientific researchers.

Ninghua Sun
Nanjing University
Winter 2021

Index

Note: Figures are indicated by *italics*. Tables are indicated by **bold**. Endnotes are indicated by the page number followed by 'n' and the endnote number e.g., 20n1 refers to endnote 1 on page 20.